Jerry Baker's

Green Grass
MAGIC

www.jerrybaker.com

Jerry Baker's

Green Grass
MAGIC

Tips, Tricks, and Tonics
for Growing the
Toe-Ticklinest Turf in Town!

by Jerry Baker,
America's Master Gardener®

Published by American Master Products, Inc.

Published by American Master Products, Inc.,
Executive Editor: Kim Adam Gasior
By arrangement with
Storey Communications, Inc., Pownal, Vermont 05261

Contributing Writers: Arden Moore and Kim Adam Gasior
Editors: Gwen W. Steege and Eileen M. Clawson
Horticultural Editor: Charles W.G. Smith
Cover and Text Design: Betty Kodela
Text Layout: Corinne Girouard (Final Proof), Deborah Daly, and Jennifer Jepson Smith
Illustrations Editor: Ilona Sherratt
Indexer: Susan Olason, Indexes and Knowledge Maps

Jerry Baker
P.O. Box 805, New Hudson, MI 48165

www.jerrybaker.com

Printed in the United States of America
2 4 6 8 10 9 7 5 3 1   softcover

CONTENTS

PART II: When Things Go Wrong

PART III: New Lawns to No Lawns ...and Everything in Between!

PART IV: Putting It All Together

To: My grandchildren, who couldn't wait to get their shoes and socks off so they could tickle their toes in Grandpa's gorgeous green grass. Thanks for showing me what it means to be young again, and for appreciating all of my efforts over the years.
Love to all of you!

On the chalkboard: $1254X^2$, $e=mc^2$, $P(M^3)^5$, *turf 101*

INTRODUCTION

Getting to Know Lawns

Howdy, lawn lads and lassies, and welcome to the wonderful world of grassies! It doesn't matter if you're green to the lawn scene or a seasoned sodmaster from way back when, I'm here to give you the inside scoop on how to get the most out of that carpet of green that surrounds your home.

A Whole Book about Lawns?!

When I told some of my friends I was working on a book about lawns, they asked, "How can you possibly fill 384 pages talking about a bunch of boring blades of grass?!" My answer is: Quite easily! You see, I *love* lawns — there's far more to them than meets the eye.

For one thing, all lawns are not created equal. I'm sure you know someone who's out there mowing and feeding his lawn every other day — and his lawn looks better than the putting greens at the local golf course. Then again, just around the corner is the lawn that gets mowed about once a year — only one cut above the plot in front of the old, abandoned house down by the railroad tracks! The moral of this story is that it takes all kinds of people to make the world go 'round — and the grass grow green. But whatever your style is, and no matter how much you know, there's always room for improvement. Hey, I've been at this for 40+ years, and I still learn new tricks every day!

Did You Know?

Wearing golf shoes or aerating lawn sandals when mowing your yard can put your grass on par with the best around. (See pages 9 and 112 and you'll find out why.)

Positively Pleasing Payoffs

Now, most folks would probably agree that growing a gorgeous green lawn around their homes is a terrific idea. I wouldn't be surprised if you already picture your lawn as a living, wall-to-wall carpet, bringing a certain amount of character, order, texture, and color to your yard. But, hey, that's not just a bunch of fluff! If you're a practical person like I am, you'll quickly see that a well-cared-for lawn is less likely to be brought to its knees by bugs and disease. And it not only looks terrific, but a great lawn increases your property value and improves the looks of the neighborhood. Plus, it's so nice to come home to. Let me show you what I mean.

First Impressions Count

As my Grandma Putt always said, you never get a second chance to make a first impression, and that's especially true when it comes to your lawn. After all, it's the first thing folks see when they drive up to your house.

If your lawn features a motley assortment of grasses, a rampaging weed population, and overgrown edges, it's a real eyesore. But that's not all. An unkempt lawn is also an open invitation to nasty bugs and fast-spreading diseases, all of which just make the lawn look worse.

But when your lawn is lush, green, and healthy, it's not only beautiful all on its own, it also provides the perfect backdrop for trees, shrubs, flowers, and other dazzling landscape features. And all of this sets your house off to a "T", making it look like a masterpiece — safe, beautiful, *and* valuable.

Did You Know?

In one single growing season, a half-acre of lawn produces more than 5,500 pounds of grass clippings.

Grow for the Green

Yup, it's true! A well-cared-for lawn actually increases your property value. If you're thinking of selling your home, there's nothing like gorgeous green grass to grab the interest of potential buyers. A beautiful lawn says that here's a person who not only lovingly works on his yard, but he also takes special care of the inside of his home. Realtors call this "curb appeal."

Tax Facts

And there's another hidden bonus: Great-looking landscaping raises the value of your property, *without* increasing your property tax. When figuring out how much in taxes you owe, assessors consider additions like a new bedroom, a third bathroom, a garage, and a deck, but they skip over landscaping amenities. Talk about more bang for your buck — it doesn't get any better than this!

The Environmental Benefits

Lawns also do their part to help the environment — and us. Without getting into too much detail, all green plants, grass included, produce oxygen from carbon dioxide during photosynthesis. (Remember Biology 101?) They get this carbon dioxide as a waste product when we exhale.

Lawns step in, absorb carbon dioxide from the air, and convert it to the oxygen we need in order to live. Lawns also trap dust, dirt, and pollution, and they provide a strong root system to fight soil erosion.

Jerry Baker Says

"So a healthy lawn helps create a healthy environment, and that's good for everyone."

Gets You Grinnin'

Believe it or not, a well-kept lawn can even boost your outlook on life. A beautiful, eye-pleasing yard will put a smile on your face and a feeling of contentment in your soul — lickety split! Picture this: It's a lazy Saturday afternoon in July. The sun is shining, the air is balmy, and the grass is freshly mowed. It's the perfect time to invite the neighbors over for a cookout and a picnic, or maybe you'd like to pitch a tent and camp out in the backyard with your 8 year old. You could also put that gorgeous green grass to the test and set up a game of croquet. Or maybe you'd just like to kick off your shoes and tickle your toes, then curl up with a good book and read — and snooze — in the hammock. The choice is yours — enjoy!

A Giant Grass Garden

By now, you've probably guessed that lawns are one of the things in life that I like the most. I look at it this way: The healthiest lawns I've seen are those whose "owners" have treated them with as much care and attention as some folks give their flower or vegetable gardens. Fair enough, you say. But how do I really get this dream lawn? Is it magic? Does it take a lot of hard work? Do I have to be a genius to figure it out? What's really the scoop?!

Well, let me put it this way: Lawn care's no mystery if you know what to do and when to do it. And that's where I come in. You see, I've been working hard in the yard for the past 40+ years or so, coming up with a huge array of tips, tricks, and tonics that make lawn care a snap! I'm going to share my lifetime of lawn know-how and experience with you in this book.

Jerry Baker Says

"If you really stop and think about it, a lawn *is* just a giant garden. But instead of yielding a bumper crop of whopper tomatoes or row upon row of gorgeous roses, a lawn generates zillions of blades of green grass."

The Three-Legged Stool of Lawn Care

We're going to start off in Part I with some terrific tips about what I like to call the three-legged stool of lawn care: feeding, mowing, and watering. Sure, it takes a little bit of effort to properly mow, trim, fertilize, and water your lawn, but you don't have to become a lawn pawn or a slave to sod. No siree! If you follow my commonsense guidelines, I guarantee that your lawn will make others green with envy!

Feeding your lawn the right way at the right time with the right ingredients is the first step to a lush lawn. Chapter 2 is all about "chow" time, and it's jam-packed with my world-famous tonics for green grass success. You'll find everything you need to keep your lawn well fed year 'round — from tonics that get your lawn off to a great start in the spring, to those that keep it purring right along through the summer until it's time to put your lawn "to bed" for the winter.

When it comes time to mow, my tips will keep you a big cut above the average Joe. Whatever kind of lawnmower you choose to use, if you follow my basic techniques, your lawn will be a whole lot healthier for it. Just take a peek at Chapter 4 for the rundown on what's what in lawn mowers and all you've ever wanted to know about mowing.

The same goes for watering, which is the third leg of that critical three-legged stool of lawn care. In Chapter 5, we'll discuss the ins and outs of proper watering. You'll learn how to do it, as well as what's best for the kind of grass and the kind of climate you have in your own backyard.

We Can't Be Good All of the Time

I hate to admit it, but even the best turfmasters sometimes get hit with problems in our lawns. You might give your lawn the tenderest loving care it needs, and yet it can still get damaged by weather, disease, or insect and animal pests (both the two-legged and the four-legged varieties!). If your Aunt Edna backs her car right into the softest, wettest part of your lawn, leaving big tire tracks in her wake, or if a battalion of moles decides to camp out in your yard, check out Chapters 7 and 8 in Part II for the lowdown on how to get your lawn back into tiptop shape. Then we'll move on to the other bad guys, showing you how to get the bead on weeds (Chapter 10), drub the grubs, and make fleas flee (Chapters 11 and 12). If you follow the quick-and-easy steps I outline in this section, you'll no longer shake in your boots at the first sign of trouble.

Getting Down to Basics

Up to this point, we've covered everything you need to know to make sure that the greenest grass on the block ends up on your side of the fence. But if you don't have a lawn yet, what do you do? Well, that's what Part III is all about. The first thing I want you to know is how to understand and improve your soil (that's in Chapter 13). You'll then discover my tricks for putting in a new lawn, step-by-step, whether you do it by sowing seed or by laying sod.

You'll also learn how to make the most of your soil by planting the kinds of grasses that will grow best in it. The long and the short of it is that grass planted in the wrong place is more prone to disease, insects, and weeds. Check out my suggestions for the best grasses for *your* conditions, all listed and described in Chapter 15.

And if you ever get to a point where you want to cut back on the size of your lawn, I've got lots of handy hints about life beyond lawns, including everything from ground covers to gravel, decks, and patios to meadows full of native plants or wildflowers. After all, even for the biggest grass fanatics among us, there's a whole lot more to life than lawn care!

The World Goes 'Round and 'Round

And last, but certainly not least, I've put together a Tonic summary section and special lawn-care calendar in Part IV of this book. The calendar gives advice season by season, with special notes for you, whether you're growing warm-season or cool-season grasses, or a mixture of both. Flip to this calendar regularly throughout the year and you'll know exactly what to do and *when* to do it.

Did You Know?

A can of beer and a little dish of soap make a terrific twosome for whatever ails your lawn. (See page 324-26 and you'll learn why.)

The Tonic summary brings all of my famous lawn tonics together in one place to use as a handy reference whenever you get the urge to work on your lawn. I guarantee that you'll be dog-earring these pages as you refer to them again and again and again.

☆   ☆   ☆

Whew! As you can see, we've got a lot of ground to cover (you didn't think that I'd lost my penchant for bad puns, did you?), and 384 pages doesn't look like so much after all, does it? Writing this book was really a labor of love, which is how I want you to think of lawn care. Sure, it's going to take a little work, but as my Grandma Putt always said, nothin's worth doin' without doin' it right. So, I think that you'll find a *little* bit of work done at the right time will save you a *lot* of work in the long run and pay off big with a terrific new lawn you'll be button-bursting proud of.

Well, now that I've gotten you thinking about how terrific it will be to have the lawn of your dreams on your side of the fence, it's time to get to the heart of the matter — your lawn and how to care for it. So grab a nice tall, cold one, and turn the page!

Part 1

Jerry's Secrets for the Lawn of Your Dreams

CHAPTER 1

A Bird's-Eye View of Lawn Care

This is a rather unusual way to start a book about lawns, but one of my favorite childhood stories was "Goldilocks and the Three Bears." Remember how frustrated Goldilocks was that Mama Bear's and Papa Bear's beds were either too soft or too hard, and that their porridge was either too hot or too cold? Baby Bear's bed and porridge, though, proved to be *just right!* Well, getting your lawn to look "just right" is certainly no fairy tale, but in order to live happily ever after, you first need to make some observations and do a little planning. Here's an overview.

Lawn Matchmaking

The lawn of your dreams must meet your needs, your personality, and your abilities to maintain it. It all boils down to addressing these four major issues:

- **Time** - **Money** - **Climate** - **Terrain**

Time

Time marches on — in life and in lawns. Just as you schedule work appointments, you need to determine how much time you can — and will — devote to maintaining your lawn.

When we bought our first house, an old neighbor friend told me that lawns need a lot of attention. "If you can get one weekend a month free of any lawn worries, count yourself lucky," he said. With my lawn-maintenance program, you won't spend anywhere near that amount of time on your lawn. After all, if I can't make it fast, fun, and easy for you, then I'm not doing my job!

Money

The second consideration is money. Sheds and garages all over this country are jam-packed full of tools, fertilizers, and other lawn necessities, and believe you me, none of these come cheap! Maintaining a lawn can cost a pretty penny if you don't know what you're doing.

If you've just won the lottery or are a very good budgeter, you can take the easy way out and hire a professional lawn service to take care of all of your landscaping needs. If not, and you still want a beautiful lawn, then there are lots of terrific tips in this book that will save you a ton of time, effort, and, most important, money, and still keep your lawn healthy. And that, my friends, you can take to the bank!

Climate

There's no bartering with Mother Nature — she calls the shots when it comes to the climate, and you have to take what you can get. Like the old adage, "If you can't beat 'em, join 'em," you'll just have to learn to work with her. But you can "up your chances" by selecting grass types that are best for the temperature and rainfall in your area.

Terrain

Finally, size up your terrain. Do you have a nice, flat piece of property, or does it ramble here and there, filled with slopes, hills, or irregular boundary lines? Does your property drain off excess water easily, or are you constantly standing in pools of water? Is your soil rich and moist or dry and cracking? I'll show you some simple ways to handle each of these problems so that you'll end up with a beautiful, low-maintenance lawn that's the envy of the whole neighborhood.

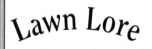

Lawn Lore

Tracing the roots of the modern lawn is a tricky business. Did Adam and Eve own the very first lawn? We know they had a snake-bitten garden, but I wouldn't bet on the lawn issue since no one really knows when and how lawns originated.

What I *can* tell you is that many centuries ago, the Chinese grew grass plants. Grass also merited a couple of mentions in the Bible.

The Fabulous Four of Lawn Care

I'm not one to beat around the bush, so let's get right to basics — down and dirty! There's no mystery to maintaining a happy, healthy lawn. It's not rocket science. You've just got to understand a few basic principles and know how to use a few common household products to keep your grass clean, green, and growin' mean! If you do nothing else to your lawn but apply my All-Season Clean-Up Tonic (page 327) and All-Season Green-Up Tonic (page 328) at the regularly recommended intervals, you'll be 75 percent on your way to having the greenest grass on the block.

Guaranteed! The rest, as they say, is icing on the cake.

But wait, I'm getting ahead of myself. In subsequent chapters I'll go into much more detail, but for now, I want to introduce you to what I call the Fabulous Four of Lawn Care. Maestro, a little drumroll, please!

- **Feeding**
- **Mowing**
- **Watering**
- **Aerating/Dethatching**

Quite an impressive lineup, wouldn't you say? Definitely an all-star cast by a *yard!* And *for* yards!

"But Wait . . . There's More!"

Okay, you ask, what about weeds and bugs and disease? And what if the weather doesn't cooperate and we shrivel up in a drought or, just as bad, drown in too much rain? Don't fret. I've devoted Part II of this book to these and other lawn menaces.

And, for those of you about to start a new lawn from scratch, flip to Part III. There you'll find all of my inside tips, tricks, and terrific tonics that will help you get your soil in tip-top shape and give you all the lowdown on fixing up old, tired lawns or starting a brand-new one.

The Facts on Fertilizers

Popeye the Sailor Man kept his muscles bulging by eating his spinach. But among lawn grasses, mateys, it's fertilizer that helps maintain an even keel. To keep your lawn fit, trim, and in tip-top shape, you need to regularly feed it.

Your job as turfmaster is to cater to your lawn's taste buds. That means providing the right kind of fertilizer in the right amount and at the right time.

When it comes to lawn food, the choices seem endless. There are quick-release fertilizers that are inexpensive and work fast, but they don't last very long. On the opposite end of the aisle are slow-release fertilizers, the slow-but-steady types that cost more but last a whole lot longer. The time of year that you are fertilizing will also influence which type you should choose and use.

Now, here's where I come in. For over 40 years, I've been preaching the gardening gospel according to St. Jer: If you use common household products like **Epsom salts, beer, soda, ammonia, and liquid dish soap,** you can treat your lawn to quite a feast. It's true! Through a lot of hard work, I've perfected some can't-miss lawn-feeding tonics that I'll share with you in Chapter 2. But for now, let's continue with the overview of lawn care basics.

Beyond Speed

Fertilizers are classified by how they are made — either organic or synthetic. Personally, I like to go with organic fertilizers whenever possible, what I call the *au naturel* of lawn chow. They are made of 100 percent manure, fish emulsion, or other high-quality natural ingredients (and no chemicals!) that provide plenty of digestible nitrogen, the all-important nutrient for green grass. They won't burn plants *and* they provide long-lasting nutrients for your lawn to grow on.

Go with the Mow

Lawn keepers, start your engines! The local garden center's showroom is full of mowers that appeal to the fits and fancies of every grass clipper imaginable. For those who crave peace and quiet, the classics — the two-wheeled, push-it-yourself mowers and the four-wheeled, hummingbird-quiet electrical rotary mowers — are ideal for small lawns or folks who are looking for a workout.

Then there are the economy models — the gas-powered rotary mowers that are easy to maintain *and* easy on your pocketbook. They're the dependable workhorses of the lawn care lineup and can handle nearly all types of terrain.

Don't Get Mowed Over

For Ponderosa-size lawns, consider the mighty (but pricey) riding mowers. They can cut up to 60 inches of grass in a single swipe and boast the highest horsepower. They'll bring a large lot quickly down to size, but they do have some drawbacks: They can be tough to maneuver in close quarters, and they don't ride real safely on a steep incline. In that case, you'll need a backup push mower or trimmer (or a goat!) to keep those grassy slopes in shape.

The Next Steps

Selecting the proper mower is only the first step to green grass glory. Guaranteeing that your lawn sports a fabulous haircut each and every time you mow depends on how well you maneuver the mower. A bit further on, I'll explain my "One-Third Rule" and how it keeps valuable nutrients in your lawn and helps the roots grow thick and strong. Check out Chapter 4 for a lot more of my marvelous mowing magic.

Turf Trivia

A turf farmer named Jay Edgar Frick, of Monroe, Ohio, is credited with owning the world's widest mower. Dubbed "The Big Green Machine," the 5-ton, 60-foot-wide, 27-unit gang mower can trim an acre in 60 seconds flat!

Water: Worth Its Weight in Gold

Water can be a lawn's best friend or its worst enemy; it all depends upon timing and quantity. Too little water, and your lawn will dehydrate; too much water, and your lawn will drown. The time of day, week, and season that you water your lawn is also critical.

Lawns, in general, love a deep, steady, lingering shower about once a week. And they're not particular — they don't care if the water comes from clouds or from a sprinkler system. Lawns should have 1 inch of water a week to keep them looking lush and to give them the extra "oomph" they need to withstand droughts and heavy rains.

If you really want to pamper your grass, I strongly urge you to resist the temptation to water daily. Overwatered roots shrink in size and strength, and your best efforts will only end up jeopardizing the health of your lawn.

Shower Power

Flip to Chapter 5 and you can dive right into plenty more watering tips. I call it "Shower Power," and it's all about the wonders of water for your lawn.

Scheduling Know-How

The type of soil your grass grows in will also influence your watering schedule. For instance, because clay soils hold more water than do loamy or sandy soils, they dry out more slowly. Sandy soils, on the other hand, don't hold water, so they can dry out in the wink of an eye. This means that those of you with the sandy variety may have to water twice as often as your friends who have clay soil.

Help Your Lawn Breathe a Little Easier

Poking a little fun at your lawn is okay, but poking holes in the soil is even better! I like to think of aeration as acupuncture for your grass! Soil that has a little breathing room is better able to absorb water, oxygen, nitrogen, and other nutrients from fertilizer than hard-packed, trampled-down ground is. And aerated soil makes the best home for the most desirable tenants your lawn can ever have: burrowing earthworms.

Give Her Air, Please

My general rule is that you should aerate your lawn twice a year. This, of course, depends upon the type of soil you have and the condition of your lawn.

The biggest, best, and most expensive way to aerate is to use a machine called a core aerifier, which yanks up thin soil plugs and scatters them on top of the lawn. I, myself, prefer to go natural and use an even easier method: aerating lawn sandals or golf shoes. Yep, wear your golf shoes when you do your yard chores.

When you walk about from the front to the back of your yard, the little golf spikes penetrate the invisible barrier between the blades of grass and the soil that is known as surface tension. And, besides, golf shoes give you more secure footing when you're walking. Want to learn more about aerating and dethatching? Then check out Chapter 6.

Equally important for the overall health of your yard is regular baths. No, not for you — I'm talking about your lawn! A little liquid dish soap and some other handy household items mixed in a 20 gallon hose-end sprayer will go a long way towards making your lawn squeaky clean *and* super-healthy! Throughout Part I are plenty of terrific clean-up tonics that'll do just that.

Just What Is Grass?

You're probably saying, Aw, c'mon, Jerry, everyone knows what grass is — right? But do you *really* know grass? Down to its roots? If you don't, you need to sign up for the Jerry Baker Grass Anatomy 101 class. Don't worry — *this* book is the only textbook required! No final paper due. No final exam. And I'm a real easy grader!

Bermuda Mama

One Bermuda grass plant, with a stolon and a rhizome, can spread to cover more than 1,000 square feet of turf in 10 years — but only if you give it the right combination of nutrients, water, and soil conditions!

Anatomy of Grass

The next time you're in your yard, I want you to kneel down and peer closely at your grassy soil. See if you can find these grass parts:

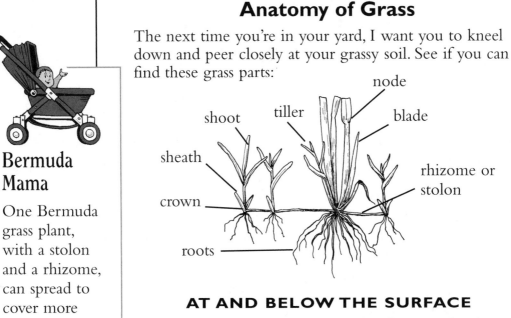

AT AND BELOW THE SURFACE

Crown and roots. Take your index finger and poke below the soil surface about an inch or so. Most likely, you'll notice the place where the grass plant is anchored into the soil. The base of the plant is called the *crown.* Those hairlike fibers that branch out from the crown and wiggle below ground are the *roots,* where the plant absorbs nutrients and water from the soil.

Rhizomes and stolons. The rootlike branches that grow parallel and just below the soil surface are called *rhizomes.* Their counterparts that creep vertically just above the ground are called *stolons.* Both feature branching systems.

ABOVE THE SURFACE

Sheath, blade, and shoots. The *sheath* is the part of the grass leaf located at the lower end that hugs the stem. The upper part of the grass leaf — called the *blade* — grows upward and away from the stem. Before I forget, I need to mention the primary and secondary shoots. The *primary shoot* is the main grass stem that grows upward from the crown and develops the germinating seed. The *secondary shoots* appear after the primary shoot and account for most of the grass blades in your lawn.

Tillers. They may sound nautical, but *tillers* are secondary shoots that grow from the grass plant's crown. For you avid lawn buffs, bunch grasses are major tillers. This group includes the ryegrasses and such fescues as chewing, hard, and tall.

Nodes, ligules, and auricles. Ready to learn about the nodes? Good! *Nodes* are bulbous joints on the stems from which the sheaths and blades grow. Now, take a deep breath — you're in the homestretch. The collar represents that spot on the grass plant where the sheath and blade meet. Paper-thin membranes called *ligules* usually poke out of the sheaths and from the earlike lobes called *auricles* that help grass experts accurately identify the grass plant.

Turf Trivia

Each stolon and rhizome has the ability to root, grow, and develop into an individual grass plant.

AT THE TOP

Flower and seed heads. Last but certainly not least are the *flower* and *seed heads.* Perched on stems held above the grass blades, flower and seed heads emerge many times during the season to produce and spread their seeds for future grass-plant generations. When you mow your lawn regularly, you generally trim the plant stems before they have a chance to develop seed heads.

SEED HEAD

How Grass Grows

Along with knowing the anatomy of grass, it's equally important to learn how grass grows. This will help you understand why certain mowing methods work better than others, why a particular grass will grow better in your yard, and when and why to use a specific fertilizer or pesticide. Remember the old phrase "growing like a weed"? When we hear that, the reference is usually being made to girls and boys who are getting a whole lot taller a lot more quickly than other children the same age. Well, different grasses grow at different rates, too — and in different directions as well!

Four Ways That Grass Spreads

It may surprise you to learn that grass plants spread by four methods:

- **Go to seed.** Grasses that are not cut short will flower and spread seeds to grow new plants.

- **Add new shoots.** This method is used by clump grasses, which add new shoots to the original plant's base.

- **Spread by rhizomes.** Underground stems create new plants within arm's reach of the mother plant.

- **Spread by stolons.** Stems above the ground take root and send up shoots vertically across the soil surface.

With any of these methods, roots and shoots form and anchor themselves in the soil. The crown of the plant develops, followed in rapid succession by grass blades and secondary shoots, finally climaxing with flowers and seed heads.

Photo-What?

To understand how grass grows, you need to recall the process called *photosynthesis*. Every living thing grows, whether animal or plant. To get bigger, organisms use materials, such as carbohydrates, to make cells, bones, and organs. Some living things, like people, get the material they need to grow from other living things, like plants and animals. They can't *make* the materials they need, so they have to take them from others. Plants, on the other hand, use a process called *photosynthesis* to make their own building blocks for growth.

Photosynthesis is the production of food and oxygen through a chemical reaction powered by sunlight that combines carbon dioxide and water. Carbohydrates are combined with nutrients to produce fatty acids, proteins, and other elements necessary for the plant to be healthy and thrive.

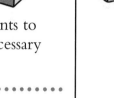

Food Factory

When you fertilize your lawn, you're adding nutrients that travel from the soil through each grass plant, which uses them and the carbohydrates produced during photosynthesis to make the proteins, fats, and amino acids it needs for proper growth and health.

Leaves can also absorb nutrients through a process called foliar feeding, which is done by simply spraying a diluted solution of fertilizer directly on the leaves using a hose-end sprayer. Many commercial products work well, or you can use my All-Season Green-Up Tonic (for the recipe, see page 328). Foliar feeding doesn't replace "regular" fertilizing, but it does provide nutrients to the grass plants, lickety-split.

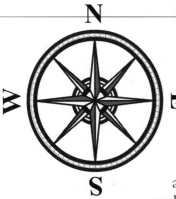

Regional Differences

Is the grass always greener on the other side of the street — or across the country? I'm blessed to have faithful followers on both sides of the Mason-Dixon Line. Folks in Minnesota are shoveling snow in January, while their cousins in Florida are working on their suntans — and mowing their lawns! So you need to remember that temperature, humidity, and soil-type needs differ among grasses of the North and South. And each area requires different types of grass.

- **Northerners** do best with cool-season grasses that grow strong enough and deep enough to cope with hot, blazing summers and bitter cold winters. These grasses grow fastest during spring and fall. They also fare well in coastal areas where temperatures rarely climb above 90°F and where there is an adequate amount of rainfall.

- **Southerners** do best with warm-season grasses. These sun-tough grasses thrive in tropical breezes, high humidity, and scorching hot temperatures.

Grasses by Climate

Cool-Season Grasses

Bent grass
Bluegrass
Fescue, red
Fescue, tall
Ryegrass,
  perennial

Warm-Season Grasses

Bahia grass
Bermuda grass
Buffalo grass
Centipede grass
St. Augustine
  grass
Zoysia grass

The Power of the 4 Ps

Folks, there is no way that you can fertilize your lawn only once a year and expect it to thrive. You need to feed, water, and mow regularly, and then practice my four Ps of Lawn Care, which I learned from my wise old Grandma Putt:

- Pride
- Patience
- Persistence
- Prayer

If you follow this advice, keeping your lawn a nice, healthy green color will be fast, fun, and easy, and it won't cost you an arm and a leg, either!

Ask Jerry

Q This may sound silly, but we live on a dusty road and our lawn often gets a lot of dust on it. Does the dust do any damage?

A Cars and trucks can kick up quite a dust storm. This settles on the lawn and blocks some of the sunlight from reaching the grass. Believe it or not, even a light covering of dust reduces the rate of photosynthesis that goes on within the grass plants. To keep your grass growing strong and looking good, too, give it a dose of my **Terrific Turf Tonic** (page 339) whenever your lawn looks like it needs a cleaning.

Q Okay, Jerry, I put on my golf shoes and walk all over my lawn to help aerate the soil. I even rented a core aerifier to poke more holes in the lawn. Now that the lawn is aerated, do you have a tonic that'll help keep the lawn from becoming compacted again?

A Do I have a tonic for aerating the lawn? Absolutely, and it's easy and effective to boot! After walking around the lawn in your golf shoes for awhile, mix up a batch of my **Aeration Tonic** (page 327) and spray away. Your lawn will be delirious!

Q I don't think I'm *too* picky about my lawn, but the one thing that drives me nuts is when my grass goes to seed, and the seed heads stick up above the rest of the grass. Do some types of lawn grasses produce more seed heads than other types, and if so, which should I avoid using?

A You need to be sure that the combination of grasses you use includes grasses with similar growth rates. Some older varieties of tall fescue and Bahia grass grow tall fast — faster than many other popular grasses. The result is that these grasses may go to seed while other grasses in the mix are still much shorter. You then end up with an entire lawn that looks a little ragged, even if you mow frequently. If seed heads really bug you, steer clear of Bahia grass and tall fescues.

Q We get frequent droughts in our area, and frequent restrictions on watering the lawn. Is there something we can do in the spring when water is usually available to help make our lawn more tolerant of dry weather later on?

A Some grasses are naturally more drought tolerant than others, but you can make just about any grass better prepared to weather hot, dry times by using my **Spring Wake-Up Tonic** (page 337). This mix has just the right ingredients to actually improve the soil while getting the plants off to a strong start.

Q I live out West where wild fires are a real hazard. Are there any lawn grasses that are less of a fire hazard in dry weather?

A Yes, there are. Many lawn seed mixes made of native grasses can reduce fire hazard. These are often available at local nurseries and are blended for your region. Many non-native grasses can also provide some protection, and they are sometimes easier to find. A nice blend is a combination of Canada bluegrass, wheat grass, sheep fescue, and blue gramma grass.

Q A section of my yard is pretty shady, and the grass that is growing there is okay, but not quite as nice as the rest of the lawn. Are there any tips to make the shady area look better without reseeding?

A I've discovered a few secrets over the years to make shady areas look great. First, let the grass in shady spots grow longer than the grass in the sunny places. Prune out some of the more dense branches of trees to let in more light, and paint nearby fences and structures a light color to reflect as much light into the shady areas as possible.

Well, there you go — you're now officially a graduate of Jerry Baker's Grass Anatomy 101 class. As you can see, geography plays a part in determining the fate of your lawn, but healthy habits play an even bigger role. Remember, you don't have to move to have a great lawn — just follow my step-by-step suggestions throughout this book, and you'll end up with a lawn that looks like a putting green! Now, where did I put my golf clubs?

CHAPTER 2

Come and Get It: Chow Town!

Unfortunately, lawns can't come and get it — they need your help to look their best. Plain and simple, all lawns must have certain nutrients to survive and thrive. You have to remember that healthy lawns are living, breathing entities. Just like you, they need a steady supply of carbon, oxygen, and hydrogen. But lawns also need a balanced diet, which, in their case, means giving them 12 key nutrients. In this chapter, I'll walk you through each of these nutrients and show you some timesaving ways to treat your lawn to a super smorgasbord of healthy chow.

The Big Three of Lawn Chow

Too little or too much of any one of 12 key nutrients will cause your grass to look yellowish, stunted, coarse, or sparse. But don't panic! The most important of these 12 — nitrogen, phosphorus, and potassium — are pretty easy to supply once I show you how. Let's start with those.

N-P-K Savvy

Nitrogen (N). Nitrogen zeroes in on all of the green parts of grass, promoting strong vegetative growth and dark green leaves. Too little nitrogen, and a lawn looks stunted and yellowish. Too much, and you must contend with rapid, weak growth and delayed maturity. Some of the best organic sources of nitrogen are *blood meal, fish emulsion,* and *manure.*

Phosphorus (P). Rock phosphate, a calcium phosphate mineral ore, is converted into a form that's usable by grass and other plants. Lawns need phosphorus to grow and mature and to develop hardy roots. Too little phosphorus, and grass blades will have a reddish, purplish, or grayish green cast. Too much, and it can interfere with the lawn's absorption of other essential elements. *Bonemeal, superphosphate,* and *rock phosphate* are sources of this mineral.

Potassium (K). Lawns must have potassium to complete photosynthesis, strengthen plant tissues, prepare for cold winters, and protect themselves against diseases. Too little potassium, and a lawn loses its vigor, yellows, and falls prey to plant diseases. Too much potassium interferes with the absorption of magnesium and calcium. Quality sources of potassium include *greensand, wood ashes, seaweed,* and *muriate* or *sulfate of potassium.*

In a Flash

You gotta love Mother Nature. She knows how to spoon-feed a lawn when she orders up a thunderstorm. During these cloud bursts, lawns chow down on much-needed nitrogen they draw from the air.

Whenever it rained when I was a kid, my Grandma Putt would tell me that Mother Nature was feeding the lawn, providing it with much-needed nitrogen, the chow of choice for growing lawns. When I took chemistry in high school (three times!), I found out that she was right.

Here's what my scientist friends tell me: Nitrogen molecules in the air are made of two nitrogen atoms bound tightly together. Plants can't use this nitrogen until lightning works a little magic. During a thunderstorm, every time there's a bolt of lightning, the electrical energy breaks the bonds of some of the nitrogen molecules in the

Primary Nutrients at a Glance

Name	Function	Effect of Too Much
Nitrogen	Assists in vigorous growth and helps in chlorophyll production	Rapid growth and retarded maturity
Phosphorus	Helps grass grow and mature and develop hardy roots	Interference with lawn's absorption of other essential elements
Potassium	Helps to complete photo-synthesis, strengthen plant tissues, prepare lawn for cold winters, and protect against disease	Interference with the absorption of magnesium and calcium; lawn becomes uneven

air. The nitrogen then quickly attaches to oxygen, forming nitrogen dioxide. Nitrogen dioxide dissolves easily in water, forming — abracadabra! — nitric acid, which then becomes nitrate, and nitrates are *great* lawn fertilizers. The nitrates fall to earth in the form of raindrops that seep into your lawn and help make your grass greener.

Turf Trivia

Many football teams have yanked out sod and replaced it with artificial turf, but the historic Soldiers Field in Chicago still keeps mowing real grass for those Monsters of the Midway, the Bears. And what true-blue baseball fan would ever want to spend a beautiful sunny Saturday afternoon in a domed stadium watching a double play on plain old artificial grass?

EFFECT OF TOO LITTLE	BEST SOURCES
Grass looks stunted and yellowish	Air, blood meal, fish emulsion, manure
Grass blades are reddish or purplish; cell division is stunted	Bonemeal, superphosphate, rock phosphate
Lawn loses vigor; falls prey to plant diseases	Greensand, wood ashes, seaweed, muriate or sulfate of potassium

Tasty Lawn Side Dishes

Now that you know all about the "Big Three," let's move on to the secondary feeders. Your lawn doesn't need an awful lot of any one of these, and in most areas you don't run into any problems. But you just may find that your lawn isn't getting enough (or it's getting too much) of one of these, and with a little more care, you can provide just the right balance of nutrients that gets your lawn up and growing.

Magnesium (Mg)

This nutrient assists in photosynthesis and is a key ingredient in chlorophyll. Too little, and your lawn develops chlorosis and grows poorly. It becomes thin due to premature dropping of leaf blades. Too much interferes with the absorption of calcium and potassium. Epsom salts (a.k.a. magnesium sulfate) are an excellent source.

Sulfur (S)

Yes, this smells-like-a-rotten-egg element has a purpose in the life of lawns — it helps build proteins as well as enzymes, amino acids, and vitamins. A shortage of sulfur turns grass blades pale green; too much can burn tender blades. A good source is superphosphate.

Calcium (Ca)

Just as humans need calcium to build strong bones, lawns need it to fortify cell walls and for normal cell division. Too little calcium can put the brakes on growth. Leaf blades begin to curl or die at the tips, and the roots become weak and stubby. Too much can block a lawn's intake of potassium and magnesium. Sources of calcium include gypsum, limestone, oyster, and eggshells.

Zinc (Zn)

Your lawn needs zinc for cell division. A zinc shortage can make your grass yellow and thin looking. Leaf blades are distorted and small, sometimes with tiny, white dead spots on the blades. Zinc, like many other trace elements, becomes toxic if oversupplied. The best source is zinc sulfate.

Iron (Fe)

This mineral is a component of proteins and enzymes and acts as a go-between for other nutrients and grass blades. Without it, young leaf blades turn streaky yellow. I don't know of any concerns for too much iron. Best sources are iron sulfate (a.k.a. copperas) and chelated iron.

Manganese (Mn)

A lawn needs this element to assist its enzyme system. Growth becomes stunted, and streaky chlorosis of leaf blades can occur with too little manganese. Too much manganese causes small dead areas in the blades and yellow borders around them. Best source: manganese sulfate.

Copper (Cu)

Copper is an enzyme activator. A reddish brown, gummy substance oozes from grass stems if the soil is short of copper. Too much copper interferes with the absorption of iron, and also can stunt the roots. The best copper sources for your lawn are copper sulfate and neutral copper.

Molybdenum (Mo)

This tongue-twisting nutrient (it's moe-LIB-den-um) is a constituent of nitrogen-containing enzymes. The best source is sodium molybdate.

Boron (B)

This nutrient improves absorption of the other elements. Too little boron, and your grass will have small leaf blades with dead spots on them. Too much, and the blades will turn yellowish red. The best source is borax.

FOR YOUR CONVENIENCE:
A TABLE OF SECONDARY NUTRIENTS

NAME	FUNCTION	EFFECT OF TOO MUCH
Magnesium	Assists in photo synthesis; key ingredient in chlorophyll	Interference with absorption of calcium and potassium
Sulfur	Helps build proteins	Grass blades burn
Calcium	Fortifies cell walls	Plant has difficulty taking in potassium and magnesium
Zinc	Aids in cell division	No symptoms
Iron	Acts as a go-between for other nutrients and grass blades	No symptoms
Manganese	Assists enzyme systems	Small dead areas and yellow borders on grass blades
Copper	Acts as enzyme activator	Interference with absorption of iron; stunted roots
Molybdenum	Helps utilize nitrogen	Lawn becomes poisonous to livestock
Boron	Improves absorption of other nutrients	Grass blades turn yellowish red

Effect of Too Little	Best Sources
Lawn thins; can't decompose old leaves	Epsom salts (a.k.a. magnesium sulfate)
Grass blades turn yellow	Superphosphate
Growth is stunted	Gypsum, limestone, oyster shells, eggshells
Grass turns yellow and thin looking	Zinc sulfate
Grass turns yellow	Iron sulfate (copperas), chelated iron
Growth is stunted; mottled chlorosis of leaves develops	Manganese sulfate
Reddish brown, gummy substance discharges from stems	Neutral copper, copper sulfate
No symptoms	Sodium molybdate
Grass develops small leaves, multiple buds, heart rot	Borax

Choosing the Right Fertilizer

All soil — and the grass growing on it — can use a little help in keeping fit as a fiddle, and that's when fertilizer and my terrific lawn tonics come in handy. I tell you, it's easy to be confused by all of the choices of commercial fertilizers available at your local garden center. Equally puzzling is trying to figure out exactly what to do and when to do it. But don't worry: I'm here to help you sift through the confusion so you can get your lawn growing in the right direction.

Slow as a Tortoise or Quick as a Hare?

Most lawn fertilizers come in bags and are manufactured to be slow release or quick release, or a combination of both.

Quick-release fertilizers are most often dry granules that dissolve fast after being spread on the lawn, providing a lot of nutrients in a short amount of time. Because they dissolve fast, they also work quickly.

Slow-release fertilizers have the same nutrients as quick-release products but are manufactured in a different way. These fertilizers have their nutrients locked in beads that slowly dissolve, releasing nutrients into the soil. Slow-release fertilizers can last for months, providing a steady supply of fertilizer to your lawn the whole time.

Combination fertilizers give your lawn the best of both quick- and slow-release action. These fertilizers have granules that dissolve fast mixed with beads that release their nutrients more slowly. Together they give your lawn what it needs now and what it will need for weeks to come, all from one application. Pretty easy, eh?

So how do you decide what to use? The box "Fertilizers 101" on the opposite page will help you choose.

A Shopping Word to the Wise

Now you're in the home stretch. Here are some other common fertilizer terms you should know.

Organic fertilizers, as their name implies, come from something that was once alive. They aren't made in a chemical lab. Top organic materials for lawns include manure, fish emulsion, and sewage sludge. They release nitrogen at a slow, easy pace and can be applied almost any time. They work terrifically with earthworms and healthy bacteria inside the soil. The only drawback is that the nitrogen release is sometimes unpredictable. Oh, and one other thing — the (phew!) smell. You may have to put a clothespin on your nose to apply organic fertilizer!

Synthetic fertilizers, as *their* name implies, are chemical creations. They're easier to apply, more readily available, and cheaper than organic fertilizers. And they also don't stink as much! With synthetics, you run the risk of burning grass in areas where too much of the fertilizer is applied to the lawn. Also, over time, they can damage the soil structure. Always wear gloves to protect your hands, and goggles and a mask to protect your face, and thoroughly wash your hands after using a synthetic fertilizer.

Fertilizers 101

Quick-Release Pros
- Rapid response
- Less expensive

Quick-Release Cons
- Only last a short time
- Can quickly leach through soil, especially sandy soil
- More likely to burn grass

Slow-Release Pros
- Provide a steady supply of nutrients for a long time
- Less prone to leaching through soil
- Less likely to burn grass

Slow-Release Cons
- Slower to show results
- Temperature and moisture affect rate of nutrient release
- More expensive

Combination Products Pros
- Work quickly
- One application lasts a long time
- Less likely to burn grass

Combination Products Con
- Can be expensive

Before You Start

No matter what type of fertilizer you choose to use, I want you to always hose down your lawn with a soap and water solution (1 cup of liquid dish soap in a 20 gallon hose-end sprayer) before *and* after you apply any type of fertilizer. This simple step does a number of things: It removes dust, dirt, and pollution from the grass blades; it helps the fertilizer adhere better, wherever it lands; and it slows down soil compaction, improves penetration, and helps to prevent burning your grass. Two more things to remember: Sweep up any spilled fertilizer and dispose of it properly, and never apply dry fertilizer during a hot spell.

Jerry Baker Says

"When it comes to using fertilizer, don't assume that more is better. Too much fertilizer can burn your grass. The trick is to apply just the right amount of fertilizer at the right times to keep your lawn growing its best."

A Good Diet Means Good Health

Did you know that the more you use the right amount of fertilizer, the less you will need to mow your lawn? You'd think that a healthy lawn would grow so fast that you'd be out there all the time mowing. But the truth is that healthy, well-fed lawns need less mowing than uncared-for lawns — and they look a whole lot better!

Problem Solver

Problem: My grass is burned in some spots.
Clues:
• When did you first notice the brown spots?
• Did spots appear just after you applied dry fertilizer?
• Are the spots in areas where you poured fertilizer into a spreader and spilled some on the lawn, or areas where you overlapped the fertilizer?
Solution: It's probably excess fertilizer. Most fertilizers contain salts that will burn grass if they're improperly applied. Never apply during a hot spell, and use my Baker's Dozen Rules on pages 34–35.

It's in the (Fertilizer) Bag

All fertilizer manufacturers are required by law to list all of the elements (and the amounts of them) that are in their bags of fertilizer. This is what they call "guaranteed analysis," and it's done in the form of three numbers on the bag. No, those are not the odds on your lawn living or dying (you bet your lawn and lose your grass!). The numbers designate the percentage of nitrogen, available phosphorus, and water-soluble potassium that's in the bag.

A Crash Course

Plop a bag of fertilizer in front of you and follow along as I give you a quick lesson on label reading. See where it says FERTILIZER GRADE?

Let's say your bag reads "10-6-4 grade fertilizer." That translates into 10 percent nitrogen (N), 6 percent available phosphorus (P), and 4 percent water-soluble potassium (K). Get it? All fertilizer companies always list these ingredients in the same order.

Example. Now, let's take that example a little further. A 40-pound bag of 10-6-4 fertilizer contains 4 pounds of nitrogen (10 percent of 40), 2.4 pounds of phosphorus (6 percent of 40), and 1.6 pounds of water-soluble potassium (4 percent of 40). Congratulations! Your high school math teacher would be so proud of you!

So how much of this 10-6-4 fertilizer should you buy for your lawn? You'll want to apply no more than 1 pound of nitrogen per 1,000 square feet at any one time. To figure how much to use, first determine how many square feet of lawn you have. "Go Figure" on page 30 shows you how.

How Big Is Your Lawn?

You might ask, Why should I want to know how many square feet of turf grass I have? Well, I'll tell you why. Knowing the square footage is vital when you're getting ready to buy bags of grass seed or fertilizer, trying to determine how much of my surefire tonics to put down, or planning an all-out assault on invading insects or diseases. You need to figure out how much material to use so that either you don't have to make several trips to the store, or you don't end up with a stockpile of products in the garage. Ditto if you want to replace your old lawn with a newer, healthier type of grass. Knowing the square footage will tell you exactly how much sod you need to buy.

Go Figure . . . Square Feet, That Is

No need to race to your computer or hire a team of MIT professors to figure out just how big your lawn is. Determining the square footage is a lot easier than you may think. You'll probably have several different areas and different shapes to measure — front and backyards, as well as side yards. I like to take separate measurements of each area, and then add them all up to get my total amount of lawn. If any buildings, walks or driveways, pools, or garden beds are in the middle of a lawn area, measure them and subtract them from the total.

Square and rectangular-shaped areas. Let's start with the easiest type of spaces to do calculations on. Take a tape measure (the longer the better — I like the 100-foot kind) and measure the length of the lawn area. Now measure the width. Multiply the length times the width, and voilà! You've got the square footage of that lawn area. To illustrate, let's say the length is 80 feet and the width is 60 feet. The equation: 80 × 60 = 4,800 square feet of lawn.

Square Feet for Odd-Shaped Lawns

Circular lawns areas. Take the radius (the distance halfway across the center, represented by the symbol *r*) and multiply that number by itself (r^2), and then multiply by *pi* (3.14). For a circular lawn that has a radius of 20 feet, the equation is: $(20 \times 20) \times 3.14 = 1,256$ square feet of lawn.

Triangular lawn areas. Measure the longest length of your yard and consider this the "height" of your triangle. Measure the length of the side of your lawn at right angles to the "height" and consider this the "base" of your triangle. Multiply the height times the length of the base and divide by 2. Here's a sample equation: 70 feet height $\times$ 40 feet base $= 2,800$ square feet. Divide by 2 and your final answer is 1,400 square feet.

Irregularly shaped lawn areas. Measure the distance across a wide area of lawn and call this your length line (L). Every 10 feet along this line, measure the width at a 90-degree angle to L. Now add all the widths and multiply by 10. You'll have your square footage, give or take 5 percent, and that's darn close. So let's try an equation. If your widths measure 30 feet, 28 feet, and 22 feet, the area is $(30 + 28 + 22) \times 10 = 800$ square feet of lawn.

The result. Once you know your lawn's square footage, divide that number by 1,000 to determine how many pounds of nitrogen you need. Finally, multiply the pounds of nitrogen by 10 to determine how much fertilizer to buy.

Let me illustrate: If you're using a 10-6-4 fertilizer on a 50-foot-by-100-foot lot, the formula is $50 \times 100 = 5,000$, divided by $1,000 = 5$, multiplied by (N) $10 = 50$ pounds of fertilizer.

A Phosphorus Boost, Please

Soils don't store phosphorus very well. That's why you need to fertilize regularly with a material that has a high percentage of phosphorus.

Making Sense Out of Percentages

A bag labeled 5-5-5 has equal amounts of nitrogen, phosphorus, and potassium. A product labeled 10-5-5 has twice as much nitrogen as phosphorus or potassium. A bag marked 20-5-5 has four times as much nitrogen.

But 5-5-5 and 10-10-10 fertilizers are not the same. True, their proportions are the same, but they provide different amounts of nutrients by weight. In the 5-5-5 case, 5 percent of the total weight of the bag is nitrogen (or phosphorus or potassium), while in the 10-10-10 case, the amount of each nutrient is 10 percent of the total weight of the bag. So, it takes a 20-pound bag of 5-5-5 fertilizer to deliver the same nutritional punch as a 10-pound bag of 10-10-10 fertilizer.

Live and Let Live

Like all of God's other creatures, earthworms deserve respect, too. These wiggling wonders loosen the soil and feed the grass with their castings. Grandma Putt used to call them "the poor man's fertilizer," and her motto was "live and let live"; the more, the merrier!

SELECTING THE PERFECT LAWN FERTILIZER

It's a good idea to test your soil every so often (see Chapter 13). Based on the results, use this handy guide to help you choose the right fertilizer for your lawn.

TYPE	WHEN TO USE
20-5-10	For regularly scheduled lawn care
5-20-10	When lawn tests low in phosphorus
5-10-10	When lawn is not regularly fertilized, or to prep seedbed for a new lawn
10-10-10	When lawn needs extra phosphorus and potassium
15-10-10	When lawn is regularly fertilized but still needs more phosphorus
15-8-12	When lawn is regularly fertilized but has too much phosphorus
20-10-5	When lawn needs a pick-me-up or has too little potassium

How to Spread the Chow

Fertilizers come in dry and liquid forms. The best way to apply dry, granular fertilizer is to use a broadcast spreader or a gravity drop spreader. I know these sound like something NASA would send to the moon, but let me assure you, you don't have to go that far! You can find both in your local lawn and garden store or mail-order catalogs. (For more about these tools, see pages 60–61).

Broadcast spreaders (also known as rotary spreaders) have the advantage of being able to cover a lot of ground in a short amount of time. But for speed, you sacrifice accuracy. The granular pellets are more prone to be carried away by the wind, so you don't get as uniform an application, and you can end up with splotchy areas, especially if you're applying a high-nitrogen fertilizer.

The gravity drop spreader doesn't work as fast as its centrifugal cousin, but it's more accurate. It's great for dishing out granular fertilizer, because you'll get a more even spread. Just be sure to overlap each preceding row as you apply it to be sure you've covered the entire lawn. If you don't overlap, you'll end up with a lawn that has alternating stripes of yellowish brown and emerald green — stripes are nice on neckties, but not on lawns!

Ends First!

Yes, the broadcast spreader sweeps across a wide berth — that's good! But less fertilizer reaches the ends of its range — that's bad. Try this trick: Apply half the fertilizer walking back and forth in one direction, then apply the rest walking at right angles to the first pass so you don't miss anything.

Hose Time

When it comes to liquid fertilizers, they are applied using a variety of hose-end, handheld, backpack, and even tank sprayers. The trick to applying liquid fertilizers is to pay very close attention to the label directions so that you don't drown your lawn or, conversely, *do* spray enough fertilizer on it.

My Baker's Dozen Rules
for Spraying Success

To clear up any confusion and make sure you're spraying right, just heed these 13 commonsense rules:

1. Select the right sprayer for the job. Spend the money up front and get the best sprayer you can afford. Also, make sure you buy one that gives you full control of the spray mix and application.

2. Read all directions before you spray. Give your new sprayer a test drive to see how well it performs.

3. Follow directions and mix your spray ingredients according to the instructions. You may enjoy improvising in the kitchen with your favorite dishes, but stick to the script when it comes to spraying ingredients on your lawn.

4. Select the right pressure. Use low pressure for heavy, wetting, nondrift spray (best for weed killing) and high pressure for a fine, penetrating mist (ideal for general use).

The Hose in the Know

One of the very best (and my favorite) lawn tools is the 20 gallon hose-end sprayer. Now, I know what you're thinking: How can I lug 20 gallons of heavy liquid tonic all around my front, back, and side yards? Well, the fact of the matter is . . . you don't have to. This sprayer's plastic container holds just 1 quart of liquid. It attaches to an ordinary garden hose with a mechanism that allows 20 gallons of water to flow through the container and to act as the carrier for whatever ingredients you place in the sprayer jar.

5. Spray only to the point of run-off. Never drench — you're just wasting valuable ingredients.

6. Spot spray only in trouble spots when tackling weeds. See Chapter 10 for more tips on weed control.

7. Use an adjustable nozzle. This produces a fine, cone-shaped mist for close-up applications. Or go with a coarser spray for long-range spraying.

8. Spray in the cool part of the day. The best time is before noon or after dinner.

9. Never spray on windy days. Mother Nature's breezes can cause your spray to drift off target.

10. Dress for the part. Wear gloves, a hat, and goggles as well as a long-sleeved cotton shirt and pants when you're spraying your yard.

11. Drain your sprayer completely when you're done, clean it with a solution of mild soap and warm water, and wipe it dry.

12. Store all sprays, dusts, and plant chemicals out of reach of children and pets.

13. Keep store-bought sprays in original containers with labels intact. Mark all homemade sprays with nail polish.

My Bags Are Sealed

I like to mix up all of the opened dry fertilizer I have on hand in October and give everything in my yard a last light feeding. If you can't do that, place the opened bags on boards or pallets to keep them off of the cold, concrete floor, because dampness can seep through and ruin the fertilizer. Or buy some plastic trash cans and seal the bags in them for the winter. That way, you can guarantee that those partially filled bags of fertilizer will survive the winter in your garage and be ready for spring.

Jerry's Year-Round Feeding Program

Remember that old saying, "You are what you eat"? Well, that same saying applies to your lawn as well as the plants, trees, and shrubs in your yard. And here's another saying to keep in mind: "Timing is everything."

In this section, I'm going to show you how to s-t-r-e-t-c-h the value of commercial fertilizers *and* save you some time, money, and effort with my easy-to-make tonics. Then I'll provide you with a foolproof feeding schedule so that your lawn is always well fed and never experiences either empty stomach rumblings or uncomfortable indigestion caused by overeating.

Spring Start: Step 1

Springtime is the right time to get your lawn off on the right root, and there's no better way to do it than to apply my Spring Wake-Up Tonic as early as possible, but no more than 2 weeks before your first dry feeding. Then follow up with a dose of my Get-Up-and-Grow Tonic. This will help aerate the lawn, while giving it something to munch on until you start your regular feeding program.

Next, at the start of each growing season (and remember that there are two growing seasons, one in the spring and the second one in the fall) you should feed your lawn with a dry fertilizer. To get the best results, here's what to do:

First thing in the spring, as soon as you feel like getting out in your yard, I want you to add 3 pounds of Epsom salts to a bag of your favorite slow-release, dry lawn food (enough for 2,500 square feet). (20-5-10 is fine.) Dump the Epsom salts into the bag, close it, and give it a few good Elvis-like shakes to really mix it up. Now apply half of this mixture at *half* the recommended rate with your spreader set on the medium setting. Move north to south in rows across your yard. Set the other half of this mixture aside — you're going to use it for Step 3.

Get-Up-and-Grow Tonic

To energize the Spring Wake-Up Tonic, overspray it with a mixture of:

1 cup of baby shampoo
1 cup of ammonia
1 cup of regular cola (not diet)
4 tbsp. of instant tea

Combine all of these in your 20 gallon hose-end sprayer and apply to the point of run-off.

Spring Wake-Up Tonic

Mix:

50 lbs. of lime (pelletized)
50 lbs. of gypsum (pelletized)
5 lbs. of bone meal
2 lbs. of Epsom salts

Combine all these ingredients in a wheelbarrow and apply the mixture with your handheld, broadcast-type spreader.

Applying Fertilizer

As a rule of "green thumb," always apply lawn fertilizer, both dry and liquid, early in the morning, before noon. This allows your grass to digest the food right away, before the hot afternoon sun can burn it and give it an upset tummy. And be sure to water the area the day before and then give it a light dousing after any application with my soapy water solution (see page 28).

Two Days Later: Step 2

Within 2 days of putting down the dry fertilizer/Epsom salts main meal, it's time to energize the meal with a snack for your lawn! Mix up a batch of my Snack Tonic and let 'er rip. The best time to apply it is early in the morning, any time before noon. Folks, if you follow Steps 1 and 2, your yard will be off and running for a great growth spurt during the summer. Just watch out, because your grass is liable to grow right up your pant leg!

Snack Tonic

My Snack Tonic gets your lawn up and growing in both the spring and fall when you need aggressive root action and thatch breakdown.

1 can of beer
1 cup of liquid dish soap

Put these ingredients in a 20 gallon hose-end sprayer jar and fill the balance of the sprayer jar with ammonia. Apply the Tonic to your lawn to the point of run-off. This amount of Tonic, like all of the others in this book, should cover 2,500 sq. ft. of lawn area.

One Week Later: Step 3

One week later, I want you to apply the other half of the Epsom salts/dry lawn food mix from Step 1, this time spreading it in rows going east to west. This guarantees that every inch of turf gets fed, and you won't have any embarrassing light green lines in your lawn that indicate your "misses." While you're at it, don't forget to spread some of this chow around your trees, shrubbery, and beds to give them the benefit of this extra early feeding as well. Because you've used slow-release fertilizer, your lawn will have something to munch on all season long.

Through the Summer: Step 4

Once you've completed this early season feeding, it's time to begin your lawn's regular light meals that will carry it through the rest of the growing season (until fall). The best meal for my money is my All-Season Green-Up Tonic. Nobody likes to eat big, heavy meals when the weather warms up, and the same goes for your grass, too. That's why this tonic works great year 'round, and best during the summer months. It provides a light, refreshing diet of food that sustains the growing plants without filling them up and slowing them down. Apply this tonic every 3 weeks right through the first hard frost, and your lawn will come through the hot summer months with flying colors! If you prefer not to make this tonic, then you can always substitute a good liquid lawn food or fish fertilizer in its place. Just remember to keep it "lite."

Fall Feeding: Step 5

Your final fall feeding should be a mirror of your first spring feeding. So once again mix 3 pounds of Epsom salts into a bag (enough for 2,500 square feet) of slow-release, dry lawn food, (use a 10-10-10 mix this time) and apply half of the mixture at half the recommended rate, moving north to south.

Two Days Later: Step 6

Now, once you've got your final dry feeding down, I'm going to share with you a little secret known among professional greenskeepers. You need to activate the dry food so that the plants can digest it better. So, within 2 days of applying your final dry lawn feeding, I want you to overspray your lawn with my Snack Tonic again. This will give your lawn something to digest immediately and help energize the dry food mixture.

All-Season Green-Up Tonic

Here's my world-famous recipe that'll keep your lawn growing great from early spring until fall:

1 can of beer
1 cup of ammonia
½ cup of liquid dish soap
½ cup of liquid lawn food
½ cup of clear corn syrup

Mix all the ingredients in a large bucket, pour into a 20 gallon hose-end sprayer, and spray everything in sight — your lawn, trees, shrubs, flowers, and even vegetables. Apply this tonic every 3 weeks throughout the growing season, and you'll end up with the most spectacular yard in town!

The Secret behind My Homemade Tonics

My Snack Tonic is a tried-and-true tonic that encourages healthy growth and greens up your grass in a flash. Here's the secret behind each ingredient:

- **Beer** acts as an enzyme activator to stimulate the health and growth of beneficial micro-organisms in the soil.

- **Liquid dish soap** cleans the blades of grass and softens the soil so plants can absorb nutrients through both their roots and foliage.

- **Ammonia** is what I call a thunderstorm in a bottle — it is an instant, digestible form of nitrogen to feed your grass plants.

A Strong Fall Finish

Congratulations! If you've fed your lawn at just the right times with just the right foods during the spring and summer, your yard should be gorgeous going into the fall. Steps 5 and 6 (pages 38–39) are the big fall finish! It's very important to give your lawn a substantial feeding before it hibernates for the winter. It gives it something to munch on during the late fall and provides a healthy supply of nutrients when it wakes up the following spring.

Hole in One

Here's a little trick I learned a long time ago: Always keep a white golf ball in your 20 gallon hose-end lawn sprayer. It acts as an agitator while you're spraying, keeping the ingredients thoroughly mixed up for even application. And while you're at it, put a red or orange golf ball in your weed sprayer; that way, you won't confuse the two. The weed sprayer, of course, contains strong chemicals that kill, so you want to make sure that you select the right sprayer for the right job. On a golf course, we duffers know how much a golf ball can aggravate us, but inside a sprayer, it's just par for the course!

LAWN QUIZ TIME!

How many pounds of actual nitrogen for every 1,000 square feet are needed per year to keep your northern lawn (like Kentucky bluegrass, for instance) healthy? Give up? The answer is 2 to 3 pounds. Southern lawns, especially those made of Bermuda grass, need twice as much.

Insider Tips for Different Regions

Here are some additional tips based on whether your lawn is made of warm-season or cool-season grasses.

• **Warm-season grasses** like St. Augustine and Bermuda do best when fed in late spring and again in early fall. If you apply fertilizer too early, you're likely to fill the bellies of weeds. But if you wait too long, your grass won't be fortified as well and will be more vulnerable to cold-weather damage.

• **Cool-season grasses** like tall fescue and Kentucky bluegrass need heavy feedings twice a year — in early spring and late fall. If you wait too long, the grass won't have anything to grow on, and you'll trigger a super growth spurt just as the hot weather hits.

Compost for Healthier Soil

The discarded grass clippings you've been adding to the compost pile in the backyard can be called into active duty once they've decomposed and become compost. This "black gold" is great for your lawn! (See page 332 for my Grass Clipping Compost Starter.)

Compost fortifies the soil, helps slow water evaporation, cools down soil temperatures, and suffocates weed seeds. Use compost when putting in a new lawn, patching bare spots, or even as a yearly top-dressing. For new lawns, work compost into the soil prior to seeding or sodding. Not sure what type of soil you have? Then it's time to take my soil test in Chapter 13.

COMPOST APPLICATION	
AMOUNT OF COMPOST (PER 1,000 SQ. FT.)	
Sandy soil	250 pounds
Loamy soil	400–600 pounds
Clay soil	1,200 pounds

Grandma Putt's Homemade Organic Fertilizer

Back in the good old days, Grandma Putt made her own lawn fertilizer. She'd mix up:

1 part dehydrated manure
1 part bonemeal
5 parts seaweed meal
3 parts granite dust

She'd combine all of the ingredients in a large, old wheelbarrow. Then she'd get out her spreader, apply it evenly over the turf, and stand back and watch the results. They were always outstanding! So if you get a hankering and you can find the ingredients, try it — you just might like it!

Ask Jerry

Q My neighbor sprayed his lawn with some kind of sudsy solution made from an antibacterial dish detergent instead of soap. Now his lawn has yellowish streaks all over it. What happened?

A This story contains two good lessons: Don't substitute detergent for soap, and, in particular, don't use antibacterial detergent. Here's why. Detergent is not the same thing as soap. Soap is made from fats and oils, while detergent is often made from synthetic materials that can damage the green portions of plants. On top of that, antibacterial detergents contain an added ingredient that is even more likely to damage plants than regular detergent. To get rid of the yellow, your neighbor should spray his lawn with my **All-Season Green-Up Tonic** (page 328), and the grass should recover quickly.

Q I've seen lawn seed mixtures that have white clover as an ingredient. I thought white clover was a weed, so what is it doing in a lawn seed mix?

A White clover is not a grass, but it is included in some grass seed mixes because it is a legume. Legumes can take nitrogen right from the air, and that means you need to put less fertilizer on the lawn. That's good. The down side of white clover is that it makes the lawn look untidy. That's bad. It all depends on what you want. If you don't mind an informal look for your lawn, white clover might be a good idea. If you like a smooth, beautiful lawn, stick to grass seed blends that are made of just grass seed. Whatever lawn seed blend you choose, remember to use my **Spot Seed Tonic** (page 337) to get the seeds off to a quick, strong start.

Q I grow a lot of different things, and I would like to attract more earthworms to my yard. Does the kind of fertilizer I use on my lawn make a difference to worms?

A Believe it or not, the type of fertilizer you use *can* make a big difference in whether worms find your lawn hospitable or not. If you use organic fertilizers, it's like hanging out the welcome sign for worms.

Q I know you say it's good to spread a thin layer of organic matter on the lawn every now and then. Normally I use screened compost, but a neighbor says I should try mushroom compost. Exactly what *is* mushroom compost and is it okay to use on the lawn?

A Mushroom compost is the stuff that mushrooms grow in on mushroom farms. It's made of lots of different things, like horse manure, straw, and even small amounts of gypsum and limestone. And your neighbor's right: Mushroom compost is *great* for your lawn. Just apply it as you would regular compost and watch your grass grow. By the way, mushroom compost will work even better if you spray my **All-Season Green-Up Tonic** (page 328) over the lawn right after applying the compost.

☆   ☆   ☆

Well, now you know all there is to know about fertilizers, lawn foods, and when and how to feed your lawn for glorious results. So let's move on to the next chapter, where I'll tell you how to be a savvy shopper for the tools you'll need to make lawn care as streamlined as possible.

CHAPTER 3

Welcome to Tool Time

Ever poke your head inside of the garage or shed of a neighbor whose lawn makes you green with envy? Chances are better than even that his or her place is loaded with a bunch of lawn-care goodies. I bet that they all are in good condition, too. Well, let's find out what you really need in the way of tools to keep that lawn of yours in tip-top shape.

Shop Around

Folks who have gorgeous green grass know how to buy and maintain just the right tools of the terrain. No need to be jealous. You, too, can create a stellar lawn without taking a big bite out of your wallet. Here are four simple ways to s-t-r-e-t-c-h the most out of your lawn-care dollar.

Jerry Baker Says

"Rome wasn't built in a day, and neither was your tool shed. Practice a little patience and take your time buying just what you really need."

No. 1: Best Buys

First of all, look around for the best buys at hardware stores, garden centers, and Internet e-tailers. The front and back ends of the growing season usually yield the best deals. In early spring, suppliers have the best selection and seem willing to answer questions and give advice about equipment. In late fall, suppliers want to reduce their inventories, so they are more willing to slash prices to get rid of stuff they don't want to carry through the winter. So, as always, timing is everything.

No. 2: Tag Sale Time

Second, don't forget about yard and garage sales. Many of my buddies have gotten some real deals by buying lawn tools from folks (especially us senior citizens) who are downsizing — moving out of homes with big yards into town houses or condominiums.

No. 3: Forget the Joneses

Third, don't think that bigger is necessarily better. This is no time to try to keep up with the Joneses! A hand tool may serve your needs just as well as a power tool, and save you a whole lot of money to boot! Remember, the more parts to a tool, the more maintenance it needs.

No. 4: Don't Be a Tool Fool!

Fourth, do some lawn-care homework. (Don't worry; there won't be a test or a term paper!) You, too, can be the sharpest tool in the shed! Talk with your friends and neighbors who have similarly sized lawns. Ask what tools work best for them and, more important, what tools are worthless or never used.

Take a tip and learn from their mistakes and experience, and you'll never be a "tool fool." You will become a savvy selector of essential lawn tools instead of neglected dust and dirt collectors.

Lawn Mowers 101

Let's start with the one must-have tool: the mighty lawn mower — unless, of course, you're planning on keeping a herd of grass-loving Holsteins in your backyard. Now, that would be a *moo-ving* experience of an *udderly* foolish kind! For a perfect mowing experience, forget about cows and focus on selecting the right mower to meet *your* individual needs.

Mowers, as you know, come in all shapes, sizes, and prices. You might say, the lawn's the limit. But basically, there are two main types: *reel* and *rotary*. Both have a number of spin-offs as well. Whichever type you decide on, you benefit from technology. Why, a century ago, those folks who didn't have cows or goats had to take on fast-growing grass with a handheld scythe. Even tiny lawns took hours to cut! Yes, mower, you've come a long way, baby!

Getting Down to Reality

So which lawn mower is right for you and your yard? Before you go shopping, ask yourself:

- Is my yard itty-bitty or LARGE?

- Is my yard flat, or hilly and steep?

- Is it wide open, or filled with trees, gardens, sprinkler heads, and play-ground equipment?

- Do I want to sweat off some calories, or do I want to get the job done pronto?

- What's my noise tolerance — do I like to listen to the birds or imagine I'm at the wheel of a roaring race car?

- Do I want to keep things simple, or do I like to tinker with the latest gadgets?

Super-Special Shopping Tips

Don't be wowed by a mower's physical appearance. Run through this checklist *before* you sign the check.

- ✔ Does the mower have a blade shut-off switch? In my book, that's a *must* safety feature. (New models have kill switches; if you have an old one, take care.)
- ✔ Can the mowing height be raised and lowered easily?
- ✔ Is it easy to start?
- ✔ Is it easy to push?
- ✔ Does it turn easily?
- ✔ Is it too heavy, too light, or just right?
- ✔ Is it a name brand that can be serviced locally?
- ✔ Is the catch bag a hassle to use?
- ✔ Is it easy to clean?
- ✔ Is it easy to disassemble to make minor repairs?

People Power

Remember that old push mower that your dear ol' dad or grand-dad shoved around the yard? The only hum you heard came from his trying to remember the words to a favorite song. The mower acted more like a mime — doing its task steady and slow at a near-silent clip.

That two-wheeled, push-type mower, powered by people, not gasoline or electricity, is the most familiar type of reel mower.

In the world of reel mowers, this is its creed: *Simple is best.* And it's the cheapest, costing between $100 and $250.

This type of mower is the perfect choice for anyone seeking a healthy workout. Reel mowers are ideal for lawns of 1,000 square feet or less (unless you really want to spend the entire day mowing) that are dip- and bump-free. You see, the reel spins slowly, so it's no match for small mounds or hills, and with only two wheels, it can fall prey to dips and holes. Either one can spell D-I-S-A-S-T-E-R!

The Reel Deal

Reel mowers feature five or more curved blades that cut grass in a spinning, scissorlike motion. The blades chew up and spit out grass blades to both the front and rear. The cut is clean, leaving your lawn with a neat, well-manicured look.

Win the Weight Game

Who needs to pay a hefty membership fee when you have the best gym in the world in your own backyard? What am I talking about? Cutting grass with a push-type rotary mower burns 400 calories per hour! That figure is based on a 150-pound person, so it could be higher or lower, depending upon where you tip the scales.

Mowing offers a better workout than trimming hedges, raking leaves, stacking firewood, or even washing and waxing your car! And other than scrubbing floors, mowing beats all other indoor chores such as ironing, making beds, washing dishes, and vacuuming — hands down!

Motorized Reels

Now, mowing — er, moving — right along, you come to the second type of reel mowers: the motorized ones. They are less common than the push type, but they do exist. They're light, typically electric, and start pronto! With these mowers, you don't have to worry about oil changes, keeping a steady supply of gasoline in the shed or garage, or a lot of engine maintenance.

Expect a price tag starting at $500.

Of course, there are downsides to electric reel mowers. First off, you have to fiddle with a snakelike power cord as you march up and down your yard, and hope you don't accidentally run over it and cut it. Goodbye, power! Electric reel mowers also rarely deliver more than 3 horsepower, so they're easily outmuscled when you're attempting to cut thick or slightly damp grass.

The Softies

Whether you choose a push or an electric reel mower, keep in mind that each provides the best haircut on soft grasses, which include Kentucky bluegrass, ryegrass, and fescues. But reel mowers are no match for tough-bladed grasses, like St. Augustine and gramma grasses, or tall lawns. Read all about the different grass types in Chapter 15.

Gang Warfare

Professional lawn-care folks use gas-powered reel mowers — usually with a three-reel gang mower. You might consider one of these if you have a large lawn and you want it to look professionally maintained.

Join the Rotary Club

If the reel mower ain't your deal, relax — you've got plenty of company. Truth be told, the rotary type is the top seller around. Most of your neighbors have this kind.

So how do you know if it's a rotary? Simple. Just take a look underneath at its belly (when it's completely turned off and has cooled, of course), and you'll see a long, horizontal blade that spins in a circle, like a fan blade. For the Einsteins among you, the principle is this: It spins fast enough to create a slight vacuum, lifting the grass for a split second before cutting it.

The Family Tree

Now, just as with your family and mine, there are many "personalities" within the rotary mower family. There are ones with gas or electric motors. There are self-propelled and mulching mowers, and there are self-propelled mulchers as well. Then there is the grande dame of rotaries: the riding mower.

Generally speaking, rotary machines are simple to maneuver, easy to maintain, and able to chew up even tough grass blades and wicked weeds in hilly terrain. In other words, rotary mowers just love a good challenge!

On the downside, rotary mowers lack the buzz-cut precision of a reel mower and can be guilty of scalping an uneven or bumpy lawn even if you're careful. So they're not perfect.

Susie
Jane
John
Liz
Grandma
Tommy
Bob

Weighty Advice

Want to wager a guess as to how many pounds of grass clippings the average half-acre lawn produces in a single season? Give up? The answer is 5,500 pounds! That's why a mulching mower has become such an environmentally friendly alternative.

The Lowdown on Mowers

Each type of rotary mower has its own pros and cons. Here's a quick rundown:

Electric. This pollution-free grass gobbler is a friend of the environment and lets you listen to nature while you clip along. But you must wrestle with a long cord or remember to recharge its batteries.

Gas-powered. You want plenty of power at a reasonable price? Say somewhere between $200 and $400? Then this is your pick. For the normal-size lawn with few or no challenges, a 3.5-horsepower mower will do the job. But you must contend with smelly gas fumes, remember to change the oil, and accept its constant roar (and ringing in your ears).

Self-propelled (both electric and gas powered). This type provides easy maneuverability because the pulleys and gears connect the engine to the front or rear wheels. It's ideal if you have a lot of corners, tight spots, or hilly areas that will leave you huffing and puffing if you use a push mower. But the ballpark price: between $400 and $700.

Support the BBC

I'm talking about the latest safety feature, called Blade-Brake-Clutch, not Queen Elizabeth's favorite television network. When you pull the clutch, it starts the blade spinning. As soon as you release it, the blade stops, but the engine keeps going. This allows you to bend over and pick up large sticks, rocks, or trash in your yard without completely shutting off the engine. How many times have you stopped the mower only to have it act like a stubborn mule and refuse to restart? The BBC eliminates that hassle!

Mulching. The mulching mower's cutting blade is designed to trap the cut grass blades inside the deck longer, so they get diced into tiny pieces. These itty-bitty bits of grass drop to the lawn and quickly decay. You benefit by not having to put down as much fertilizer, bag large clippings, or add to the local landfill. As an added bonus, mulching mowers grind up fallen leaves to save you the back-aching chore of raking each fall.

But mulchers cost nearly twice as much as gas-powered rotary mowers and can choke on long, thick grass. You also need to mow more often and more slowly.

Riding. Sit up high and mow down an acre or more in no time at all without working up a real sweat. The engine is typically in the rear, with the deck slung beneath the mower between the front and back wheels. Decks range from 30 to 48 inches in width, and engines range from 8 to 18 horsepower. But these babies don't come cheap (between $1,000 and $5,000), and they require much more maintenance to keep them in tip-top shape.

Garden tractor. Bring the farm to your lawn with this beauty. These heavy-duty workhorses feature 10-gauge steel frames and cast-iron front and rear axles. Not only are they designed to cut up to 60 inches of grass at a time with up to 20 horsepower, but they also can accommodate attachments such as rototillers, snowblades, snowblowers, chippers, and other lawn-care equipment to be true multi-taskers. But you pay a steep price for all these options: up to $10,000.

Jerry Baker Says

"Riding mowers are great, but beware! Riding mowers are not inclined to tackle steep inclines — they can tip over, and you just might be on them!"

Jerry's Top 12 Tips for Pampering Your Lawn Mower

No lawn is a deserted island, but it can feel that way at times — especially when you're about halfway through and your mower conks out. No need to feel *lawn-ly*. Being left with a half-manicured lawn is about as much fun as eating a half-baked potato. But if you practice these 12 tips, I guarantee you'll breeze through mowing your lawn without a single hitch.

1. **Don't be a gas hoarder.** Never store more than a month's worth of gas in your garage or shed. Gas older than that is prone to having water in it from condensation. This will gum up a carburetor when the volatile components in it evaporate. If this happens, the gas turns into something with the consistency of varnish.

2. **Let it breathe clean air.** Keep a close eye on your air filter and replace it when it gets dirty. Dirty filters won't be able to prevent dirt from sneaking into the engine, wearing down vital parts, and making starting a real hassle.

3. **Give the blades plenty of elbow room.** Before you start any mower, look underneath it. Clear the blades of any built-up grass or other debris. This way, you guarantee that the blade will rotate easily and cut your lawn cleanly.

4. **Plug in.** For cordless electric mowers using batteries, remember to charge them overnight after each cutting. For you northern folks who have snow on your lawn during the winter, to keep the battery from losing power, charge it overnight one last time, then disconnect it until you decide your lawn needs its first haircut in the spring.

5. **Remember the oil.** Depending on how much lawn you have and how often you cut it, change the oil at least once a season. I always do it on July 4th. And check the oil level each time you get ready to mow. Too little oil can put a death grip on your engine — a costly fate for you!

6. Keep the cooling fans clean.

7. Check the belt condition and tension each time before you mow.

8. Sharpen the blade every third mowing. Keep at least two blades handy and razor sharp with a grinding wheel or file. Also, keep them perfectly balanced by driving a long nail into your garage wall and using it as your "balance beam" to sharpen mower blades. (For tips on how to sharpen your mower blades, see page 78.)

9. Wipe down all the rubber and plastic parts with Armorall once a month to keep them from drying out, cracking, and disintegrating.

10. Wipe down all chrome and metal parts with WD-40 every few weeks. This dandy product will keep them from rusting and sticking.

11. Check all safety controls before each use.

12. Think winter, not spring. At the end of the cutting season, be sure to follow my "End-of-the-Season" maintenance chores described on page 66.

Jerry Baker Says

"Before you mow, take a stroll out over your lawn and pick up any and all debris. Even a small twig can put a choke hold on the reel blades if you're not careful."

DID YOU CATCH THAT?

When I feel the need to bag the clippings, my top choice is a rear-bagging mower. Why? Because rear bags can hold more clippings than side bags, and they allow the mower to trim closely in whichever direction you're mowing. I've also found that the clippings don't block the discharge chute. Even more important, you don't have to worry about accidentally smacking the bag, as you do with a side bag, into trees, walls, and other obstacles. The advantage of side bags? They tend to be lighter and less expensive, too.

Beyond Mowers

Congratulations! You've got yourself a mower. Now what? To give your yard a truly manicured look, you're going to need some other tools to complete the chore. Otherwise, your lawn will look like a shaggy dog. Appearances aside, lawn tools beyond the mighty mower are necessary to keep weeds from running rampant, grass from turning brown, sidewalks from cracking, holes in the ground from upending your mower, and leaves from killing your grass. Let me explain.

Rakes: Leaf Gatherers

So how do you rate a rake? There are three basic garden-variety types: bamboo rakes, metal leaf rakes, and steel garden rakes. Bamboo and metal leaf rakes feature pliable teeth that grip and gather leaves and grass clippings from your lawn. They have a wooden or fiberglass handle. These rakes are also called fan rakes because of the arrangement of the teeth. They really rake in the lawn loot!

Steel garden rakes have long, skinny, wooden handles and immobile steel teeth. As you may have guessed, steel garden rakes are best suited for smoothing soil, weeding, spreading compost, and covering seeds. They're definitely not the choice to sweep up fallen leaves! When shopping for this kind of rake, take the time to count the number of slightly curved teeth. The best buys are those that have between 14 and 18 teeth — a full set of garden choppers!

TOOLS OF THE TERRAIN

No lawn job is complete without the aid of these tools:
- Rakes
- Spades
- Edger
- Trimmers and clippers
- Wheelbarrow and/or cart
- Hose-end sprayers
- Drop or broadcast spreader
- Aerator
- Lawn blower

Putting Some Teeth into It

Whoa! Don't discard that old steel garden rake. The metal-teeth part makes a nifty rack on the garage or shed wall to hold small garden tools such as hand spades, hand clippers, and trowels. Just drill some holes into a garage wall and use nails or hooks to hold the metal rake teeth in place. Have the teeth facing out to use as holders for your small tools. A word of caution, though: Put the rack above head level; it's not much fun walking into one of those teeth!

Spades: Calling a Spade a Spade

If you've been dealt hard soil or need to loosen up some sod that's in the wrong spot, the long-handled spade is an ideal ally. A spade features a flat, squared-off blade that's sharper than a shovel. It's especially useful when you need to dig into compacted soil.

And don't forget its cousin, the spading fork. This tool comes in handy when you need to break stubborn clods of soil or sod and when you want to spread compost or manure on your yard or garden.

Edger: The Border Patroller

An edger adds that finishing touch to lawns. Sidewalks and driveways look their Sunday best when you follow up with an edger after mowing the lawn.

Whether you use a hand-held edger (it looks like a shovel with a thin, flat head) or a motorized (gas or electric) one, you can keep weeds and grass from spilling over into your nongrass surfaces. Hand edgers are lightweight and easy to use, plus, they're terrific calorie burners! Power edgers are heavy and can be cumbersome, but they save you time. Motorized edgers are expensive and usually not needed if you have a string trimmer.

Trimmers: The Lawn Manicurists

String trimmer. Got a patch of tall grass surrounding your favorite oak tree? Unable to maneuver your mower close enough to the border of your flower garden or sprinkler heads? Time to reach for a string trimmer. Trimmers make mincemeat out of unruly grassy corners and spots that are out of reach of your mower. They can be gas powered or you can get an electric one.

Gas models aren't guzzlers, but they are the noisiest of the bunch. They are also the most powerful and fastest of the trimmer clan, and the most portable. You can go from here to there, hither to thither, with no problem. Gas trimmers, however, cost the most and require the most maintenance.

Electric trimmers are lighter and quieter — and cheaper — than gas trimmers. The cord types allow you to roam up to 100 feet. The types that require their batteries to be recharged usually last for up to 45 minutes.

Jerry Baker Says

"Always keep a spare reel of trimmer cord on hand. It will save you an unscheduled trip to the store when you are in the middle of yard duty and your trimmer runs out. Guess what made me learn to do that?!"

HOW STRING TRIMMERS WORK

Most trimmers feature a spool of rotating nylon cord or nylon blades that work exceptionally fast to bring tall grass and weeds under control. The nylon cord gets worn down quickly by the job of having to cut all that greenery, so the cord has to be periodically lengthened, either by hand (you, that is) or automatically.

Personally, I like a trimmer with an automatic or semiautomatic feed system for the nylon whip. It saves time over (and is a whole lot safer than) the cheaper models on which you must tug the cutting line by hand every time it wears down.

Hand Clippers

Good old-fashioned hand clippers, with their scissorlike action, will also do the job of snipping shaggy grass down to size. It just takes longer, and if you've got a lot of edges to keep trimmed, your hands can get mighty stiff. But hand clippers are quiet and relatively inexpensive, and because they're slower, you have more control: You're much less likely to snip off that prize perennial that's a little too close to the garden edge. Just be sure to keep your clippers sharp and well oiled, and they'll work much better for you.

The Eyes Have It

Always, always, always wear safety glasses whenever you use a string trimmer.

And put on some jeans to protect your shins from rocks and other flying debris spat out from underneath a trimmer.

Staying within the Lines

Some trimmers have a pivot head that turns them into an edger. Other trimmers can do edging by turning the cutting strings vertically, instead of the usual horizontal. You can make use of these features when you want to make a perfectly neat edge along your flower beds, walkways, and driveways. Just remember what your elementary school teacher taught you about staying within the borders when drawing with crayons. This same principle works just fine when you use an edger to create those neat, confined borders.

Boot 'em Out!

Trimmers were created to help homeowners boot out unwanted grass or weeds in hard-to-reach places. It's my guess that they were invented by someone who was tired of an aching back. Who wants to constantly bend over and yank weeds by hand? Or, just as bad, use hand clippers to get rid of that grass on the edge of flower beds!

COLOR CRAYONS

Hose-End Sprayers: At Your Service

When it's chow time for your lawn, as I mentioned in Chapter 2, you'll need a tool that can handle the job quickly and evenly. Hose-end sprayers are the ideal choice for liquid applications. I use a 20 gallon hose-end sprayer for most lawn jobs, a 6 gallon model for bug control, and a 10 gallon version for weed applications. With these sprayers, you mix your solution in a quart jar that attaches to the sprayer head, which in turn attaches to your garden hose. The water then flows through the sprayer head, siphoning up the contents in the jar and carrying them out over the lawn at a set rate. Check the directions for the sprayer and the fertilizer container and make sure you apply it at the correct rate. Be sure to give the sprayer a thorough cleaning and let it dry completely before you store it away after use. For my tips on Spraying Success, see pages 34–35.

For my tips on Spraying Success, see pages 34–35.

Please, Just Stay Calm

Broadcast spreaders work best on calm, windless days, for obvious reasons. So hold off fertilizing on those days when you feel like you're walking down the wild streets of the Windy City.

Broadcast and Drop Spreaders

To apply dry fertilizer, lime, sulfur, herbicides, and other pelletized or granular lawn products, you have two applicator choices: drop spreaders and broadcast spreaders. Both types feature adjustable settings that match the application rates typically found on the back of fertilizer bags. Here's the lowdown on each one.

Broadcast spreader. Now air this! Some broadcast spreaders are handheld, while others are wheeled. They're also known as rotary spreaders in some parts of the country. Easy to operate, this type of spreader features a bucketlike container on top and a spinning wheel underneath. It works by spitting out the fertilizer over a wide area using a whirling wheel. It's great for large lawns because it can spread the fertilizer in up to a 6-foot-wide swath in one pass. Pay attention to its width so you will know how close to space your passes.

A broadcast spreader is fast but not as accurate as a drop spreader. (For more information about using broadcast spreaders with fertilizers, see page 33.)

Drop spreader. Just as its name implies, this type of spreader drops fertilizer from small, adjustable holes at the bottom of the bin. When you use this spreader, the fertilizer sifts out from the bottom in a neat, orderly fashion. Since it's so accurate, it's a better bet for herbicide applications because you'll be able to stay clear of trees, shrubs, and vegetable gardens more easily than if you use a broadcast spreader. Gravity drop spreaders also work with ground limestone.

I find that drop spreaders work best on medium and small lawns because they cover about a 2-foot swath. The key to success is to overlap your passes just enough that no strips of lawn are left underfed. Here's a tip: Overlap the wheel tracks so you are assured of applying fertilizer on the entire lawn.

Jerry Baker Says

"Know how great it feels to inhale a deep breath of fresh air on a cool, crisp, autumn morning? Well, believe it or not, your lawn likes to inhale a little fresh air, too."

Aerators: To Aer Is Divine

Air and water have a tough time reaching the grass roots. Rather than tilling up the turf, you can create some needed air pockets with an aerator.

Now, if you happen to have a Ponderosa of a yard, consider renting or buying an engine-powered aerator from your local lawn or garden store. This type looks a whole lot like a lawn mower, only you'll be poking holes, not clipping grass, with it. Or, better yet, put on your golf shoes or a pair of my aerating lawn sandals. As I told you back in Chapter 1, these "spiked soles" will keep your lawn on par with the best of the bunch!

Lawn Blowers:
Make Yard Work a Breeze

I used to think that a lawn blower looked like the long nose of an elephant. All that was missing was the trunk — and some unshelled peanuts! Lawn blowers are noisy machines that put out a steady blast of air to clear your sidewalk and driveway of grass clippings and leaves; they're also fairly expensive. I don't own a lawn blower because I like to keep my pavement clean with a broom. It works a whole lot quieter and easier, it's bargain priced, and my neighbors aren't mad at me for blowing my leaves into their yards!

Tool-Care Secrets Revealed

You can stretch the life span of many lawn tools simply by practicing what I call *TLC: Tool Loving Care*. Now, I'm not talking about sending your rake a birthday card or buying a cake for your lawn mower. The best way to show that you really care is by practicing proper storage habits and providing regular maintenance.

TLC

Mother Nature's Wrath

I'm sure all of us are reminded of a time or two when we found our favorite hand shears or clippers out in the backyard, rusted after a few days of rain. Every tool deserves to have its own place in your shed or garage, far from the ravages of Mother Nature. Prolonged exposure to the elements rusts metal parts and dulls the edges of cutting tools, spades, rakes, and hoes. Tools die an early death, and your wallet takes a wallop when you replace them.

Right Side Up

I've found that the best way to store tools with long handles is to hang them upright on wall racks. For the bigger pieces of equipment like lawn mowers, wheelbarrows, and carts, you'll have to reserve spaces against the wall. Keep their wheels in place with cleats on the floor and their handles upright with hooks attached to the wall.

Bath Time for Tools

Know how good you feel after a thorough soaking in the bath or shower? Well, your lawn tools deserve good hygiene, too. Now, I'm not suggesting that you share your bathtub with a shovel or clipper. But before you get ready to scrub yourself, you've got to take time to really clean your tools to s-t-r-e-t-c-h their life span.

Here's the best method I've found: Keep a box of old rags in the garage or shed, and wipe away any moist soil that's clinging to the metal parts of your lawn tools. This is a whole lot easier to do while the soil is still fresh, rather than when it has dried and hardened. Remember, dirty tools fall prey to rust. After wiping off the dirt, use a lightly oiled rag to dry your tools thoroughly after each use.

A Handy Sandy Trick

Here's a little secret of mine: Save a quart of used motor oil the next time you change the oil in your car, and mix it into a 5-gallon bucket filled with sand. Then plunge your dirty tools up and down in the sand a couple of times after using them. You'll clean and oil your tools all in one fell swoop.

Sharp Advice

You always want your spades, hoes, scythes, weeders, and sickles to keep their edge. Sharp blades shoulder more of the workload than do dull ones, so use files, grindstones, or other sharpening devices at regular intervals during the lawn season.

Sharpen edges by following the angle of the edge and smoothing out the rough spots. If you don't feel confident enough to do this yourself, it's money well spent to have a professional do the job for you. Then to keep them sharp, slit old pieces of worn-out garden hose and slide them over the sharp edges. They'll protect both you and the blade.

Spoil 'em with Oil

Halfway through the mowing season, treat your mower and other lawn machinery to a little lubrication. Oil keeps a machine humming along. Lack of oil causes a machine to wear out way before its time.

Hibernation Time

Just because winter's on the way doesn't mean that you can stash your lawn-care tools away and forget about them. If you treat 'em right when you put them away in the fall, they'll be all ready to go once spring rolls around again.

PUT A LITTLE SHINE ON YOUR TOOLS

Here's another use for that old oil from your car: At the end of the season, let your tools sleep through the winter by thoroughly cleaning them with kerosene to remove caked dirt, dirty oil, and grease. Then swab them with an oily rag before storing them away till spring.

Finish in Style

Before winter hits, act like an inspector general and line up all of your tools. No need to march or salute! Examine each and every one closely, looking for worn or broken parts. If you're the handy type, sharpen, repair, repaint, and restore each to its proper condition. Or if you're all thumbs when it comes to mechanical tasks, have your local lawn-care professional do the deed, especially on your mower. By getting your tools shipshape at the end of the season, they will be fit as a fiddle come spring.

Be a Scrooge

As cold weather approaches, become a bit stingy on the gas if you've got a gas-powered mower. What I mean is, don't fill the tank completely if you've got only a little bit left to cut. Your goal is to drain the tank as completely as possible on your final cut of the season. After all, you don't want to have to drain a full tank — waste not, want not!

Plan Ahead

Winter is the ideal time to tune up your lawn mower — or have it done at your trusted service center. Believe you me, it's worth the investment. Have the blades sharpened, gas tank drained, working parts lubricated, filters replaced, spark plugs cleaned or replaced, and oil replaced. If you wait until the snow melts in spring, you may find that a varnishlike film has formed on the carburetor (from the old gas left behind in it), your blades are rusty, and your spark plugs have lost their spark. This is not the time to procrastinate: Come spring, everybody and his brother will be bombarding the centers with mowers in need of service. You don't want to be put on a waiting list while your grass keeps growing and growing and growing.

End-of-the-Season Checklist

By following some simple maintenance steps, you'll have a mower that will be ready and revving to go come spring!

1. Before you store your mower, empty the gas tank. Over time, old gas turns into a varnish-like film that can cause serious problems for the mower's carburetor.

2. Drain and replace the engine oil.

3. Remove the spark plug and squirt about 15 drops of lubricating oil in the hole. Then crank the engine a few times to spread this oil all over the inside of the engine.

4. Check the spark plug. Clean and regap it if it's in good condition; replace it if it's old.

5. Sharpen the blade. First smooth out jagged spots, then sharpen with the angle of the edge.

6. Dip an old rag in oil. Rub the oily rag all over the blade to prevent rust from starting. Spread some oil on all exposed metal parts. Finish by greasing all moving parts.

7. Tuck that mower into your garage or shed. Let it hibernate in peace until next spring.

Ask Jerry

Q I have a bet going with my neighbor that I'd like you to settle. I use a mulching mower partly because I've heard that the mulched clippings help fertilize the lawn. He says I'm nuts and that the clippings don't have enough nutrients to do the lawn any good. Who's right?

A You win. Mulching mowers are a great invention to a point, because they drop the chopped up clippings right down to the soil level where microorganisms help them decompose — fast. A typical grass clipping contains about 4 percent nitrogen, 1 percent phosphorus, and 3 percent potassium. That's about the same as many organic fertilizers. And here's another tip. Every time you mow, remember to spray the lawn with my **Grass Clipping Dissolving Tonic** (page 332). It will help those clippings turn into valuable fertilizer even faster.

Q I just moved into a house that has a very small, hybrid Bermuda grass lawn. I thought I'd get a reel-type push mower to cut it rather than a big, noisy, rotary one. When I went to the store, I was confused — some of the mowers had more cutting blades on the reel than others. How do I choose?

A Reel-type mowers have different numbers of blades on the reel for a good reason. The shorter you cut your lawn, the more blades you need to cut it cleanly. When you have a hybrid Bermuda grass lawn, you're going to want to cut the grass shorter than most other grasses — and also more frequently. So buy the mower with the greater number of cutting blades on the reel. Be sure to keep the blades sharp. Rake up the clippings after each mowing, add them to the compost pile, and spray them with a dose of my **Grass Clipping Compost Starter** (page 332).

Q A day or two after I mow my lawn, the grass doesn't seem as green as it was before I mowed. It has a tan cast to it. Am I doing something wrong?

A It sounds like your mower blades are dull. Here's what happens when you don't cut with a nice sharp blade. When a blade of grass is cut, the cut edge turns a light brown as it heals. A sharp blade cuts the tops off of each grass blade, leaving only a thin, tan line along the edge. A dull blade tears the grass, leaving ragged edges and a big wounded area that turns brown. The difference between a lawn cut with a sharp blade and a dull one is striking. A few days after mowing, the lawn cut with a sharp blade is still green, while the one cut with a dull blade is brownish green.

Get in the habit of sharpening your mower blades every third or fourth mowing. And for even more insurance that your grass will stay green and gorgeous, be sure to spray it with my **Kick-in-the-Grass Tonic** (page 333) after each mowing.

Congratulations! You've just graduated from the Jerry Baker School of Lawn Tools. You now know how to tell the difference between a reel mower and an "unreel" (rotary) one. You can impress your friends by explaining the pros and cons of drop vs. broadcast spreaders. And you know how to save yourself a whole lot of money and aggravation by keeping your tools in great shape all year long. Remember, in all aspects of life — including lawn care — knowledge is power. And with the knowledge you've gained in this chapter, you're now ready to tackle that lawn.

CHAPTER 4

Mowing Magic

Lawn care — most folks hate the work but love the results. Well, everything worth doing requires some effort, and lawns are no exception. By practicing proper mowing habits, you will make your lawn more resistant to pests and diseases, plus you can turn your less-than-perfect dog patch into a lush, velvety green carpet. You just have to follow a few simple guidelines and use a little common sense, so that when problems arise, you can get rid of them in a snap!

Premowing Ritual

Haste makes waste, so never be in a hurry when you cut the grass. Think like a tortoise, not a hare. A rushed maneuver or a trip to daydream land can result in serious injury. Always pace yourself and pay attention to the task at hand. Remember, you're using mighty sharp tools that can do a lot of damage.

Take a Hike

No need to don your hiking shoes and a backpack. I just want you to spend a few minutes walking through your front and backyards, and do it s-l-o-w-l-y, scouting potential hazards.

- **Keep your eyes peeled for sticks, stones, and other items** that could be thrown by the mower blades and injure the mower or anyone within range of the whirling blades.

- **Check the mower for signs of trouble** — loose screws, loose nuts and bolts, and so on — and tighten them up.

- **Bring along a little bag with you to collect litter.** No lawn should look like the aftermath of a New Year's Eve party, with paper scattered about, shredded like confetti.

- **Toss small sticks and stones onto the walk or driveway,** far away from your mower's path.

- **Make sure mulch chips and wood** are where they belong, not in the path of your mower.

- **Look out for anthills**, especially those fire ant mounds. Agitated by being booted out of their cozy homes, they retaliate by swarming and biting your feet, ankles, and legs.

Sun Safety

The perfect time to mow is in the early evening, when things have cooled down and you don't have to worry about the sun's hot rays beating down upon both you and the newly cut blades of grass. You won't get as tired, and the grass will recover from the shock of cutting much faster than if you mow in the middle of the day. If you've got to mow in the middle of the day, be prepared! Even if the sky is overcast, be sure to put on sunblock. Mr. Sun can still burn you from behind the clouds. Read the label and go with sunscreens that protect against UVA and UVB rays.

Your Lawn Wardrobe

Don a hat and sunglasses. Even during the dog days of summer, wear a long-sleeved cotton shirt and pants, not a tank top and shorts. Cotton's a great fabric — it "breathes," and that's important because it keeps your skin from overheating. The long sleeves and long pants give you an added layer of protection from mean Mr. Sun.

Jerry Baker Says

"I've had friends who shrugged off a mowing preinspection of their yard, only to pay dearly later to have their damaged mowers repaired. And I've seen folks who didn't 'have time' to do a walk-through get clobbered in the shin by a flying rock or stick that was hurled out from under the mower's deck. In a word — ouch!"

How Dry Am I?

While you're out in the yard, make sure that you drink lots of water. Keep a water bottle (with a cap, to keep out thirsty insects) on the front stoop or back porch, and take breaks to visit it regularly. Heat exhaustion can sneak up on you if you're not careful about the sun's effects, and before you know it, you'll be down and out.

For Your Good Health

Hot, sunny weather is good for plants, but it isn't always good for us gardeners. Heat rashes, sunburns, heat exhaustion, and heat stroke can hit before you know it if you're not careful. So it's very important to know the signs of heat exhaustion and heat stroke. If you experience these symptoms, get medical attention . . . ASAP!

Symptoms of Heat Exhaustion

- Cool, pale, clammy skin
- Profuse sweating
- Dry mouth
- Headache/dizziness
- Muscle cramps
- Weak and rapid pulse
- Nausea/vomiting

At the first sign of any trouble, get out of the sun immediately, or your body temperature will continue to rise. Call your doctor as soon as you can.

Symptoms of Heat Stroke

- Very high temperature (104°F or higher)
- Dilated pupils
- Hot, dry, red skin
- Convulsions
- Confusion/delirium/hallucinations
- Loss of consciousness

Heat stroke can be life threatening, so get emergency medical care immediately. Medical conditions like diabetes, as well as vomiting or diarrhea, can put you at an even greater risk of developing heat stroke.

A Horsey Remedy

If someone faints due to heat exhaustion and you happen to have some horseradish handy, crush a small piece of it under the person's nose — it's a powerful eye-opener.

Keep Cool

Here are some tips to keep you cool and comfy while you're out working in the yard:

- **Stay out of the midday heat** as much as possible. Your outdoor chores will be much more enjoyable if they're done in the mornings and evenings.

- **Drink lots of fluids**, and don't wait 'til you're thirsty. Your body needs water before that. If you sweat a lot, add ½ teaspoon of salt to 1 quart of water, and drink this instead of regular water. It'll quickly replace the fluids you lost from all of that hard work. Fluid loss leads to heat exhaustion and heat stroke, so drinking lots of water is extra-important!

- **Keep yourself and others around you cool** by misting all exposed areas on the face, arms, neck, and legs with my Chillin' Out Brew.

Chillin' Out Brew

A few spritzes of this brew and you'll feel as cool as a cucumber!

2 tsp. of witch hazel tincture
12 drops of lavender essential oil
10 drops of peppermint essential oil

Mix all of these ingredients with enough water to fill an 8-ounce spray bottle, and then spray away.

Protect Those Toes!

A final caution: Never, ever mow in your bare feet. Wear golf shoes and let the little spikes aerate the soil as you work. Keep your shoes stored near your front door so you won't have to waste time hunting for them. You won't have to do any "sole" searching if you follow this advice!

The Art of Mowing

Now, I've been mowing for decades, so I regard it more as a manicure for the lawn. What you're doing, in essence, is forcing grass plants that would naturally grow much taller to survive at a shorter height.

Soften It Up

Hate cornering? No problem. I have a solution: Alter your lawn's geometric design. Redesign your yard with soft, circular sides by placing garden beds and shrubs in such a way that you'll never have to duel with a sharp edge again.

Jerry Baker's Special Mowing Techniques

Vary your route. Don't get yourself into a rut by mowing the grass the same way week in and week out. Be creative. Each week, select a new place to start. By mixing up the route, you avoid soil compaction and tell-tale wear patterns in your lawn. It may surprise you to learn that grass grows in the direction that it is mowed. By switching directions, you keep it straighter and in better lawn posture. So try mowing at a 45-degree or 90-degree angle from your previous course. You benefit, too, by not being bored with the same route all the time.

Round your corners. If you have a big square or rectangular lawn, you can save lots of time by bypassing the outside corners. Instead, round off the corners and mow in a large oval fashion. After you've mowed the majority of the lawn, go back and finish by mowing the corners. You'll save time and have to contend with corners only once — not on every pass around the yard.

Don't scrimp on your route. Be sure to overlap each pass of your mower by at least 3 inches to get rid of wheel marks. By doing so, you're also guaranteed to have an even mowing with no skipped strips. From up close or at a distance, your lawn will flash that enviable neat and trim look, and that's what you want.

Move at an easy, steady pace. When you're pushing the lawn mower, don't imagine you're behind the wheel of an Indy race car. A steady pace, not a rush job, will actually get it done faster and better.

Go greenless around trees. You don't have to play ring-around-the-rosy with your mower and your maple tree anymore. Encircle the base of the tree with a 3-foot-diameter, 3-inch-deep layer of weed-suppressing shredded bark mulch. You won't get fed up and waste time with the need to make dime-size turns around it. This is 100 percent better for the trees, too. As I always say, the two-legged varmints with the machines do a lot more yard damage than an army of four-legged varmints will ever do!

Give your turf a monthly bath. Keep your grass looking its best by washing it down with my Terrific Turf Tonic once a month, after you mow. This tonic helps the grass plants recover faster from the mowing shock.

Jerry Baker Says

"Avoid making sharp turns with your mower because they create uneven cuts and damage grass during dry spells. They also deposit a pile of clippings at each turning point, which means more cleanup at the end. And who needs that?"

Terrific Turf Tonic

1 cup of baby shampoo
1 cup of ammonia
1 cup of weak tea water

Pour the ingredients into your 20 gallon hose-end sprayer and fill the balance of the sprayer jar with warm water. Then apply it liberally to your lawn to the point of run-off.

The Mechanics of Mowing

Believe you me, there is a method to all of this mowing madness! Selecting the correct blade height, speed, and throttle to meet your lawn's specific needs is crucial. So if you're willing to take a few moments to learn, I'll show you how to tame this shrew that you grew!

Reaching Blade Heights

During the heart of the growing season, get out your ruler and follow my One-Third Rule. What do I mean by that? Set the height of your mower blade so that you never cut more than one third of the grass blade length at any one time.

Let me illustrate. Let's say that the optimum growing height for your grass is 2 inches tall. Then you should mow it when it is 3 inches tall, removing 1 inch (one-third) of grass at that time. This method encourages the grass to grow strong, thick, healthy roots.

- **Full throttle ahead.** For peak mowing performance that saves wear and tear on the engine, adjust the throttle to its fastest setting. Fast blades make cleaner cuts, which means less stress for the grass plants.

- **Set the correct speed.** Some lawn mower models come equipped with variable speeds for the wheels. This is a nifty feature that allows you to adjust the wheel speed to best match the grass conditions. Keep pace with your lawn. Use this as a handy guide:

    Speeds 1 and 2: These slow speeds are ideal for tackling tall or thick grass.

    Speeds 3 and 4: Stick with these speeds for normal mowing conditions.

    Speeds 5 and 6: Shift to these speeds when the grass is on the thin side.

Jerry Baker Says

"When you follow my One-Third Rule, you'll have healthier grass, and healthy grass is less likely to be troubled by pests and diseases. It will also stand up better to drought."

Read Up

It should go without saying: Always read the owner/operator's manual of your mower before using it for the first time. Familiarize yourself with all of the different parts and the special features of your grass-cutting machine. Give your mower the same undivided attention you would give a new car or a VCR. If you bought a used mower, contact the manufacturer or local lawn-repair shop to order a replacement manual. They will be more than happy to oblige you. Then, at the start of each mowing season, give yourself a refresher course by leafing through the pages of the mower manual.

Stay Razor Sharp

Ever find yourself going over the same area of lawn again and again and again and not seeing any progress? That's a clear sign that your mower blades need sharpening.

And it's not just the frustration of trying to match your neighbor's putting-green lawn: Dull blades make jagged, unclean cuts that leave grass at risk for developing disease or damage by the sun. The unhealthy grass can turn a sickish gray — or brown — and potentially die. So sharpen your blades, and your problems will be over.

Ideally, rotary mower blades should be sharpened every 4 to 6 weeks, if you mow your lawn regularly. Take the mower in and have the job done by a professional, or you can do it yourself. To find my tips for how to do it, just turn the page!

Jerry Baker Says

"There's an art to mowing. Sure, it's not the same as painting a masterpiece or composing a symphony, but there is a certain flow to achieving a proper mow."

Don't Get Mowed Over!

Don't ever let your mower run unattended. Turn your back for a second, and it could be motoring in the opposite direction. Then look out for the runaway mower!

Jerry Baker Says

"Avoid buzz cuts. While the flat-top look may be fashionable among the Marines, it is definitely not fashionable among lawns."

Blade-Sharpening Savvy

If you're handy, you can save yourself some money. Blade sharpening is easy if you follow these simple steps:

1. Detach the spark plug wire so the mower engine doesn't accidentally turn over.

2. Set the mower securely over two sawhorses so you can work beneath the machine and avoid spilling fuel or oil.

3. Look under the mower deck, and you'll find the nut that holds the blade in place. It's right in the center of the blade. Remove the nut. *Tip:* If the blade keeps moving while you're trying to remove the nut, keep it still by wedging a wooden board between the blade and the mower deck. You can also buy a super handy tool called a Blade Buster that locks the blade securely in place while you remove the nut.

4. Hone the blade by drawing a coarse grindstone or file back and forth over one edge of the blade, holding the stone at about a 10-degree angle to the edge of the blade. (Instead of using a grindstone, you may want to purchase a Mower Blade Sharpener, which fits right into your power drill and keeps the grinding wheel at just the right angle for getting a good edge.)

5. Use the stone to remove burrs and even out any rough spots.

6. Finish by checking the blade's balance: Support the blade under its center and then spin it. It should spin evenly and not wobble. Mowers don't run smoothly if the blade is off kilter.

Timing Is Everything

The time of day, the weather, and the season all factor into how often you should mow your lawn. Before you take out your lawn mower for a spin, consider these timely pointers.

Go with the Flow — the Way the Grass Grows

Be flexible. During peak growth times (late spring and early fall), you may have to mow more than once a week. During off-peak times (summer), you may need to cut the grass only twice a month. That's a rule of thumb. For you folks living in the Sun Belt, weekly cuts may be necessary year round.

Avoid a High-Noon Showdown

Don't get near your mower between noon and 3:00 P.M. if you can help it. That's when the sun is at its fiercest. Grass clipped during these hours is helpless against the blazing, drying power of direct sunlight and may burn if newly mown. Instead, schedule your mowing for either late in the afternoon or early in the evening.

A FAIR-WEATHER MOWER

Wait for sunshine. Trying to mow wet grass will only create an uneven cut and make a wet mess. Wet clippings tend to clump together and sit on top of the lawn instead of nestling out of sight in the turf. In other words, wet mowing creates a yucky, matted mess! You run the risk of clogging your mower, too, by mowing damp grass.

Listen to Your Lawn

Schedule your mowing days by your lawn's needs, not by the calendar. How fast does your lawn grow? Well, it depends. Among the major factors are the type of grass, how much fertilizer you apply, and how much water it receives. That explains why it seems that grass can grow like a weed almost overnight.

TWICE IS NICE

Sometimes grass grows faster than we realize. Maybe a bunch of rainy days kept you from meeting your regular grass-cutting schedule. Or you came home from vacation to an out-of-control lawn, sporting grass that's 5 inches or taller. Resist your first temptation to race out and give it a low cut.

Instead, cut twice. Set your blade at its highest setting and take off half of what is needed. Then wait a couple of days, lower the blade to its normal setting, and cut it again. By practicing a little patience, you'll maintain the health of both your lawn and your mower!

A Weekday Date with Your Lawn

If Wednesday is Prince Spaghetti Day, why can't Thursday be Lawn Day? If you're like me, you cherish your weekends away from the office. You don't want to spend them doing yard and house chores and running errands. As long as your lawn doesn't need to be mowed more than once a week, why not cut your grass during the week after work instead of on the weekend? Then, come Saturday, you'll have more spare time to play golf, ride your bike, or kick back on the porch and relax.

A Bad Mow Is a Low Blow

Remember the One-Third Rule I told you about on page 76? If you keep your grass at its optimum growing height, you'll encourage it to grow strong, thick roots. Your lawn doesn't want a buzz cut.

Grass that's too short in the summer becomes weak and has a tougher time fighting off invading bugs, thugs, and diseases — not to mention the scorching sun!

And deep cuts expose the tender, shaded lower stems to burning sun rays and wicked winds.

A Real Shocker

Removing too much of the grass blade in any one mowing shocks the plant and stunts the growth of the all-important roots. If you set the mowing height too low or refuse to budge from your once-a-week schedule, your grass is weakened, resulting in thin spots that open the door for weeds. And it can easily fall prey to a host of diseases such as dollar spot, leaf spot, and rust.

JERRY'S RECOMMENDED CUTTING HEIGHTS

I've created this handy chart to help you figure out when it's best to cut the various types of common grasses. Keep in mind that warm-season grasses need mowing more in summer and cool-season grasses need mowing more in spring and fall.

WARM-SEASON GRASSES	BEST CUTTING HEIGHT	MOW WHEN
Bahia grass	2"	3"
Bermuda grass	½"	1"
Blue gramma grass	2"	3"
Buffalo grass	2"	3"
Carpet grass	1"	2"
Centipede grass	1"	2"
St. Augustine grass	1"	3"
Zoysia grass	½"	1"

COOL-SEASON GRASSES	MINIMUM HEIGHT	MAXIMUM HEIGHT
Bent grass	¼"	¾"
Bluegrass, Canada	3"	4"
Bluegrass, Kentucky	1½"	2½"
Bluegrass, rough	1½"	2½"
Fescue, chewings	1½"	2½"
Fescue, hard	1½"	2½"
Fescue, red	1½"	2½"
Fescue, sheep	2"	4"
Fescue, tall	1½"	3"
Ryegrass	1½"	2½"

Jerry Baker Says

"Puzzled over whether you have Kentucky bluegrass or St. Augustine grass? Dig up a handful and head to your local nursery or County Extension agent. They'll gladly help you clear up the mystery."

A Mowing Schedule by Season

Spring. In spring, don't rush out and mow the lawn for the first time. Instead, let the grass grow a little taller than the recommended growing height before cutting. This gives the lawn a jump start and makes it stronger. When it's time to mow, set the mowing deck to trim the grass back by about one-third. Then gradually lower the mowing deck height week by week until you're mowing at the recommended height for your type of grass.

Summer. Let your grass grow beyond its maximum height by one-third. Then cut it back to its maximum height, *not* its minimum height. Summer is the hottest time of the year and the season when your grass is most vulnerable to sunburn. Letting your grass grow to its maximum height slows its growth, conserves moisture, and inhibits weeds.

Fall. Aim high for your final cut. To prepare your lawn for the long winter season, mow grass at its maximum height until it stops growing or goes dormant. Then drop the blade one notch and mow one last time.

Winter. Okay, the mower may be stored for most of you Northerners, but for the folks living in the Sun Belt, mowing is a year-round activity. Thank goodness, the need to cut the green isn't as frequent during the winter months. So even Southerners get some breathing room.

Jerry's Dos and Don'ts of Mowing

- **Do** mow slight slopes on a diagonal.

- **Don't** mow up and down on a slope.

- **Don't** try to mow minor slopes when the ground is damp. All it takes is one slip and you're toast.

- **Don't** attempt to mow steep slopes (those greater than 15 degrees) with a push or riding mower.

- **Do** keep your lines straight when you mow.

- **Do** fuel only when the engine is cool. Wait at least 10 minutes before adding a second round of fuel.

- **Don't** add gas or oil to your mower while it's sitting on top of the grass. Any spill can kill the lawn in that area. Add gas and oil in the garage or on the driveway.

- **Do** stay mentally sharp, and keep your mower's blade sharp, too. A sharp blade makes a clean cut through the grass and leaves the lawn with a uniform cut.

- **Don't** try to muscle your mower through thick, wet, or tough grass. Slow down a bit.

- **Do** keep your pets and children out of range of any object that may fly out from under the mower.

- **Don't** let children mow the lawn until they are physically strong and tall enough to handle the mower, and also mentally mature enough to understand and practice sound mowing techniques.

- **Do** wear goggles or sunglasses to protect your eyes. Wear long pants to protect your shins from flying objects.

The Dope on Slopes

To get a steep slope from looking overgrown, plant a fast-spreading ground cover or other plant that doesn't require mowing. If you really must have grass, use a string trimmer on steep slopes.

Giddyap!
Using a Riding Mower

Okay, I know what you're thinking. You can drive a car. Some of you can even shift gears on a manual transmission. A riding lawn mower should be a breeze, right? Not necessarily.

Even though this is not your family sedan, the riding mower deserves your respect. It's heavy and potentially dangerous. Riding mowers also don't come cheap, so think it over carefully before you rush out and buy one. You get the biggest bang for your hard-earned buck if you own a large lawn — one that is half an acre or bigger. Don't waste your money on a riding mower if you have a tiny yard.

KEEP YOUR DISTANCE

Forget about trying to get too close to borders, trees, sheds, and other objects with your riding mower. The fact of the matter is that it's impossible. Save those spots for a push mower or your string trimmer.

Sitting Pretty

When you use a riding mower, *it* works up a sweat, not you. It cuts a wider swath than does a push mower. But a riding lawn mower has its own set of special considerations. Keep in mind that the two of you — you and the mower — are putting a lot of pounds on your lawn. So don't mow damp ground. This will create tire ruts, and you can also slip and slide all over the place, which is dangerous.

Resist the tempting pleas of small children to catch a ride with you while you tool around the yard. This is not a giant toy. One unexpected bump on this workhorse, and you both could be bucked out of luck!

Grass Clippings: Uses for Lawn Locks

You've just given your lawn a healthy cut, and now the clippings are strewn about your yard like locks of hair covering the tiled floor of a beauty salon. Now what? Should you rake the clippings, tuck them in plastic bags, and set them on the curb on garbage-pickup day?

No way! Here's your chance to be an environmental hero. Recycle the clippings and reap the rewards by choosing one of these options: leave 'em, compost 'em, share 'em, or mulch 'em.

Option 1: Leave 'em

By leaving clippings on your freshly mowed lawn, you can actually cut the amount of fertilizer you need by up to 25 percent! Yes, 25 percent! That's because the nutrients in clippings break down and become organic material for your grass plants to feed on.

Leaving a *light* layer of clippings also prevents thatch from developing on your lawn, because the clippings quickly decompose and nourish the growing grass. Just make sure that it's not a heavy layer of clippings, which can smother the growing grass.

Grass Clipping Dissolving Tonic

If you don't pick up your grass clippings, give your lawn an inexpensive "facial" to help it breathe better. Spray it with my Grass Clipping Dissolving Tonic twice a year. Here are the vital ingredients:

1 can of beer
1 can of regular cola (not diet)
1 cup of ammonia
1 cup of liquid dish soap

Mix all of these ingredients in a bucket and pour them into your 20 gallon hose-end sprayer. Apply to the point of run-off. This'll really help speed up the decomposition process for any clippings left littering your lawn.

What's in It for You?

If you were to dissect grass clippings, you'd discover that they contain 90 percent water; the remaining 10 percent consists of nitrogen and other lawn-friendly nutrients.

Option 2: Compost 'em

Okay, but what about those times when you've been a little bit delinquent in mowing the lawn? By the time you're ready to mow, the grass blades are twice as long as normal. Yikes! It's time to bring out the rake, gather up these heavy clippings, and compost them. Otherwise, you'll pay dearly later when your lawn becomes the new home for bugs that like to hide in the clipping-covered turf.

To start a compost pile, pick a place in your yard that's out of the spotlight. After each mowing, rake the yard or collect the clippings in your grass catcher, and then empty them on this pile. Also add small prunings, discarded plants, and other healthy yard fodder. Then, give the pile a good dose of my Grass Clipping Compost Starter. Afterward, add an alternating layer of soil and brown matter, like leaves.

Grass Clipping Compost Starter

Every time you add a new batch of grass clippings to your compost pile, spray the pile with the following mixture. It'll speed up the decomposition process. Every once in a while, toss the pile with a garden fork, just like it's a big garden salad.

1 can of regular cola (not diet)
½ cup of ammonia
½ cup of liquid lawn food
½ cup of liquid dish soap

Pour these ingredients in your 20 gallon hose-end sprayer and soak each new layer of grass clippings and yard fodder.

Option 3: Share 'em

Okay, let's say you have more than you need. Resist the temptation to throw them in the trash. Make friends with your neighbors and coworkers by giving your extra clippings to them for use as mulch. Spread the wealth and do your part to improve lawns in the community.

Option 4: Mulch 'em

Lawn clippings that are used as organic mulch help your soil by slowing down water evaporation and reducing soil temperature. They also suffocate weed seeds, thus preventing them from germinating and spreading. So, after mowing, rake up your grass clippings and use them as mulch around the base of trees, shrubs, flowers, and even vegetables.

DON'T GET MOWED OVER!

Whoa! Don't ever use contaminated clippings as a mulch! If you just applied a chemical control to your lawn, wait at least a month after each such use before tossing any grass clippings onto the compost pile. That way, you'll give the controls a chance to do their stuff and work their way through the plants' systems.

Edging: The Finishing Touch

I certainly don't want to keep *you* on edge, but you do want to keep your *lawn* on edge. Edging gives your lawn that look of completion. It's more than a beauty issue, though. Edging saves you time and hassle when you're maneuvering the mower around trees, flower beds, and sidewalks. Edging also keeps weeds and plants from creeping and spreading into parts of the yard where they don't belong. So, your mowing job isn't finished until you trim.

For a really well-groomed look, get out your edger and use it wherever your lawn runs into walkways, driveways, or flower beds. Then follow up with your trimmer or clippers to cut back any stragglers. You'll be amazed at how that final touch sets off your newly mown lawn. Then grab a cool drink and head for the hammock to survey your masterpiece. You've earned it!

Timesaver Tip

Flip over to page 109 in Chapter 6 to get the lowdown on how to use trenches or bricks to create edges that can cut your edging chores down to almost nothing.

Ask Jerry

Q After I mow my lawn, I rake up the clippings and toss them onto the compost pile. But instead of nice brown compost, I get an ugly, greasy-looking mat. What am I doing wrong?

A Good compost piles need good air circulation. Before you add anything else to the pile, go out and give it a good turning. Think of the pile as a big, tossed salad. Mix it up well. Then, when you add new clippings, apply a dose of my **Grass Clipping Compost Starter** (page 332), turn the pile again. Continue to turn the pile once a week, so oxygen gets into the center of it. You'll be surprised at how soon you'll have that dark brown compost you want.

Q I've been trying to make compost from my grass clippings, but the pile smells awful! Should I give up and take the whole thing to the town landfill?

A Absolutely not! Grass clippings make terrific compost material, but their high nitrogen content causes them to smell pretty bad when they're decomposing. The secret is to use them with other ingredients like leaves, which are high in carbon and which break down more slowly, but less odiferously. Use a ratio of about 3 parts leaves to 1 part clippings. Try that and your compost pile will be cookin' with grass — and odor-free — in no time!

☆   ☆   ☆

Well, now you know how to mow, the mechanics of mowers, how important timing is, and what to do with the clippings! With that major part of lawn care covered, it's time to move on. What's next? Water, my friends! Read on. . . .

CHAPTER 5

Shower Power

It's a fact of life — all living things need water. For some, it's easier to tap into than it is for others. When we're hot and parched, we simply pour ourselves an ice-cold glass of water to quench our thirst. Our dogs and cats know to head to their water bowls. But lawns must depend on Mother Nature and the kindness of strangers — us — to receive a steady supply of water. In this chapter, we'll cover everything you need to know to make sure your lawn receives the proper amount of water at the proper time.

Weathering All Seasons: When to Water

It can be a vicious or a victorious cycle as your lawn moves from one season to the next. In summer, your lawn is hot and thirsty. In spring and fall, it's as full as a tick on a coonhound. Briefly, let's run down the effects each season has on lawns.

Spring Has Sprung

During the spring, most parts of the country are bursting out in bloom. That's because the plants (including grasses) are waking up from their long winter's nap and are looking around for soil moisture to grow and grow.

Water does more than just quench a lawn's thirst. Grass must take in almost all of its nutrients dissolved in water. Without enough water in the soil, a lawn won't get enough nutrients to grow, reproduce, and defend itself against bugs and diseases. On the flip side, too much water, and the lawn can drown.

The Sponges Among Us

I want you to think of the soil underneath your lawn as one gigantic sponge. Healthy soils hold water like a sponge but let the excess water drain away. Poor soils either let water slip away swiftly (sandy soils) or put up a challenging barricade (clay soils).

Jerry Baker Says

"All of us have been known to recite the old adage 'April showers bring May flowers.' But in my book, April showers bring gorgeous, green grass, too!"

Turf Trivia

Annual ryegrass is often included in lawn seed mixtures because it sprouts and grows fast, elbowing out weeds until more desirable grasses fill in. Because of its protective qualities, it's sometimes called *nurse grass*.

Summertime, and the Livin' Ain't Always Easy

Next comes summertime, and the livin' is often far from easy for your lawn. Hot weather and little rain are a lethal combination. The soil can dry out, and a shallow-rooted lawn can die unless you give it a weekly watering. This is no time to depend on Mom Nature to satisfy your lawn's thirst. A heavy summer shower might nourish the lawn for only a few days before the soil quickly becomes as dry as a crocodile's skin again.

Wash away your worries by pouring on the H_2O, pronto! Once the grass returns to its green hue, hold off on the mowing until it's at least 3 inches tall. The reason for this wait is that the leaf blade is where the lawn makes food. Once it has some food, it will be strong enough to push its roots deeper into the soil to reach for the water below.

For areas with water restrictions, be sure to water only during your designated time. Over an extended period of restriction, I'm afraid there's not much to be done — you'll just have to accept the fact that some grass may die and need to be replaced with sod or seed later. (For strategies on how to cope with drought, see pages 142–45.)

Fall and Winter: Time to Cool Off

Autumn signals a time of cooler temperatures, more frequent rains, and piles of fallen leaves. Lawns that endured summer's dry, hot blast will resume their rich green looks again. Just like I told you back in Chapter 1, winter is a time of dormancy for most lawns outside of the Sun Belt.

Whether to Water: What's the Weather?

Seasons aside, climate can be atypical at times. For that reason, you should always water according to the weather. Water more when there are warmer temperatures, bright sunlight, breezy times, low humidity, and rainless spells. Water less when the temperature's cooler, days are overcast or there's no wind, and humidity is high, and, of course, if it's rainy.

Problem Solver

Problem: My lawn always feels brittle and crunchy.

Clues:

- Has the green color of your lawn faded into a silvery blue and/or brown?
- When you walk on the grass, are footprints noticeable?
- Is the soil light brown and crumbly?
- Is your grass starting to curl?

Solution: Unless you live in the middle of a desert, the problem is probably related to insufficient watering.

Bath Time

You may love taking a bubble bath before heading for bed, but *nighttime* is the *wrong time* to water your lawn. You don't want to go to bed with a wet head, and neither does your lawn. Nighttime watering encourages fungi to grow on the grass and encourages diseases such as summer patch, dollar spot, and brown patch to develop.

It's best to water your lawn early in the morning, between 5:00 and 8:00 A.M. During this time there is less evaporation into the air and the greatest penetration into the soil. For all you sleepyheads or party animals, at least try to roll out of bed and quench your lawn's thirst by no later than 2:00 P.M.

Wetted Bliss: How Much to Water

When it comes to watering a lawn, one size *doesn't* fit all. There is no one-and-only formula for watering wisely. Climate is one variable that makes a huge difference. Soil condition, grass type, and the size of your lawn matter as well. But there are some general guidelines that *do* apply.

Two Wise-Watering Rules

Water infrequently. It may surprise you to learn that the healthiest lawns are those that are watered infrequently, *not* every day. At first blush, this doesn't seem to make sense. But actually, lawns need only about 1 inch of water per week, which is plenty of water to reach deep into the soil where the root systems can drink it up. Grass plants aren't fussy about where the water comes from — rainfall, sprinklers, or a combination of the two.

Water slowly. Lawns should be watered slowly and deeply to moisten the soil to a depth of 6 to 8 inches below the surface. This deep watering encourages deep root growth, and deep roots help the plants survive better in times of drought.

Dry Grass? Don't Worry!

Allow your lawn to dry out between waterings. Most lawn grasses can tolerate dry conditions over a reasonable period of time.

Lawn Freshener Tonic

A good way to determine whether it's time to water is by walking on the grass. If it doesn't spring back to life, it's definitely thirsty. To help it along, strap on your aerating lawn sandals or golf shoes and take a stroll around your yard. Then follow up with this Tonic:

1 can of beer
1 cup of shampoo
½ cup of ammonia
½ cup of weak tea water

Mix all of these ingredients in your 20 gallon hose-end sprayer and apply to the point of run-off.

The Catch-Can Test

Take this "catch-can test" to check how much water is being put down on your lawn. Place empty soup or coffee cans in the path of your sprinklers. Run the sprinklers for about 15 minutes, then stick a ruler in each can and measure the level of water inside. This will help you figure out how long it takes for a can to "catch" 1 inch of water.

If the cans measure ¼ inch of water after 10 minutes, how long would you need to keep your sprinklers on to apply a full inch of water? If you answered 40 minutes, give yourself an "A"! If you didn't, well, there's always medical school. By the way, it usually takes between 30 minutes and an hour of watering to get 1 inch of water for your lawn.

Jerry's Ten Wise Watering Commandments

To ensure that you have the greenest grass on the block, follow these can't-miss watering rules.

1. Short waterings work the best. Give your lawn about ¼ inch of water, wait 10 minutes, then give it another ¼ inch. Continue this water-then-wait approach until you've applied a full inch of water. When you put in a little water at a time, the soil is better prepared to absorb water and help grass develop strong roots.

2. Don't give your lawn a daily drink. Running a sprinkler for 5 or 10 minutes each day will do more harm than good. Roots grow only where there is water, so they tend to be shallow and near the surface. Your ever-wet lawn will also easily fall prey to diseases.

Footnote

Try to keep all feet off of the lawn after a heavy downpour. Walking around on the soil can leave the *wrong* impression on the lawn. It can tear up the grass and cause a muddy mess!

3. Know your soil. Sandy soils need to be watered more often than do loamy soils. Generally, water lawns that are on clay and loamy soils once a week; water lawns on sandy soils about twice a week.

4. Stop watering if puddles or run-off occurs. Let the water soak into the soil completely before you resume watering.

5. Avoid buzz cutting your lawn, thinking you won't have to mow as often. A close-cropped lawn tends to make roots shrink and shrivel. Try to keep your grass about 3 inches high, depending on the type grass you have (see page 81).

6. Don't water your lawn during high winds. Strong gusts can distort your sprinkling pattern, blowing some water off of the lawn completely.

7. Pay attention to location, location, location. Real estate agents know all about this. Shaded areas need less water than sunny spots.

8. Give a newly sodded lawn a good soaking every day for about 2 weeks. This gives the root system a chance to become firmly established in the soil.

9. Keep a newly seeded or sprigged lawn moist, but not soaked, during the germination period. Overwatering causes disease and poor growth. You don't want that! As the new lawn starts to grow, reduce the *frequency* of watering, but increase the *amount* of water. In 4 to 6 weeks, your new lawn should be ready for a regular watering program.

10. Increase the watering distance of your sprinklers by simply raising them up on a box or an overturned bucket. The higher they sit, the bigger the area they will cover, and the less you'll have to water.

Jerry Baker Says

"Inch by inch, you can help your lawn thrive. Just remember to follow the 1-inch watering rule!"

Turn of the Screw

Are you not sure whether your lawn's thirst needs quenching? Here's a foolproof way to find out. Push a long screwdriver into the soil. If it is difficult to push 6 inches or so down into the ground, it's time to give your lawn a drink of water. Also, thirsty grass will start to curl before it turns brown. These cues are friendly reminders to get back to my watering schedule.

All Water Is Wet — But All Water Isn't Alike!

All water may look alike, but the various trace elements in rain and snow can have more to do with the health of your lawn than you might think.

Rainwater. Grandma Putt used to catch every last drop of precious rainwater in rain barrels placed at strategic spots all around her yard. She knew that the best and purest water available runs down your rain spout and out into the street every time it rains! What a pity to waste it, since rainwater contains a lot of nitrogen, along with other elements. In fact, scientists have found that some water actually has a "fertilizer" analysis of 78-21-1.

Well water. After rainwater, well water is next best, because it has many trace elements, such as iron, which are important to grass plants just as they are to people.

City water. Water from a municipal water system also has many trace elements, but it also may have many unwanted chemical additives. For instance, fluoride is put in some community water to give kids strong teeth. Chlorine is used to kill germs. And if you soften your water, you're adding that old villain, salt. Too much salt isn't good for you, and it certainly doesn't do your lawn any good. In fact, lawns can be harmed by an overload of salt.

Soil Types

People drink in many different ways. There are sippers, gulpers, and lots of folks in between. In the world of soils, there are also sippers and gulpers. Knowing your basic soil type alerts you to how much water to give your lawn so that you don't soak or underwater it.

You can learn how to figure out what type soil you have and all of my strategies for different types of soils in Chapter 13. But for now, let me give you a sneak preview that should help you know how to handle the water situation best for the kind of soil you have.

Soils range from sandy to rock-hard clay. Your sprinklers can be working anywhere from 30 minutes to 5 hours at a time, depending on the condition of your soil. Use my handy chart below to help you figure out how long you need to water your lawn to reach the desired depth of 4 to 6 inches. Be sure to stop watering if you notice any run-off.

SOIL RUN-OFF

SOIL TYPE	INFILTRATION/HOUR	TIME FOR 1" TO SOAK IN
Sand	2"	30 minutes
Sandy loam	1"	1 hour
Loam	.05"	2 hours
Silt loam	.04"	2 hours, 15 minutes
Clay loam	.03"	3 hours, 20 minutes
Clay	.02"	5 hours

Lawn Lore

Elfego, New Mexico, hosts a challenging one-hole golf tournament. From a tee on top of 7,243-foot-high Socorro Peak, golfers attempt to land their shots on a patch of 60-foot-diameter green, 2.5 miles away, and 2,500 feet below. The best score to date: 11.

It's All in the Family

Families of grasses also have different water needs, depending on climate and their true roots. Here is a rundown of the major types of grass:

Wet Soil–Tolerant Grasses: They Love a Good Soaking!

- Bluegrass, Canada
- Bluegrass, rough

Grasses That Need Weekly Watering: 1 Inch, Please

- Bent grass, colonial
- Bent grass, creeping
- Carpet grass
- Centipede grass
- Perennial ryegrass
- St. Augustine grass

Drought-Tolerant Grasses: The Camels of Lawns

- Bahia grass
- Bermuda grass, common
- Bermuda grass, hybrid
- Blue gramma grass
- Buffalo grass
- Fescue, chewing
- Fescue, creeping red
- Fescue, hard
- Fescue, sheep
- Fescue, tall
- Kentucky bluegrass varieties
- Zoysia grass

From Too Dry to Too Wet

Weather always makes a great conversation starter. It seems like folks are never satisfied — it's always too hot or too cold, too wet or too dry. But the fact is, it really *can* be too dry, as well as too wet, for your lawn. In Chapter 8, I go into detail about how I handle too little and too much rain. But here's an overview to get you thinking about the weather and how it affects your lawn.

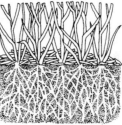

"Wet" Your Lawn's Appetite

Because lawns are more vulnerable to drought than are deeper-rooted perennials, shrubs, and trees, the best defense against drought is to develop a deep-rooted lawn. As grass grows, its root system matures so that it can replace the water that it has lost from the leaf surfaces. When water is readily available near the soil surface, the plant's roots grow only 2 or 3 inches deep. That's a small amount of soil to act as a water reservoir for the roots.

In contrast, healthy grass roots that stretch 6 to 8 inches below the surface are better prepared to handle dry times. They pick up moisture from a large amount of soil, and water loss from evaporation is much less.

Be a Good Scout

You can't cajole Mother Nature into unleashing needed rain showers. Almost every year, droughts occur in some parts of this country, and it only seems to be getting worse. Unfortunately, it's out of your control. But you can exercise an ounce of prevention to reduce the risk of losing your lawn during dry spells. What's the secret? Proper watering, plus a dose of one of my tried-and-true tonics.

Like the Boy Scouts, practice the motto "Be prepared." Water your lawn deeply and then leave it for several days, depending on the air temperature. If you alternate between giving your lawn a good soaking and letting the top layer dry out, you're helping the grass to develop deep, dense roots that will save your lawn if or when a drought occurs.

During those dog days of summer when the sun is blazing, spray your lawn a couple of times with my Drought-Buster Tonic. It'll help prevent drought damage and provide nourishment at the same time. (For recipe, see page 330).

What to Do When It's Raining Cats and Dogs

In some parts of the country, it may rain for days and days. You may feel a bit like Noah and have the urge to build an ark. As the water table rises, you see your hopes of maintaining a lush lawn dashed. You can't stop the rain, but in Chapter 8, you'll find some helpful tips, tricks, and tonics to mop up the mess once the sun returns (see pages 146–47).

Watering Equipment

All kinds of tools, equipment, and supplies can help lighten your watering chores. If you have an itty-bitty lawn, probably the best (and cheapest) investment you should make is in a good-quality garden hose. It can more than handle the task of being your lawn's water supplier. But there are a number of other, more high-falutin' attachments and systems that may catch your fancy. Let's start with a simple hose.

Hoses

When you shop for a garden hose, select a decent-size one, ¾ inch or bigger in diameter. You want a quality hose that spews forth instead of sputtering. Look for one made of laminated filament or high-grade rubber. And for goodness sake, buy one that rolls up easily and is kink resistant! If you're not sure how to recognize these characteristics, ask your garden center salesperson to help you.

Ideally, you should select a hose that can reach your entire lawn. If your lawn's very large, consider buying two or more hoses and attaching them to outside faucets in the front and backyards.

Bury It

You can create a simple "underground" sprinkler system with just a hose, a portable sprinkler head, and a little dirt. Here's how to do it.

1. Place your hose where your lawn always seems to dry out quickly.

2. To keep from tripping over the hose, run it along the edge of the lawn, maybe bordering a flower bed. That also keeps the snaking hose from leaving dead grass in its wake.

3. Cover the hose with about ½ inch of soil or mulch. Leave only the end of the hose exposed, so you know right where it is when you need it.

4. Keep the sprinkler attachment hooked to the end and hide it behind nearby shrubbery until it's time to water.

Portable Sprinklers: Pro and Con

Portable sprinklers are easy to move from one place to the next in small yards. They are fine for lawns of 1,000 square feet or less, but they can cause an uneven distribution of water on your lawn — watering too fast or too little in spots. They can also be a source of irritation if you live in an area with dry summers, and you find yourself having to drag the sprinkler around to a different location every 30 minutes or so.

IRRIGATE, DON'T IRRITATE

I have a simple solution to eliminate the headache of having to screw a hose onto and off of a faucet all summer. Go to the store and buy a two-headed Siamese faucet head for each and every outside water hookup. These strange-sounding contraptions are definitely the cat's meow when it comes to hoses.

Attach the hose to one of the heads and leave the other open for when you need the water faucet to fill up a bucket.

Sprinkle, Sprinkle, Thirsty Yard

For medium- to mega-size lawns, permanent sprinkler systems are definitely the answer. There are dozens of styles, including oscillating, impulse, revolving, traveling, and in-ground. Whichever style you choose, make sure it distributes water evenly over your entire lawn. Otherwise, you're left with some areas that are too wet and others that are too dry, and both can look like heck! Here's a quick rundown on each kind:

Oscillating sprinklers like to throw water all around. They shoot streams from a slowly sweeping arm in, typically, a rectangular pattern. Their range is usually decent, but high winds can distort their water patterns for uneven distribution.

Impulse sprinklers feature an internal jet nozzle and external hammer that work together to spew pulses of water in a circular pattern, which can be widened or shortened. Folks with large lawns (even golf courses) rely on this type because it spreads water more evenly over a large area.

Revolving sprinklers release streams of water from a pair of spinning sprinkler nozzles in a circular pattern. Unfortunately, you can't adjust the nozzles, so more water tends to fall on the outer edge than closer to the sprinkler. These sprinklers are best for areas under 8 feet in diameter.

Traveling sprinklers don't come equipped with suitcases! They get their name because the entire sprinkler housing travels all over the lawn in a path designated by the hose. Water falls evenly in a series of connecting circles. Just don't get in the way of its travels!

In-ground sprinkler systems are the most expensive, but you get what you pay for: convenience and on-target action. When activated manually or by a timer, spray heads pop up at strategically placed intervals in your lawn to provide full and complete watering.

Smart Sprinklers

Automatic sprinkler systems actually use less water than do hoses and movable single sprinklers. That's because you can control the shutoff on a timer, so there's no danger of accidentally forgetting that the water is running and finding a miniflood in your backyard.

I prefer the automatic systems. Once they've been properly installed, they not only save on water, but they save you time as well. After a predetermined amount of water has been applied to one section of lawn, these timed systems have the "smarts" to move on to the next, distributing water uniformly across the lawn. And the best part is you don't have to lift a finger!

Installing an In-Ground System

I want to tell you, you *can* install your own in-ground system. Now, before you start shaking your head and backpedaling, try to keep an open mind. Don't underestimate your abilities. Installing an in-ground sprinkler system is not an impossible dream!

Obviously, the optimal time for installation is when you're planting a new lawn. All that stands between you and success is a carpet of groomed dirt awaiting its dressing of grass seed or sod.

More challenging, but certainly doable, is installing an in-ground sprinkler system in an existing lawn. Yes, it can be done! If you are up for a challenge, consider the factors listed on the next page before you go full-steam ahead.

Jerry Baker Says

"I can't tell you how many times I would plumb forget that my manual sprinkler was on and get busy on another project, only to return hours later to a lawn filled with puddles! The ducks were happy, but not me!"

Put yourself through this little test before tackling an in-ground sprinkling system on your own.

✔ Do you have the time — and patience — to install it yourself?

✔ Do you have an adequate supply of water available for irrigation?

✔ Is the water pressure adequate to cover the entire lawn?

✔ Is your soil easy to dig up to install the pipes? And how deep do you have to dig?

✔ Do you know the absorption rate of soil being irrigated?

✔ Do you have steep slopes or irregular patterns anywhere in your yard?

✔ Do you know how to calculate the precipitation rate to properly space enough sprinkler heads?

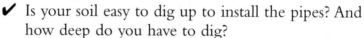

Ask Jerry

Q We haven't had a lot of rain lately, but my lawn was looking pretty good until we had a family-reunion barbecue. When the guests left, my lawn had footprints all over it. How come?

A Sounds like your lawn could use a dose or two of my **Drought Recovery Tonic** (page 330). When lawn grasses are getting enough moisture, they usually pop right back up after being trampled. But if they're already water starved, they just don't have the strength to recover. Give your lawn a good, slow drink of tonic, and I think you'll find that your grass will recover nicely. Remember that every time you water, moisture needs to reach 6 to 8 inches below the surface. This deep watering will encourage strong, deep roots that can stand up to periodic droughts.

Remember Your Zip

Your zip code comes into play when making a sprinkler decision. Folks living in the Northeast and the Pacific Northwest need only minimal watering to supplement the normal rainfall in those regions to keep the top 6 to 8 inches of soil moist and healthy. But folks living in California and the Great Plains need to give their lawns more water to counter arid or semi-arid conditions.

Q We went on a month's vacation and left our neighbor's teenage son in charge of watering our lawn. When we came home, our lawn was full of brown patches. What went wrong? And how can I get rid of the spots?

A It sounds as though your young helper was working the night shift, which is bad for your grass. Watering in the evening encourages brown patch — and other fungus diseases like summer patch and dollar spot. To get rid of the spots you've got, spray your lawn with my **Lawn Fungus Fighter Tonic** (page 334). And from now on, make sure no one gives your lawn a drink after 2:00 P.M. (To be extra safe, water between 5:00 and 8:00 A.M.)

Q I just got a new water softener, and I've heard that the salt in softened water is harmful to lawns. Is this true? And if so, how can I protect my grass?

A Yes, it is true. Too much salt can make a lawn go belly up. Fortunately, the answer to your problem is simple: Just make sure your outdoor faucets are not connected to the softener system. (Besides saving your grass, you'll save money on water-softener salts!)

Q Help! I live on the Olympic Peninsula in Washington, where it rains so much that the ducks carry umbrellas. What's the best grass for my lawn?

A Go for the blue — bluegrass, that is. Either rough or Canada bluegrass will weather your weather like a champ. And don't forget to treat your lawn to heaping helpings of my **All-Season Green-Up Tonic** (page 328) to keep it healthy and happy.

Q I've heard that a good blast of water can wash away disease problems in my lawn. Is this true?

A Nope! Watering your lawn won't cure any problem except drought. In fact, water can make it even easier for many disease germs to do their dirty work. Your best strategy for fighting diseases is to identify the problem and then apply my recommended cure. (See Chapter 12 for ways to put Dastardly Diseases in their place.)

Now that you know all about your lawn's watering needs and how to satisfy them, let's move on to what you can do to revive that old, lifeless lawn of yours. You'll learn some other terrific tricks of the trade that'll get your lawn looking really spiffy!

CHAPTER 6

Teach Your Old Lawn New Tricks

I can just see you sitting there shaking your head and saying I'll never get my old lawn in picture-perfect condition. And I say, YES, you can! Reviving a poorly growing lawn is not as difficult as you might think. The biggest culprit is neglect. So you need to counter that with what I call TLC: Trouble-free Lawn Care. You can give your lawn some TLC by doing four simple things:

✔ Edging   ✔ Aerating

✔ Raking   ✔ Dethatching

In this chapter, we'll discuss what to do and when to do it, so that your old lawn looks like new again!

Edging Tricks and Techniques

Remember how your mom always insisted that you get a haircut the day before you had your class picture taken? And how she fussed over your hair, putting down those cowlicks and brushing out snarls before the photographer pinched your cheeks and said to say "Cheese"?

Well, your lawn could use a little mothering from *you* now and then. That's where edging comes in. Regular edging stops rapidly growing grass from spilling over onto walkways and other places where it doesn't belong. Let me introduce you to the wonderful world of edgings.

Can You Dig It?

The most popular type of edging starts as a simple trench, typically 2 to 4 inches wide and 4 to 5 inches deep. Trenches are the most common way to make a border between the edge of the lawn and your flower beds or other garden areas and objects. Think of them as "mini-moats" surrounding your flower beds, trees, paths, and sitting areas, protecting them from the whirling blades of the mighty lawn mower.

Interested in this method? You can create a trench as easy as 1-2-3! Just read on!

Jerry Baker Says

"Edging gives your yard that finished look. It sets and defines boundaries. It can make mowing a lot easier — it allows you to mow close to trees, hedges, fences, and gardens. And you don't have to do hand trimming. I'm all for time-savers, aren't you?"

MORE THAN JUST PRETTY

It's extra hard to mow along places like walls, fences, and hedges. If a spot like that is your special curse, consider planting a border of perennials such as hostas (for shady spots) or daylilies (for sunny spots) as an edging. They're beautiful to behold and eliminate almost all of those boring trimming chores, especially if you give them one of the nice, neat edges I'm going to tell you about.

3-Step Edges

Step 1. Arm yourself with a square-edged spade or long-handled, half-moon edging tool. If you've got a big lawn, save some sweat by using a gas-powered or electric-powered edger. These tools make clean, straight cuts very easily and quickly. You may be able to rent one, if you don't want to buy one.

Step 2. Dig straight down with your spade and cut the soil to the recommended depth of 8 inches and a width of 4 inches.

Step 3. Place a metal or plastic edging strip vertically in the soil with the top edge below the lawn surface. Sink the strip at least 8 inches. This makes it nearly un-detectable to the eye and out of reach of the lawn mower.

Continue placing as many strips as you need. You need the 8-inch depth to stop spreading plants — including grass — from creeping under the strips and going where they don't belong.

Keep Your Gardens on the Edge

But wait — there's more! Landscape timbers and bricks also make excellent edging materials. You can lay them flat, diagonally, or on edge, right along your flower beds. Then, when you're mowing, you can run the wheels of the mower along them. This way you can easily make that last pass next to the garden, getting every last bit of lawn mowed without catching any of your favorite plants with the mower blades. You also won't need to go back along the bed with trimmers or clippers when you're through mowing.

And don't forget about paved or gravel paths. They, too, make a good boundary between a lawn and a flower bed. Plus, paths have the added advantage of being virtually maintenance-free, and there's nothing better than that!

Raking It In

I don't know many folks who actually look forward to raking. It ranks near the bottom of the chore chart. Armed with only a rake, you can easily feel like David facing a Goliath-like yard full of grass clippings or leaves.

It's a task that can't be skipped, though. Time is your lawn's enemy. Excess leaves or thick piles of grass clippings interfere with the turf's ability to breathe and interrupt your lawn's ability to make chlorophyll. So the long and the short of it is that sometimes there's no getting around it — you just need to rake. But you'll have big rewards for getting this chore done if you use the rakings on your compost pile (for more about compost, see the next page).

Jerry Baker Says

"There's gold in them thar leaves and clippings, so don't throw them out! Enrich your yard by converting leaves and clippings to compost — the soil conditioner known as 'gardener's gold.'"

Raking Tools

Finding the right rake can be a piece of cake! Go easy on your back and choose a rake made of bamboo, flexible plastic, or flexible steel. Forget about garden rakes: They are heavy and rigid so that they can smooth garden soil. They're not meant for removing leaves or grass clippings.

For large lawns, it's a good idea to invest in a lawn sweeper. Save some money by sharing this tool with your neighbors and dividing the cost among the group. Just set up a schedule for its use. You'll soon have the best-looking neighborhood in town!

Stand Up Straight

Raking helps keep lawn grasses in proper posture. If you lightly rake a freshly mowed lawn in the opposite direction of how the blades are leaning, your grass will not only stand up straighter, but it will also be easier to cut the next time around.

Clip 'n' Save

Now, some folks like to leave their grass clippings on their lawns. But not me! (If *you* do, though, see page 332 for my Grass Clipping Dissolving Tonic.) Why, I gather them right up and heap them on my ever-growing compost pile out in the back corner of my yard. Follow these tips for best results:

• **Don't segregate clippings** from other compost materials — mix 'em all in together. Left to themselves, clippings tend to mat down after a short while and start to stink!

• **Mix clippings with leaves** in a ratio of about 3 parts leaves to 1 part clippings. This gives the pile enough natural aeration so that it can very quickly decompose.

• **Toss and turn the compost** pile with a pitchfork or other turning tool twice a month to speed up decomposition.

• **Hold off using lawn clippings** that have been treated with chemicals and pesticides as mulch. Wait at least a month after the last time you used pesticides before adding those clippings to your compost.

• **Spray each batch** of new clippings that you toss onto the compost pile with my Grass Clipping Compost Starter (page 332).

Jerry Baker Says

"If thick clippings or leaves remain on the lawn, they can block sun and moisture from getting to the grasses and thus keep them from growing as well. And that's beside the fact that clumps of old clippings don't look real pretty, either."

Baby, It's Cold Outside

Never let fallen leaves blanket your lawn through the cold winter months. Rake them up and add them to your compost pile before the first snowflakes fly. You'll be helping your lawn hibernate in a healthy way!

To speed up the decomposition process, mow over the leaves several times to get them into nickel-sized pieces. Then rake them up and add them to your compost pile.

Aerating

I want you to put yourself in your lawn's place for a moment. Every day, you risk being trampled on by shoes, paws, mowers and other lawn equipment, and even tires from the occasional misguided car. With all this heavy weight coming from above, it's no wonder that the soil underneath you sometimes becomes compacted and hard. The solution is aeration.

It Can't Be Beaten

Don't let your lawn get beaten down! With a little help from you, your lawn won't ever experience this problem. Basically, aeration punctures holes in the invisible surface tension barrier at the soil line to allow food, water, oxygen, and my terrific tonics to get down to the grass roots. Golf spikes are the simplest form of aerators — that's why I'm always reminding you to wear them while you mow! Aerating lawn sandals are also very helpful; or you can rent a power aerator at your local garden center.

A Worm's Life

Lack of humus in soil and prolonged use of chemical fertilizers can result in hard-packed soil. When the air and moisture get squeezed out of the soil, lawn-friendly earthworms are unable to bore through it and keep it loose enough to absorb air, fertilizer, and water. Over time, roots slowly starve, and grass begins to die as its steady supply of oxygen and nitrogen from soil decreases.

Aeration Test

So, just how airy is your soil? Here's an easy test that'll answer this question. (The method is similar to the way you test a cake baking in the oven with a cake tester to see whether it's done.) Just poke a large screwdriver or a sturdy stake into the ground. If it goes in easily, the soil is not compacted. But if it goes in only with difficulty, that's a clear signal that your soil is compressed and needs some breathing room.

As with everything else, timing is everything. The best time to perform this test on cool-season grasses is in the fall. Test warm-season grasses in the spring.

Warning Signs

Signals that it's time to aerate:

- You notice worn-out areas where people walk frequently.

- No matter what you do, you can't seem to keep certain parts of the lawn moist.

- Puddles form and drain slowly.

- After you've had the sprinkler on for only a few minutes, water runs off the lawn and down the street.

AIR IT OUT

To aerate your lawn in a hurry, powered core aerators or rolling lawn aerators can come to your rescue. You can buy or rent these tools from your local garden store or from mail-order catalogs.

Aeration Schedule

For lawns with a thick patch of thatch, you may need to aerate each spring and fall for 2 years in a row. Then aerate every other year to maintain peak condition. Even if you're blessed with an easy-breathing lawn, you should aerate it every 3 years just to stop any compaction from getting a start.

Jerry Baker Says

"If you're stumped as to which aerator to pick, by all means ask the professionals at your garden center. They have the answers, but they need to know the questions; they're not mind readers."

Powered Aerators

For large lawns, you can buy or rent a powered walk-behind aerator. If you run the aerator in rows, just as you do a lawn mower, you will breeze through this chore. My two favorite aerator models feature hollow or open tines. Let's look at both:

• **Hollow-tine aerators.** These pull out tiny cores of soil and grass and drop them on top of the lawn.

• **Open-tine aerators.** These work by scooping out soil and grass, leaving tiny, empty holes in the surface that permit air, water, fertilizer, and tonics to penetrate deep into the heart of the soil.

Whichever model you choose, don't bother raking up the plugs of soil they pull up. These should be left on the lawn to decompose, which will help feed your turf from top to bottom.

After aerating your lawn, pamper the grass roots by sprinkling a topdressing of peat and sand along with some quality topsoil mixed with processed manure over the top of it. Fill in the tiny aerated holes with this mix by brushing it or raking it in. This way, you'll be improving both the lawn and your soil.

Jerry Baker Says

"Give your hard-working lawn a much-deserved breather. When you aerate the turf, pull the plugs and leave them on your lawn. In a week or two, they'll break down and provide your lawn with important nutrients."

Just Desserts

For best results, aerate your lawn the morning after you water it or after a heavy rain shower — the soil will be easier to penetrate.

After you've poked the holes in the soil, put some sifted peat moss, dried manure, or compost in your spreader, and apply a layer about ¼ inch thick to the whole area. Your lawn will love it — it's the lawn food equivalent to apple pie or a hot fudge sundae.

Awesome Aeration Remedies

Here are my three top ways to discourage the possibility of future soil compaction:

Remedy 1. Mow often and leave the clippings on the lawn. Overspray with my Grass Clipping Dissolving Tonic to help the clippings decompose quickly (for recipe, see page 332).

Remedy 2. Make friends with earthworms. How? Regularly use my tonics along with organic foods on your lawn. You'll make the earthworms wriggle with delight, and they'll show their gratitude by poking much-needed holes in your soil.

Remedy 3. Install paths in high-traffic areas of your lawn. Then once they're installed, use shrubs and borders to encourage walkers to use these pathways and stay off the recovering grass.

Aeration Tonic

You can slow down soil compaction and improve penetration by spraying your lawn once a month during the growing season with my Aeration Tonic. To make it, mix:

1 cup of liquid dish soap
1 cup of beer

Combine ingredients in a 20 gallon hose-end sprayer, filling the balance of the sprayer jar with warm water. Apply it liberally to the point of run-off.

Turf Trivia

Lawns did their patriotic duty during World War II. Lots of military money was poured into developing ways to convert grass plants — among nature's most common commodities — into grass-cushioned airfields so our boys would have safe places to land.

Dispatch the Thatch

Thatch is definitely not a welcome guest. It will disfigure and cripple a lawn if it is not identified and dispatched before it takes hold.

So, what exactly *is* thatch? Thatch consists of a spongy, tight mass of undecomposed organic matter (leaves and grass roots, stems, stolons, and rhizomes) that lodges itself in your lawn. Any lawn can be its victim. This lawn criminal:

- Crowds the grass crowns, hampering healthy growth.

- Blocks water and nutrients from reaching the plants' roots.

- Forces roots to grow near the surface in a search for water and nutrients, instead of growing deep into the soil.

- Makes mowing difficult, as wheels sink into the soft material.

What Thatch Is Not

Contrary to what you may have heard, thatch is *not* fresh grass clippings lying on your lawn.

Problem Solver

Problem: My grass plants look dull in color and stunted in growth. What's happening?

Clues:
- Is it difficult to separate the grass plant from the thick covering of grass clippings, leaves, and other organic matter piled on top?
- Are you having trouble actually seeing the soil underneath the grass plants?
- If you poke your index finger down through the grass, are you unable to get past the above-soil barriers to burrow an inch into the ground?
- Are the roots of your grass plants stubby and thin?

Solution: This lawn villain is thatch, and you'll have to get to work on it with my Thatch Control Tonic (for recipe, see page 339) and a good raking.

The Thatch Batch

Thatch can be a menace to any type of grass, especially in lawns treated with a lot of chemical fertilizers and controls. In the family of grasses, these are especially vulnerable:

- ✔ Bent grasses, cool season
- ✔ Bermuda grass
- ✔ Bermuda grass, warm-season hybrid
- ✔ Fescue, chewing
- ✔ Fescue, creeping red
- ✔ Fescue, hard
- ✔ Kentucky bluegrass
- ✔ St. Augustine grass
- ✔ Zoysia grasses

Why these grasses? Because they tend to send out shoots above the ground. As these shoots start weaving about and mingling, they create thatch while also keeping grass clippings from reaching the soil and decomposing.

Thatch becomes a menace when it's more than ½ inch thick. That's when it starts to bully your grass plants and take over your turf. When it's less than ½ inch thick, you can keep it under control by raking the lawn with a bamboo or metal leaf rake about twice a year. And don't forget to add compost to your lawn; it helps break down thatch naturally.

"Springy" Is a No-No

Left unchecked, thatch will thicken and block moisture from ever reaching the soil. It traps moisture and bottles it up close to the leaves, increasing the lawn's chances of developing diseases, especially in warmer climates. Soon your lawn will show signs of dry, dead patches. When you walk on your lawn, the ground will feel springy — definitely not a healthy situation!

As I mentioned earlier, thatch can be tricky to identify. Some earnest homeowners have rushed out to buy or rent machines to remove what they *thought* was a thatch invasion, only to discover that it was merely a different type of grass or even weeds.

Sherlock Holmes on all Fours

Time to be a lawn detective! One way to identify thatch is to use a long knife to slice down into the soil. Pull out a plug about 3 inches square so that you can examine a cross section. If you see a layer more than ½ inch thick of dead plant material between the green grass leaf and the soil, you've got thatch. Here's another way to determine whether you've got a thatch problem:

Step 1. Get on your hands and knees and take a good, up-close look at your lawn.

Step 2. Press your index finger firmly into the grass in several locations in the lawn.

Step 3. If you can easily touch the soil, great! If you can't, chances are good that your lawn has thatch.

Attack Thatch

Well, say you've decided that you really do have thatch. So what's the cure?

- **First, get your soil tested.** The results will help you correct the nutrient and pH deficiencies that may be aggravating the situation.

- **Remove thatch as soon as possible** so that it doesn't get any worse. Don't let time be on thatch's side! Clear it out when you spot it to save yourself from having to tackle a major job down the road.

WHEN TO DETHATCH

Ideally, you should dethatch your lawn in late summer (September 1 to 10 in most areas). The second best time is in early spring, say around April 15 to May 1, before your lawn kicks into high gear.

Thatch Attackers

Here are some ways to get rid of thatch:

- **Apply a commercial product** like my natural, organic Thatch Buster (see page 147) to the area twice a year.

- **Do it yourself,** and mix up a batch of my Thatch Control Tonic.

- **Use a thatch rake** that has specially designed blades instead of normal tines. You'll need some elbow grease to work the rake into the lawn and remove the thatch.

- **Add a dethatching blade** to your lawn mower.

- **Use a vertical mower** with metal blades that rotate vertically to cut into and yank out thatch. Set blades at a height where they barely touch the soil surface. For deep thatch, you may need to use the vertical mower a couple of times, making the second pass at right angles to the first. After each mowing, rake the lawn vigorously to remove the loosened thatch.

Thatch Control Tonic

To control thatch, mix:

1 can of regular cola
  (not diet)
½ cup of liquid dish soap
¼ cup of ammonia

Put all of these ingredients in a 20 gallon hose-end sprayer and apply to your lawn once a month to the point of run-off.

Big Guns!

For thick thatch, most ordinary tools are powerless. It's time to call in the heavy artillery! Enlist the aid of a gas-powered machine that answers to the name of dethatcher, power rake, or vertical mower. Rent one at your local garden or rental store, but be forewarned — some of these machines are very heavy and awkward to handle!

Offensive Measures

As Vince Lombardi used to say, the best defense is a good offense. So, once you've dispatched the thatch, keep it from taking over again by taking these offensive measures:

- **Apply my Thatch Control Tonic** (for recipe, see page 119) each spring as soon as the temperature stays above 50°F.

- **Bag all of your grass clippings.**

- **Alter your watering habits** by watering deeply and letting the thatch area dry out. This encourages plant roots to move downward in search of water.

- **Use a natural soil conditioner** like my organic Thatch Buster once a month during the growing season.

- **Stick with my regular maintenance schedule** of fertilizing, aerating, and mowing your lawn.

- **Avoid applying high-nitrogen lawn fertilizers,** because their excess nutrients may encourage thatch growth.

- **Aerate your lawn** every few years.

- **Select either perennial ryegrass or tall fescue** when you install a brand-new lawn or replace an old one. Both of these are thatch-resistant types.

- **Finish strong each year** by applying the dry fertilizer/Epsom salts mix that I recommended way back in Chapter 2 (see page 36). You may need to reseed the lawn as well. Be patient: It takes about 6 weeks for a lawn 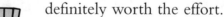 attacked by thatch to look and feel brand-new. But it's definitely worth the effort.

EPSOM SALTS

Ask Jerry

Q Help! I have a nice, young fella cut my grass when I'm away, but every time he does, he chops up a lot of the surrounding vegetation. What's the best way to protect my plants?

A That's easy! Just do what I've done at my place: Install a mower-proof edging around your planting beds. The easiest — and least expensive — edging is a strip of wood chips, about 2 feet wide, all the way around your flower beds. This makes a narrow path that not only protects your plants but lets you wander along and get up close and personal with all of those great flowers! The path gives you — and your helpers — room to maneuver and keep at a safe distance from delicate plants, and it requires almost no maintenance. (For some other simple edging ideas, see page 109.)

Q I've just bought my first house, which means I've also gotten my first lawn to mow. I'm okay on the mowing part, but is there a "best" way to rake up the clippings?

A You bet! My secret is to rake my new-mown lawn in the opposite direction of the way the grass blades are leaning. It makes them stand up straighter — and makes them easier to cut the next time I mow. If you don't have time to rake, just spray the lawn with my **Grass Clipping Dissolving Tonic** (page 332) right after you mow, and the clippings will disappear in no time at all.

Q I keep hearing that compacted soil is bad for my lawn. How can I tell whether my soil is getting too caked-up?

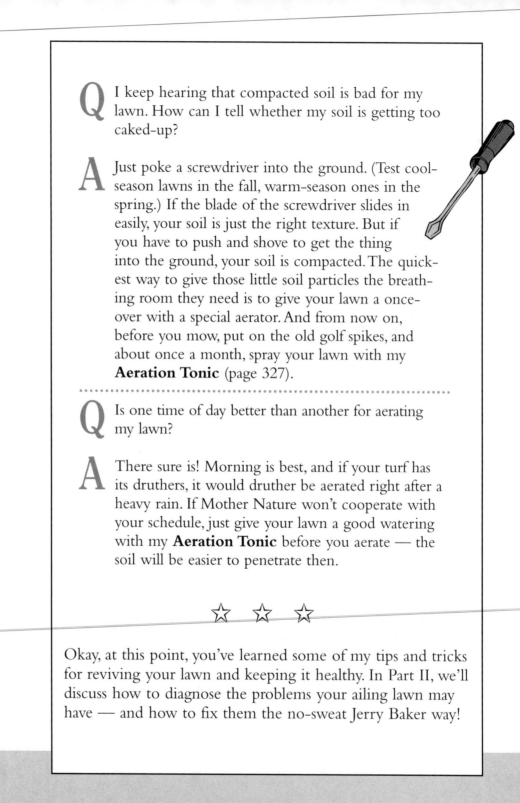

A Just poke a screwdriver into the ground. (Test cool-season lawns in the fall, warm-season ones in the spring.) If the blade of the screwdriver slides in easily, your soil is just the right texture. But if you have to push and shove to get the thing into the ground, your soil is compacted. The quickest way to give those little soil particles the breathing room they need is to give your lawn a once-over with a special aerator. And from now on, before you mow, put on the old golf spikes, and about once a month, spray your lawn with my **Aeration Tonic** (page 327).

Q Is one time of day better than another for aerating my lawn?

A There sure is! Morning is best, and if your turf has its druthers, it would druther be aerated right after a heavy rain. If Mother Nature won't cooperate with your schedule, just give your lawn a good watering with my **Aeration Tonic** before you aerate — the soil will be easier to penetrate then.

☆ ☆ ☆

Okay, at this point, you've learned some of my tips and tricks for reviving your lawn and keeping it healthy. In Part II, we'll discuss how to diagnose the problems your ailing lawn may have — and how to fix them the no-sweat Jerry Baker way!

Part II

When Things Go Wrong

CHAPTER 7

Environmental Enemies

Spilled gasoline, too much fertilizer, and toxic herbicides can leave ugly, brown dead patches in your lawn. Those miniponds of standing water caused by poor drainage can cause dips in your lawn and leave you with a real "sinking" feeling. And traffic of all kinds can sure wreak a whole lot of havoc!

This chapter will help you identify and then show you how to repair lawn damage caused by spills, ruts, high traffic, poor drainage, bumps and holes, slopes, bald spots, and a host of other environmental woes. Ready for the treatment tips? Let's dig in!

Splendid Spill Solutions

Lawn chemicals, gasoline and oil, and road salt can all do serious damage to your green pride and joy. But don't panic! I'm going to tell you how you can fix the problems before it's too late.

The Doctor Is In

When your lawn is ailin', you can't dial 911 for a lawn ambulance. I can't tell you how many times I've wished there was a lawn ER to handle the crisis. But with my help, you can train yourself to be a house-call lawn doctor who makes the right diagnosis to guarantee a healthy prognosis.

Your most important skill? Paying close attention. Catching trouble before it festers into a full-fledged lawn emergency will save you time, worry, and money.

A Gas Crisis

Sometimes you're in a hurry or you're just daydreaming a bit, and all of a sudden, you've overfilled the lawn mower with gasoline. The excess gas spills over and splashes onto the grass. Don't just stand there! You've got an ecological disaster on your hands because your yard has just been attacked by a powerful substance. This is the time to take action immediately.

First, drench — and I mean *drench* — the soil with soapy water (½ cup liquid soap per gallon of water). Let it soak in for a few minutes, then grab the hose and give the area a good dousing of water. If stubborn brown spots develop, cut out and remove the dead grass and soil to a depth of at least 5 inches. Fill with new soil and then reseed the area per my directions in Chapter 14.

An Ounce of Prevention

Never add gasoline or oil to your mower when it is parked on the lawn. Always do the pouring on a flat, dry surface like the sidewalk, driveway, or the garage, near the door (please keep the door open for ventilation). Use a funnel, and don't be in a hurry. Go slow with the flow and you'll minimize the risk of spills!

Fertilizer Fix

For less hazardous spills, like dry fertilizers, the solution is even simpler. Take the same initial step of drenching the area with soapy water, and then follow up with plenty of water daily for several days. Then apply gypsum at the rate of 50 pounds per 2,500 square feet of yard. (See pages 146–47.) The grass should perk up in a month or two.

Put a Halt to Salt

Plain and simple — salt kills grass! It doesn't matter whether the salt comes on coastal breezes or from a bag used to melt snow and ice on the driveway and sidewalk; either way, you get the same result.

You can help save your lawn from the ravages of salt by taking care to apply salt pellets *only* on concrete and asphalt surfaces. As careful as you are, however, it's likely that some salt will spill onto the lawn bordering your driveway and walkways or the run-off will seep into turf.

What to do? I've breezed through many an icy winter confidently knowing that I've protected my lawn against salt damage. In late fall, I liberally sprinkle gypsum in a 5-foot-wide band over all grass within spittin' distance of where I'm even thinking about using salt. Then I overspray the gypsum with my Winter Walkway Protection Tonic.

Winter Walkway Protection Tonic

To keep grassy areas around walks and driveways in good shape during winter, first sprinkle liberally with gypsum, then apply this Tonic. Mix:

1 cup of liquid dish soap
½ cup of ammonia
½ cup of beer

Combine all of the ingredients in your 20 gallon hose-end sprayer and apply it over the gypsum.

Roadblock Ahead

Think of my Winter Walkway Protection Tonic as sort of a roadblock for salt. One week later, follow up by applying an anti-transpirant like my Weatherproof, which locks in moisture but locks out harmful elements while protecting against sunscald, windburn, and salt and pollution damage. Try it, it really works!

Melt Down

This winter, why not try some terrific natural alternatives to melting the ice — like clean kitty litter or sand? Both provide traction on slippery surfaces, and they're cheap, effective, and lawn friendly. There's also a whole slew of new ice melters that are salt-free. Some even contain fertilizers that provide nutrients to your lawn as they wash away the ice.

Another way to protect your lawn is to grow salt-tolerant grass such as warm-season St. Augustine or cool-season fescues.

Pollution Solution Tonic

To give your lawn some relief from the dust, dirt, and pollution that accumulate over the winter, apply this mix with a handheld broadcast spreader as early as possible in the spring.

50 lbs. of pelletized lime
50 lbs. of pelletized gypsum
5 lbs. of Epsom salts

Spread this mix over 2,500 sq. ft. of lawn area, then wait at least 2 weeks before applying any fertilizer to the area.

Turf Trivia

Did you know you're the lucky recipient of a great big gift from modern scientific research?

New grasses are more resistant to diseases, pests, and weeds — some even require less mowing and watering! Plus, the variety of heights, shapes, foliage colors, and textures means that grass just plain looks better.

Good Riddance to Ruts

I remember one summer afternoon when I had invited a bunch of friends over for a cookout. It rained hard almost every day for the whole week before. On the day of the barbecue, the sun broke through and the sky was a beautiful, cloudless blue. Trouble was, my lawn was still soggy — like a sponge. After my driveway filled with cars, the latecomers parked on the front yard. I didn't think much about it until the next day, when I saw the tire tracks carved into my lawn! I took a deep breath, exhaled, and set about fixin' the ruts. My technique works well for all kinds of tire ruts on damp lawns, including those from wheelbarrows, bicycles, and lawn mowers.

Spinning Your Wheels?

Trying to get rid of tire tracks in your lawn, but feel like you're spinning your wheels? Let me share my secret on how to curb tread damage in a hurry. Wait for the area to dry out a bit, and then punch holes in the turf or walk on it with aerating lawn sandals. This allows the soil to expand somewhat. Then sprinkle gypsum over the damaged area at the recommended rate and overspray it with my special Tire-Track Remover Tonic.

Tire-Track Remover Tonic

Combine all of the following ingredients.

1 cup of ammonia
1 cup of beer
½ cup of baby shampoo
¼ cup of weak tea water

Mix in a 20 gallon hose-end sprayer, filling the balance of the sprayer jar with warm water. Apply to the point of run-off and repeat this treatment every 3 weeks. Quicker than you can say "Jumpin' Jack Flash," your lawn will be on the road to recovery!

A Holey Mess

Try as you might, you can't always keep your lawn out of harm's way. Your usually smooth-as-silk lawn sometimes develops holes and/or bumps that could drive you nuts. Here's how to deal with those problems.

Repairing Bumps and Holes

If you live in an area with changing seasons, the alternate freezing and thawing over winter can create bumps and holes in your lawn. Temperature changes cause the ground to repeatedly rise and fall. And how many times have you spotted tortured turf that was ripped to shreds  by an overzealous snowplow scooping up chunks of your lawn along with snow?

Also, your lawn may have gotten off kilter because you've done some landscaping or added a new garden, or your drain pipes or underground sprinklers are undermining a certain area. The result of any of these can be poor drainage, and before you know it, pools, puddles, and natural birdbaths appear in low spots in your yard. If your lawn has major drainage problems, you may need to undertake a wholesale attack to get things on an even keel. Flip ahead to pages 242–46 and I'll give you the lowdown on how to get going. But many dips, holes, and bumps can be fixed fairly easily if you know what to do.

Down with Dips

If your lawn needs a minor grading adjustment, the ideal time to make the repairs is when the soil and weather are most cooperative, usually in spring. If you can't get to it then, do it as soon as you can — anytime, that is, except when the ground is frozen. Your treatment method depends on how serious the problem is.

8 Steps to Dip-Free Lawns

Jerry Baker Says

"Get to the root of the problem if your lawn has exposed tree roots. Forget trying to mow this bumpy terrain — plant ground covers instead."

For the most minor problems, simply sprinkle some new topsoil on the low or damaged area. The grass will grow right up through the topsoil.

If the area is compacted and has standing water, you will need to aerate the turf before you fill it and reseed. Aerating opens up avenues in the soil and grass that allow food, water, oxygen, and chemical controls to get where they are needed the most — to the roots. Here's my step-by-step method:

Step 1. Remove the grass in the low or uneven area with a shovel or spade. Dig about 2 inches deep into the soil.

Step 2. Save healthy sod by rolling it up, tucking it away in a shady area temporarily, and keeping it moist. Buy some replacement sod as needed.

Step 3. Churn the soil with a spade to aerate it. For bumps, remove enough

soil to restore the proper level. For holes, fill in with good, clean (weed-free) topsoil to make the area level again.

Step 4. Rake the area until it is smooth.

Step 5. Water the site lightly; this helps the soil to settle.

Step 6. Unroll the good sod and return it to its original spot, or add a fresh piece of sod cut to the size of the bare spot.

Step 7. Lightly water the area daily for a week to 10 days, depending on the weather; this helps the sod to stabilize.

Step 8. Now for the finishing touch. After you've worked the kinks out of your lawn, it's time for a little treatment to keep it in tip-top form. Give it a good healthy soaking with my Kick-in-the-Grass Tonic. Until the soil and grass mend in the area, tread lightly around it.

Kick-in-the-Grass Tonic

After you've repaired your lawn, apply this tonic to help get it off to a rip-roarin' start.

1 can of beer
1 cup of antiseptic mouthwash
1 cup of liquid dish soap
1 cup of ammonia
½ cup of Epsom salts

Mix all of the ingredients in a large container, and then pour into your 20 gallon hose-end sprayer. Apply liberally to the point of run-off, wait 2 weeks, then apply it again.

Bare Spots

Even when you're giving it your best, unexpected problems can pop up on your home turf. It's almost a guarantee — like a sudden rain shower during the middle of a July picnic. Or a flat tire on a country bike ride when you're miles from home.

Anywhere grass grows, bare spots usually appear at least once a season. The culprit can be anything or anyone.

Out, Damn Spot!

One likely cause of bare spots is heavy foot traffic. And high-traffic areas with thinning turf are an open invitation to weeds. For high-traffic areas *in* the house, a lot of folks put down rugs or runners to handle the footwork. Be turf-wise and apply a similar strategy for heavily used areas outside.

No, I'm not recommending carpeting for outdoors: To prevent wear and tear and keep weeds at bay, plant durable, traffic-resistant grasses in these areas.

• **In warm-season regions,** go with Bahia grass, Bermuda grass, or zoysia grass.

• **For cool-season regions,** the best choices are Kentucky bluegrass, tall fescue, and perennial ryegrass.

The Path to Success

Give up on trying to grow grass in high-traffic areas. Instead, install bricks or paving blocks or make a simple path of gravel, coarse bark chips, or pine needles.

Stop Turf Scalping

During a dry spell, it is highly advisable to check the height setting on your mower. A close-to-the-turf setting can scalp a chunk of lawn quickly, leaving little bald spots. Fortunately, the grass will recover in time, but it's best to avoid this problem in the first place. As I've said before, never cut more than the top third of the grass blade at any one time.

Buzz Cuts Are Definitely Out!

Don't subscribe to the short, cropped, manicured look for your lawn. The buzz cuts some folks give their lawn keep roots from burrowing deep into the nutrient-rich lawn soil, which brings on a whole host of problems.

E-Trouble

If you've ruled out heavy traffic, overmown grass, your playful pup burying bones, your children pretending to be pirates looking for hidden treasure, lawn diseases, weeds, and bugs, then the likely cause is environmental, what I call E-trouble. No, it has nothing to do with the Internet or the World Wide Web.

Don't underestimate the grass-destroying powers of Mother Nature with her unwelcome droughts, heavy rains, bitter cold, and sweltering heat. So what's a lawn enthusiast to do? Never fear, 'Ol Jer is here!

Jerry's 10-Step Repair Plan: Reseeding Made Easy

When you see bare spots in your lawn, don't panic. I'm here to walk you through my surefire, grass-growing repair plan. Ready? Let's grow!

Step 1: Remove all dead grass, weeds, grass clippings, rocks, and debris from the injured area. Rely on a rake for most jobs. For tougher jobs, you'll need a shovel.

Step 2: Once you've cleaned the area, it's time to loosen the soil surface. Use a hoe or rake to stir things up a bit and churn the soil.

Step 3: Guarantee seeding success by spraying the soil with my Soil Prep Tonic (for recipe, see page 134).

Step 4: Give the platoon of replacement seeds a good soaking in my Seed Starter Tonic (for recipe, see page 134). Then dry the damp seeds on a smooth, flat surface such as a clean-swept area of your driveway or sidewalk. Lightly run a broom back and forth over the seeds to speed the drying process.

Step 5: Mix the seeds with a little professional planting mix and sand, and then spread the mix on the bare areas in your lawn. Top it off by sprinkling the area with some of my Plug Rejuvenating Tonic (for recipe, see page 335).

Step 6: Lightly cover the seed mix with soil by top-dressing or raking. Make sure you create a slight mound; you can bet that the soil will settle over time, and you don't want telltale dips in your lawn where you've made earlier repairs.

Step 7: Cover the whole area with a light layer of organic mulch. I prefer fresh straw.

Step 8: Use the back of a lawn rake and gently press down the seeded area to make the surface firm. Then lightly overspray it with my Spot Seed Tonic (for recipe, see page 134).

Step 9: The final, but an important, step! Keep the soil surface moist (not too wet, but not too dry) until the new seedlings are strong and thriving. Then resume your normal lawn-watering schedule.

Step 10: Give yourself a big pat on the back! Once you've followed these steps, no one — not even you — will be able to point to the former bald spots in your lawn. Your lush, thick lawn will be back . . . and this time with a vengeance!

Jerry Baker Says

"For successful spot repairing in the middle of the hot summer, follow my 10-Step Repair Plan plus one more: Give the area ample water. During the summer, the soil tends to be drier and to dry out faster than in spring, and you don't want the germinating seeds to dehydrate and die."

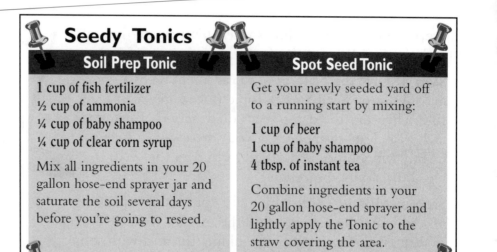

Seedy Tonics

Soil Prep Tonic

1 cup of fish fertilizer
½ cup of ammonia
¼ cup of baby shampoo
¼ cup of clear corn syrup

Mix all ingredients in your 20 gallon hose-end sprayer jar and saturate the soil several days before you're going to reseed.

Spot Seed Tonic

Get your newly seeded yard off to a running start by mixing:

1 cup of beer
1 cup of baby shampoo
4 tbsp. of instant tea

Combine ingredients in your 20 gallon hose-end sprayer and lightly apply the Tonic to the straw covering the area.

Seed Starter Tonic

This nifty Tonic will guarantee almost 100% grass seed germination every time. To make it, mix:

¼ cup of baby shampoo
1 tbsp. of Epsom salts
1 gallon of weak tea water

Combine these ingredients in a large container. Drop in your grass seed and put the whole shebang in your refrigerator for 2 days. The shampoo softens the seed shells, and the Epsom salts and tea provide nourishment to the emerging plants. The chill makes the seeds think that it's winter, so when they wake (warm) up, they'll be rarin' to grow.

It's Not for the Birds

Whenever you sow grass seed, watch out for birds; these winged wonders love to dine on fresh grass seed. This really terrific, bird-brain solution keeps them from the feast: Sprinkle high-quality grass seed onto bare spots and tamp into place. Take an old window screen, paint it green, and cover the newly seeded area with it. From a distance, no one can tell the screen from the grass. And the screen keeps birds from stealing the seed before it sprouts.

Sprigging and Plugging

For quick and complete repair to patchy lawns, don't overlook two powerful allies: sprigs and plugs. When I speak of sprigs, I don't mean those pieces of parsley that adorn your dinner plate at your favorite restaurant. In the lawn world, a sprig refers to a piece of specialized stem — a stolon or rhizome — that has nodes (joints) that are able to take root and create new grass plants. Plugs are tiny squares or circles of turf made up of established plants and a couple of inches of soil.

Jerry Baker Says

"When you plant grass seed in bare spots, be sure to select a variety that matches the green hue and leaf width of your lawn. You don't want the new stuff to stick out like a sore thumb!"

"Biscuit" Bushels

Now that we've gotten the introductions out of the way, let's look at sprigs and plugs in greater detail. Depending on your need, you can buy sprigs individually or by the bushel. Bermuda grass, St. Augustine, and zoysia grass top my sprig selections. Plugs, nicknamed "biscuits" by some of my lawn friends, are cut out of an existing lawn and planted 6 to 12 inches apart in the very spot that is in need of grass.

Personally, I prefer plugging. This repair method carries a higher rate of success than sprigging because plugs are packed with more roots. The more roots, the more likelihood that the plug will anchor itself into the soil and grow, grow, grow! For more about plugs and how to plant them, see pages 285–88 in Chapter 14.

Whether you opt for sprigs or plugs, you need to keep them moist and in the shade until you're ready to plant them. They will dry out and die quickly in direct sunlight. And keep them cool by mist spraying them occasionally with my Plug Rejuvenating Tonic. (For recipe, see page 136.)

Plug Rejuvenating Tonic

To keep your plugs and sprigs fresh as a daisy while you're waiting to put them in, periodically mist-spray them with the following tonic:

¼ cup of liquid dish soap
¼ cup of ammonia
1 gallon of weak tea water

When you're done planting don't let any go to waste; sprinkle the leftovers on the newly planted plugs.

Jerry Baker Says

"Here's a real money-saver: Buy a piece of sod and pull or cut it apart into individual plugs to patch up your yard."

Purchase Those Plugs!

Believe it or not, you don't have to cut plugs from your existing lawn — they can be bought from a lawn care supplier. They come in trays and are planted just like bedding plants.

In warm-season regions. Varieties you'll find are warm weather grasses like Bermuda, buffalo, centipede, St. Augustine, and zoysia.

In cool-season regions. You Northerners can make your own.

Mower Moratorium

After all your hard work seedin' and pluggin', you need to mow very, very carefully on the freshly repaired patches of grass. My best advice: Hold off on running the mower over these spots for at least 3, and preferably 6, weeks to allow the roots to get a good grip and the grass to grow. The first few times you mow, be sure to set your mower deck higher than normal so that you don't buzz-cut the new grass to death. Also, go slow and mow light because you don't want the mower wheels to sink into the freshly tilled soil.

Hope for a Slope

Mowing up and down slopes is a very tricky business. You need to be alert and keep a secure grip on your mower, which can be both physically and mentally taxing. And there are problems besides difficult mowing. Slopes are tough to drain properly; oftentimes, the crest is too dry and the bottom is too wet. Soil erosion can also be a big problem. Here's how to handle these problems.

Grasses for Slopes

Here's my number one hint: For gentle sloping areas, select grasses that require infrequent mowing, dry soil, and little to no fertilization. The idea is to keep your lawn care chores to a minimum whenever you have to maneuver on a slope.

If you think I'm about to tell you which grasses are my proven favorites for situations like this, you're right! Here they are:

- **For cool-region slopes:** hard fescue and sheep fescue
- **For warm-region slopes:** blue gramma grass or buffalo grass

Ground Covers for Slopes

If the area is very steep, consider replacing the grass with a durable ground cover that will anchor the soil and prevent rain run-off from carting away your nutrient-laden topsoil. Ground covers are real problem-solvers around the yard. And the best part about them? They look good *and* hold slopes in shape without a lot of upkeep! You might just say they suit my style. (For more on ground covers, see Chapter 16.)

Great Ground Covers

Crown vetch, daylilies, English ivy, creeping juniper, common periwinkle, St. John's wort, and woolly yarrow

Ask Jerry

Q Every time I fill up my lawn mower with gasoline, I worry that I'll spill some on the lawn. My wife says I'm just being a fuss-budget — a little gas won't hurt a healthy crop of grass. Who's right?

A You are! A gasoline spill can kill grass — or any other plant — faster than you can say "Fill 'er up." Always gas up your mower on a hard, flat surface, well away from your lawn or any other planted area. And use the same caution with chemical fertilizers, which can do almost as much damage.

Q I know I shouldn't do it, but sometimes I cheat and just fill 'er up wherever I am when I run out of gasoline. If I do spill some gas on my lawn, what should I do?

A First, mix up a big batch of soapy water (½ cup liquid dish soap per gallon of water) and drench the soil with it. Let it soak in for a few minutes, then turn a hose on the spot and give it a good shower. If some grass dies in spite of the dousing, cut out the brown spots to a depth of at least 5 inches, fill in with new soil, and reseed the area. Then give the area a light spray with my **Spot Seed Tonic** (page 337).

Q I live in big-time snow and ice country, and the city dumps tons of salt on my street. Is there any way I can protect my lawn?

A There sure is! Just spread a 5-foot-wide band of gypsum over all of the grass that borders the road. Then overspray the gypsum with my **Winter Walkway Protection Tonic** (page 340). Come spring, as soon as all the snow has melted, treat your grass to a big drink of my **Pollution Solution**

Tonic (page 335) — it'll get rid of all the dust, dirt, and general-purpose pollutants that have piled up over the winter.

Q I have a lot of big, old, beautiful trees in my yard. I love them, but the big roots make for bumpy mowing. Is there a special lawn mower I can get that will make for smoother going?

A Unfortunately, no. Your best bet is to forget grass under your trees and make a wide circle of bark mulch instead. (The mulch is actually better than grass anyway: Lawn grass competes with trees for water, and trees that get bumped by mowers suffer and can eventually die from the damage.)

Q I know that plugs are great for filling in bare spots in my lawn, but they cost an arm and a leg. Is there a less expensive alternative?

A For certain — make up your own! Just buy a piece of sod and cut it into whatever size pieces you need. Follow the same procedures as for "plugging," and don't forget to use my **Plug Rejuvenating Tonic** (page 335) when you're through planting.

☆   ☆   ☆

Well, we've covered quite a few lawn problems that you now know how to fix: damage caused by chemical spills, salt, tire ruts, frost heaves, and poor drainage. Now let's move on to a force that you'll find harder to control: the weather!

CHAPTER 8

When Mother Nature Won't Cooperate

If you're blessed with healthy soil and perfect weather conditions, your lawn can be virtually maintenance-free. Congratulations! But I doubt that you live in the Garden of Eden, so let's be realistic: Mama Nature doesn't always cooperate with ideal weather season to season or year to year.

No part of the country is spared. Sometimes, no matter where you live, at one time or another it may be too dry, too rainy, too hot, too cold, or too shady. I'm here to help your lawn survive during these less-than-picture-postcard-perfect times.

Quiz Time!

What do soda pop, the Old West, and lawns have in common? Give up? The answer is the number 6. Soda pop comes in 6-packs, the Old West was famous for 6-shooters, and in the United States, there are 6 lawn regions, based on climate. Knowing the weather tendencies where you live will help you choose the right grass for your climate. Pinpoint your lawn region on the map at the left, then refer to pages 269–70 for information about each region.

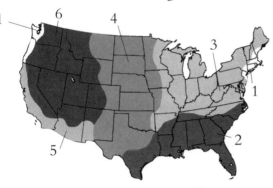

Lawn Regions in U.S.

The Backyard Climate Zones

You already know that both the climate and soil type influence the health of a lawn. Yet it may surprise you to learn that the conditions that influence your lawn's health can also vary from the front to the backyard and from sunrise to sunset. It's true, they do!

Tour Time

Try this test. Walk around your home at various times during the day and note the difference in temperature, sunlight, and shade in each location. In the morning, the warmest side of your house most likely will be on the east. Throughout most of the day, the south side will be warmed by the sun. By late afternoon, after the sun has passed its peak position in the sky, the west side of your house should be the warmest. The north side will likely be cool and shady the whole day.

Different parts of a yard behave differently and have different needs based on their contours and location. High areas tend to drain faster and require more water. Low areas tend to collect some run-off from rains or sprinklers, and so they need less water. Shaded areas need less watering than do sunny spots.

Coping with Drought

All plants (and that includes grass plants) need moisture to grow. To provide adequate moisture for a healthy, growing lawn, the top 6 to 8 inches of your soil should stay moist to support it. That obviously becomes more challenging when a drought occurs.

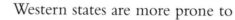

Western states are more prone to droughts, but we all know that Mother Nature can refuse to send rain anywhere, any time. Although you can't leap up and squeeze the rain out of those clouds overhead, an "ounce of prevention" will reduce the risk of losing your lawn during long dry spells.

Iron-Clad Protection

One of the best ways to protect your lawn from drought is by applying an anti-transpirant product, like my WeatherProof, which keeps the combination of hot sun and little rain from damaging your grass. It locks moisture in the plants while locking out the harmful effects of the weather and pollution. Be sure to apply it anytime *before* the really hot weather gets your lawn feeling down.

Drought Basics

So what do you do during a severe drought, especially when your local municipality orders water restrictions? You can't water as much as you'd like, but don't want to lose your lawn. Here are some tactics that've worked for me:

- **Cut back or stop fertilizing** during a drought. By reducing the amount of available fertilizer, you'll slow down your lawn's growth naturally and safely, and it will need less water.

- **Add a light coat of compost** to your lawn if you expect a dry spell. It helps retain moisture, releases nutrients, and conditions the soil. Use screened compost to be sure you have a fine, uniform product. Use a shovel and spread the compost as evenly as possible over the lawn. Put on just enough to cover the lawn with a layer about ½ inch deep. Lightly rake the area to spread the compost as evenly as possible, then water thoroughly.

- **Select drought-resistant,** deep-rooting grasses like fescues for new lawns or when reseeding.

- **Don't mow the grass** until it gets 3 inches tall, and then cut off only the top inch. This encourages roots to grow longer, hunting for moisture deep in the soil. Water loss from evaporation will also be reduced.

- **Keep your sprinkler system** in A-1 condition, and make sure it's right for your particular lawn. That way, you are not wasting water, overwatering some spots and underwatering others. Use a timer so you don't go hog-wild on the H_2O.

- **Water every 5 days** instead of every 3, but then water well. This encourages deep root growth.

- **Dethatch and aerate** in the spring to improve water penetration into the soil.

- **Step back** and assess your property. Maybe all you need is a small area of lawn instead of that Ponderosa-size spread you're now tending.

- **Use ground covers,** drought-resistant plants, patios, or decks instead of lawn grass. (See Chapter 16 for more on how to go about being lawn-less.)

- **Let your lawn go dormant** (and pray for rain!). Don't panic when the grass turns an ugly, scary brown color. It can go a few weeks without water and usually doesn't suffer irreversible damage.

- **When all else fails, throw in the trowel** and paint your lawn green. Your local nursery or lawn-care center should stock lawn paint. Then you can celebrate St. Patrick's Day year-round! For more smart watering tactics, see Chapter 5.

Give 'em a Fighting Chance

Plant more than one drought-tolerant variety when you start or overseed a lawn. Grass diversity will help your lawn survive those tough drought conditions.

Drought-Tolerant Grasses

Whether you're starting a lawn from scratch or replacing an ailing one, use this golden opportunity to select grasses that are best suited to the climate in your region. Generally, warm-season grasses can handle droughts much better than can cool-season grasses. My favorites are those grasses that tend to grow long roots that can reach out for all available soil moisture.

Best choices for warm climates: Blue gramma, buffalo grass, and hybrid Bermuda grass

Runners-up: Bahia grasses and zoysia grasses

Best for cool climates: Fine fescues, tall fescues, and Kentucky bluegrass

Deep Roots

As I told you in Chapter 5, during hot, dry spells, it's best to water deeply and then leave your lawn alone for several days, depending on the air temperature. This tactic encourages roots to grow deeper into the soil. Here's how: By soaking your lawn to a depth of 6 to 8 inches and then not watering again until the top layer dries out, you are encouraging grass roots to develop in the lower level below ground, not near the surface. It's like a camel storing water and using it to survive in the desert. Saturating this deep layer of soil activates deep, dense root growth that protects your lawn during an extended period without water.

During and After Droughts

You can minimize drought damage to your lawn by overspraying it once a week during hot weather with my Drought Buster Tonic. Once the drought is over, I want you to apply a dry, natural, organic fertilizer at half of the recommended rate, adding 1 lb. of sugar and 1 lb. of Epsom salts per 2,500 sq. ft. bag. Then overspray the turf with my Drought Recovery Tonic.

Drought Buster Tonic

Mix:

1 can of beer
1 cup of Thatch Buster
½ cup of liquid lawn food
½ cup of baby shampoo

Combine all of these ingredients in a 20 gallon hose-end sprayer jar and apply to the point of run-off. Use this Tonic in the early morning to minimize evaporation and give grass plants ample time to digest it. Then, in addition to your normal watering, water for 10 minutes at noon and again at 4:00 P.M. for optimum results.

Drought Recovery Tonic

Mix:

1 can of regular cola (not diet)
1 cup of baby shampoo
1 cup of ammonia

Combine all of these ingredients in your 20 gallon hose-end sprayer and saturate the turf to the point of run-off at 2-week internals until the grass returns to normal.

OFF-BEAT SOLUTIONS TO GETTING THE GREEN

If you're really convinced that you don't have the time to spend on your lawn, maybe there's a unique lawn solution right within shouting distance. In West Palm Beach, Florida, some folks fancy what I call the "lawn veneer" look. They rip out the sod, cover the ground with cement, and paint it green — for a never-to-be-mowed-again lawn!

Coping with Too Much Rain

"Rain, rain, go away. Come again some other day." At times, don't you wish you could repeat this childhood rhyme and make it come true?

Don't let steady showers dampen your spirits — or drown your lawn! I remember some springs when it rained so hard that I daydreamed about building an ark that would make even Noah proud. Talk about raining cats and dogs! You can't shut off Mother Nature's faucet, but you and your lawn can survive her rainy wrath.

After the Downpour

Here are some timely tips and tricks that'll restore your lawn to health once the heavy rains stop.

- **Try to stay off the grass** immediately after a heavy downpour or sprinkling. After all, you don't want to leave the "wrong impression" or tear up the turf and create a mud bath. Wait until all traces of standing water disappear.

- **Route any standing water away** from low spots in your lawn. Simple trenches in the turf should work (see page 109).

- **Aerate any damaged turf areas.** Strap on your aerating lawn sandals or golf shoes and walk around the area. This will help water percolate into the soil properly.

- **Apply gypsum at a rate of 50 pounds per 2,500 square feet** of yard. This will loosen the soil, encouraging better drainage — almost like an army of little rototillers going to work in the soil.

- **After you apply the gypsum,** wait a week and follow up with premium dry lawn food at the recommended rate.

- **Each fall, feed your lawn** with my Fall Lawn Food Mix to help get the turf in shape (see recipe below). Immediately overspray this dry feeding with my Thatch Buster™ or All-Season Green-Up Tonic (for recipe, see page 328).

- **If your soggy lawn begins to thin out,** reseed with a turf-type grass seed, like rye, as soon as you notice the problem. This quickly gets a ground cover established. Best bets: 'Derby' (a disease-resistant perennial ryegrass), 'Falcon' (a variety of tall fescue), and 'Palmer II' (another perennial ryegrass). Then next spring, reseed with a blend similar to your existing grass type. Don't forget to use my Seed Starter Tonic (for recipe, see page 336) to get the seed off and running.

- **In the worst cases, dig a series of small, deep holes in the turf.** Be sure to select inconspicuous areas in your lawn for these dry wells. They'll give the excess water a run-off route.

Fall Lawn Food Mix

3 lbs. of Epsom salts
1 cup of dry laundry soap
1 bag of premium dry lawn
  food (enough for 2,500 sq. ft.)

Apply this mix at half of the recommended rate with your handheld broadcast spreader.

Thatch Buster

Basic soil conditioning is the key to a lawn that resists problems, including soggy weather. An important tool in my soil conditioning arsenal is my Thatch Buster, which is made from organic ingredients, including humus. It controls thatch, works as a compost starter, eases summer stress, reduces the need for watering, and gives a boost to my lawn tonics.

For regular lawn care, spray your whole yard with Thatch Buster once a month.

Coping with Shade

Look around and find the shady "characters" hanging around your yard. I'm referring to the house, garage, shed, trees, fences, and anything else that creates shade. "Made in the shade" sounds good, but when it comes to lawns, inadequate sunlight causes more harm than good to lawn grasses. Without a minimum of 4 hours of sunlight a day, the rate of grass growth slows and a lawn thins and weakens. It becomes vulnerable to nasty diseases and insects, plus moss may develop. (For the lowdown on dealing with moss, see page 181).

Shade-Tolerant Grasses

Warm-season
Bahia grass
Centipede grass
St. Augustine
  grass

Cool-season
Fine fescues
Tall fescues

Select the Proper Grass

Most turf grasses prefer sunlight to shade. If you've got a lot of shade, then, if possible, for new lawns or renovated ones, select lawn grasses that are shade tolerant.

Other Shade-Fighting Tips

Beyond grass selection, there are several other things you can do to help your grass survive:

• Mow at higher levels.

• Water only in the morning.

• Water thoroughly, but infrequently (make sure that the grass dries out completely between waterings).

• Go easy on the fertilizer; more is not better!

• Discourage foot traffic in that area.

LET THE SUN SHINE IN

To clip away shade, bring out the clippers. Clear away all low-growing foliage, and prune tree branches to let in more sunlight. With a little effort you should be able to brighten up your shady situation!

If You Can't Fight It . . .

Finally, if you've decided you just can't live with a lawn that's in shade all day, I recommend replacing it with ground covers that were made for the shade! Just plant 'em, mulch 'em, and clear 'em of weeds a few times the first year. Then sit back and let them work their merry magic.

You know your lawn better than anyone else does, but the usual suspects that harbor shady lawns are north sides of buildings, tall trees and tall hedges, and fences. For these areas, consider the low-maintenance ground covers to the right. Flip to Chapter 16, and I'll fill you in on the details about ground covers and much, much more.

Low-Maintenance Ground Covers

Ajuga
English ivy
Common
 periwinkle
Strawberry
 geranium
Sweet woodruff
Winter creeper

Beat the Heat

Hot spells make us head for the shade (or inside for a little A/C) and a tall, chilled glass of iced tea. Too bad your lawn can't do the same thing. Unfortunately, it has to stay put and endure the heat. Here's what you can do to lend a helping hand.

Choosing the Heat Lovers

Most warm-season grasses handle the sun's blazing rays better than do cool-season grasses, which tend to slow down in growth and even go dormant during hot weather. Some grasses, even some usually cool-season grasses, stand up to occasional heat spells better than others. Here are my choices.

For Hot Regions	For Cool-Season Regions
Bermuda grass	Fine fescues
Buffalo grass	Tall fescues
Centipede grass	Kentucky bluegrass
St. Augustine grass	Perennial ryegrass
Zoysia grass	

Heat-Sink Surfaces

Sidewalks, driveways, and patios collect sunlight and spread the warmth to nearby lawn areas. So do walls. Light-colored walls reflect sunlight that can burn your Bermuda, and dark-colored walls reflect heat that can fry your fescue or zap your zoysia.

A good way to solve this problem is to create buffer gardens between the surface and the lawn. Sow a narrow strip of petunias along the driveway or make foundation plantings of bushy evergreens in front of a wall. These buffer gardens may also need some extra water in their warm locations. Install a soaker hose along the planting to give these gardens the moisture they need. To prevent grassy spots near these areas from drying out too quickly and dying, water them more often than you do the rest of your lawn, and every now and again, give 'em a dose of my Summer Soother Tonic.

Summer Soother Tonic

If you're like me and you enjoy watering your yard from time to time by hand, then why not kill two birds with one stone? By that I mean to water *and* soothe your plants at the same time with a nice relaxing shower.

1 cup of baby shampoo
1 cup of hydrogen peroxide
2 cups of weak tea water

Combine these ingredients in your 20 gallon hose-end sprayer, and spray everything in sight. It makes for a really delightful summer shower.

Just to Be Safe

You can't lower the temp, but you *can* do some things to lower your lawn's chances of being harmed by heat.

• **Avoid fertilizing** during hot weather, especially if it's dry. Stressed out grasses are much more easily damaged by fertilizer.

• **Be on the lookout** for summer patch, a lawn disease that loves hot, humid weather. Dose the area with my Anti–Summer-Patch Tonic (for recipe, see page 328; see also page 234).

Coping with Cold

Brrrr! Windchill, heavy snows, and alternate freezing and thawing will all take their toll on your turf by causing bumps or dips in the terrain. You folks in cold climates can minimize Mother Nature's "cold shoulder" by planting Kentucky bluegrass. Among the cool-season grasses, it ranks as one of the cold hardiest. Other cool-season grasses, such as colonial bent grass, creeping bent grass, and fine fescue, will survive severe winters, too.

In late fall, just before the really cold weather sets in, you should also give your lawn a good application of an anti-transpirant like WeatherProof, which protects not only against cold damage but also against harsh winter winds, dust, dirt, road salt, and pollution.

Create a Winter Wonder-Lawn

If you live in the North, the day will surely come when you peek out of your frosted windows on a cold, wintry day and see snow blanketing your lawn. If you've followed my regular lawn maintenance program up until that time, then you can coast through the winter without a lawn care in the world.

The condition of your turf as winter approaches is critical. The healthier the turf, the less likely that snow mold, fungus, or other problems will develop. (I'll explain those in Chapter 13.)

Keeping your lawn in good health going into the winter should be at the top of your priority list. So, first off, I want you to clean up everything with my Fall Clean-Up Tonic (for recipe, see page 152). Within a week or so of applying it, feed your lawn with the dry lawn food/Epsom salts mixture I described in Chapter 2 (page 37).

And, most importantly, follow up the fertilizer feeding by treating your lawn to what I somewhat irreverently like to call The Last Supper Tonic (for recipe, see page 152).

Fall Clean-Up Tonic

To make this Tonic, mix:

1 cup of baby shampoo
1 cup of antiseptic mouthwash
1 cup of Tobacco Tea★
1 cup of chamomile tea

Combine all of the ingredients in a bucket, and then add 2 cups of it to your 20 gallon hose-end sprayer, filling the balance of the sprayer jar with warm water. Overspray your turf, trees, shrubs, and beds on a day when the temperature is above 50°F.

★For recipe, see page 326.

The Last Supper Tonic

This Tonic helps your final fall feeding to break down and really work its magic.

½ can of beer
½ cup of apple juice
½ cup of Gatorade
½ cup of urine
½ cup of fish fertilizer
½ cup of ammonia
½ cup of regular cola (not diet)
½ cup of baby shampoo

Combine all ingredients in a large bucket and pour into your 20 gallon hose-end sprayer. Apply to the point of run-off. This Tonic softens up the dry fertilizer mix so that the nutrients can be easily digested by your lawn all winter long.

No Snow Worries?

Winter is tough on warm-season grasses, too, but in a different way. While cool-season grasses stay nice and green through the cooler weather, warm-season types feel a frost and turn brown.

To keep a warm-season lawn looking green all winter, overseed in October with annual ryegrass. This cold-hardy grass will establish itself quickly, stay green all winter long, then die away just as your warm-season lawn is trading in its old brown blades for new ones of bright green.

Jerry Baker Says

"I always prepare for winter by cutting my lawn in the fall until the blades of grass stop growing."

Wintertime Feeding

For you folks living in milder climates where snow is almost as rare a sight as a zebra walking down the road, wintertime is feeding time. But I want you to use a good, balanced, all-purpose fertilizer, like a 10-10-10 mix. For those of you who live in the no-mo-snow Sunbelt states, the winter months are the time to apply any premium dry lawn food at half of the recommended rate, adding 1 pound of Epsom salts per each 25 pounds of lawn food. Then follow it up with my Stress Reliever Tonic, which will keep your lawn relaxed during the winter months.

Stress Reliever Tonic

To keep your grass growing happy and healthy during the winter months, you folks in the milder climates should overspray your turf once a month with my Stress Reliever Tonic. Mix:

1 cup of baby shampoo
1 cup of antiseptic mouthwash
¾ cup of weak tea water
1 cup of Tobacco Tea★
¼ cup of ammonia

Combine all of these ingredients in your 20 gallon hose-end sprayer and apply it to your turf to the point of run-off.

★For recipe, see page 326.

Lawn Lore

Credit the ancient Greeks with cultivating the first crop of what is today called Kentucky bluegrass. The seeds migrated throughout Europe during the Middle Ages and eventually wound up on some seafaring vessels sailing from England to American shores during colonial times.

So, despite the Kentuckians' pride of ownership, their bluegrass is not even native to the Bluegrass State.

WEATHERING THE WEATHER: RATING THE GRASSES

GRASS	DROUGHT	HEAT	COLD	SHADE	FERTILIZER NEEDS
WARM-SEASON GRASSES					
Bahia grass	good	good	poor	good	low
Hybrid Bermuda grass	good	good	so-so	poor	average
Blue gramma grass	good	good	good	so-so	low
Buffalo grass	high	high	good	poor	low
Carpet grass	so-so	high	poor	poor	low
Centipede grass	so-so	good	poor	so-so	low
St. Augustine grass	poor	good	poor	good	average
Zoysia grass	good	good	good	so-so	low
COOL-SEASON GRASSES					
Bluegrass, Canada	so-so	poor	good	so-so	low
Bluegrass, Kentucky	so-so	so-so	good	so-so	average
Bluegrass, rough	poor	poor	good	so-so	average
Creeping bent grass	poor	poor	poor	so-so	high
Fescues, fine	good	so-so	good	good	average
Fescues, tall	good	good	good	so-so	low
Perennial ryegrass	so-so	so-so	good	so-so	low

Ask Jerry

Q I've heard that it's not good to fertilize my lawn during dry spells. Why is that?

A It's because going cold turkey on fertilizer will slow down your lawn's growth, and when it's growing slower, it won't need so much water.

....

Q What else can I do if I know a drought is headed my way?

A One of the best things you can do is spread a light layer of compost across your lawn. It'll condition the soil so it can hold moisture better. Then, once a week during hot weather, overspray your lawn with my **Drought Buster Tonic** (page 330).

....

Q I'm starting a new lawn. Any suggestions on how to protect it from drought?

A Here's my best advice: Diversify! Instead of sowing just one kind of drought-tolerant grass, use two or three different varieties. Just as it does in nature, diversity will help your lawn stand up against whatever the dry, cruel world dishes out!

....

Q Winters in my part of the country would make a polar bear feel right at home. What grasses do you recommend for *really* frosty territory?

A My all-time cold-climate favorite is good old Kentucky bluegrass. It'll take all the icy weather Mother Nature throws its way. Other good choices for tough winters are fine fescue and colonial bent grass.

Q Where I live, it stays pretty mild all winter, but when the first frost of the season hits my warm-season grass, it turns brown and stays that way until spring. Is there any way I can keep my lawn green through the winter?

A You bet there is! Just overseed your lawn in October with annual ryegrass. This cold-hardy trouper will dig right in, stay nice and green all winter long, and then fade away in spring, just as your warm-season turf is greening up.

Okay, now you've done battle with droughts, deluges, shade, heat, and cold. Feel up to taking on some more lawn enemies — the not-necessarily-visible, but oh-so-obvious ones? Let's go!

CHAPTER 9

Critter Calamities

Animals! You love 'em, but sometimes they're a real pain. Dog urine can leave ugly, brown dead patches in your lawn. Cats can chew up your favorite garden plants or make unwelcome "deposits" to mark their territory. Gophers, moles, and other critters dig deep holes that can literally turn a lush lawn into a mountainous moonscape overnight. What's a turfmaster to do? Fear not, for this chapter is filled with super strategies for dealing with lots of critters — both friend and foe.

Put a Leash on Doggie Damage

Dogs may be man's best friend, but they certainly aren't a lawn's best pal. When dogs gotta go, they seek relief outdoors. Maybe someday we'll be able to train them to use indoor plumbing.

But until then, keep this in mind: When your dog does its business on your lawn, it's *your* business to take steps to save your grass.

Dog urine is packed with nitrogen. Yes, lawns need nitrogen to feed upon, sustain soil life, and maintain a healthy green color. But concentrated nitrogen, especially when the source is Fido, leaves telltale dead-grass circles with those bright green outer rims. The grass can't handle this dose of concentrated nitrogen. Why, in no time at all, burns or bare spots start to surface.

What to Do about 'Dem Dogs?

The quickest solution: Keep the hose handy. Water down your dog's favorite target spots immediately after the deed is done to dilute the strength of the nitrogen. The more long-term solution is to train your dog to go in one place in the yard, like a back corner, so your whole lawn won't look like a minefield. Then replace the sod every so often in the severely damaged areas.

Here are two other paws-itively pleasing solutions to try:

• **Feed your dog brewer's yeast each day.** The yeast takes the pungent punch out of the dog's urine. (And while you're at it, add some bits of fresh garlic cloves to the doggie dish: Garlic helps keep fleas away.)

• **Apply my Dog-B-Gone Tonic** to places where you don't want pooches to roam.

Dog-B-Gone Tonic

To keep dogs away from your yard, liberally apply this spicy tonic to your soil.

2 cloves of garlic
2 small onions
1 jalapeño pepper
1 tbsp. of cayenne pepper
1 tbsp. of hot sauce
1 tbsp. of chili powder
1 tbsp. of liquid dish soap
1 qt. of warm water

Chop the garlic, onions, and pepper fine, and then mix with the rest of the ingredients. Let the mixture "marinate" for 24 hours, strain it through cheesecloth, then sprinkle it on any areas where dogs are a problem. If you're on the howl prowl, the hole diggers will go elsewhere!

Doggie Damage Repair Tonic

To fix those ugly brown or yellow spots in your lawn caused by dog droppings, remove the dead or dying grass in the affected area. Overspray the turf with 1 cup of baby shampoo per 20 gallons of water, and then apply gypsum at the recommended rate. Wait a week, and then mix up a batch of my Doggie Damage Repair Tonic.

1 can of beer
1 cup of ammonia
1 can of regular cola (not diet)

Combine these ingredients in a 20 gallon hose-end sprayer. Then overspray the turf every other week until the normal color returns.

The Best Grasses

When it comes to lawns and dogs, not all grass is created equal. Fescue and perennial ryegrass are resistant to damage caused by dog urine. The most sensitive turf types are Bermuda grass and Kentucky bluegrass. So choose your turf accordingly.

POOP SCOOPING

Doggie-doo is much less of a problem than urine because it is a solid, so it releases its nutrients more slowly. Just take a stroll out over your lawn with the pooper-scooper every day or so, and the problem will be solved.

The Neighborhood Canines

Let's say you've managed to train your dog on the dos and don'ts of doggie doo-doo. But what about those four-legged, tail-wagging visitors that live down the block? Check with your veterinarian about using animal-repellent sprays, or save yourself some money and try any or all of these homemade repellents:

- **Apply my All-Purpose Pest Prevention Potion** (for recipe, see page 327).

- **Spread mothballs, tobacco dust**, dried blood, or oil of mustard in areas that are favorite doggie haunts.

- **Sprinkle cayenne pepper** or mothball flakes in and around prime urination areas.

- **Spray your trash cans and bags** with a pine-scented cleaning detergent mixed with an equal amount of water. Or hang ammonia-soaked rags on the handles.

- **If all else fails, consider pricier alternatives:** Install a fence or Yard Guard electronic repeller, or plant a hedge of thorny shrubs around your yard's perimeter.

Dealing with the Damage

When any enemy of your lawn creates a dead patch of turf, follow the step-by-step, easy repair plan I outlined in Chapter 7 (see pages 132–33). It'll have you seeing green in no time at all!

Being Catty

It's been said that dogs are people oriented and cats are territory oriented. But even if you do keep your own cat indoors and out of harm's way, you can bet that there are some neighborhood cats roaming around your yard that are anything but the cat's meow. If felines claw, chew, spray, or make unwelcome deposits in your yard, try one of the natural remedies on the next page.

Avoiding Cat-astrophes

Cats are smart, so you may have to try several of these before you hit upon the right one.

- **Get a big, loud, barking dog**.

- **Give a little,** and dedicate a place in your yard where you grow catnip just for them. They'll be too busy enjoying this frisky flavor to bother with anything else.

- **Sprinkle ground black pepper**, hot cayenne pepper, mothball flakes, or dry Borax soap powder in and around the places you want to protect.

- **Fool them** by filling large pop bottles half full of water. Put a couple of long, thin strips of aluminum foil into the bottles and add a bit of bleach to prevent stinky algae from growing. Place the bottles strategically around the problem zone. The changing foil reflections are enough to frighten felines and foil catty problems.

Meow-a-lous Tonics

Cats are very scent oriented. You can make them turn up their noses and head elsewhere by overspraying the perimeter of your yard with either one of these two Tonics.

Tonic #1: Mix ½ cup of Tobacco Tea (for recipe, see page 326) or oil of mustard and ¼ cup of liquid dish soap in 2 gallons of warm water.

Tonic #2: Add 1 clove of garlic (crushed), 1 tbsp. of cayenne pepper, and 1 tsp. of liquid dish soap to 1 qt. of warm water, and purée the heck out of it.

Scat Cat Solution

If felines are digging in your yard, send them packing with my All-Purpose Pest Prevention Potion (for recipe, see page 327), or with this Tonic:

5 tbsp. of flour
4 tbsp. of powdered mustard
3 tbsp. of cayenne pepper
2 tbsp. of chili powder
2 qts. of warm water

Mix all of these ingredients together and sprinkle the solution around the perimeter of the areas that you clearly want to mark as being "Off Limits!"

Go fer Gophers

Are gophers tearing up your turf?
Gophers are active at all times of the
day, so it'll be hit or miss trying
to catch them in the act. But
keep looking, and when your
ID is certain, experiment with one
or more of these tactics to try to persuade them to move on out
of your neighborhood:

- **Place fish heads, human or dog hair,** bleach, mothballs, used kitty litter, or dry ice in their tunnels.

- **Block all exits** except the main tunnel entrance; then stick in a hose, turn it on, and try to flood them out.

- **Gas them out with gopher gas bombs** available from local garden centers or garden catalogs.

- **Use my Gopher-Go Tonic** at the very first sign of trouble.

Gopher-Go Tonic	Goodbye Gophers and Move On Moles Tonic
I've had amazing results with this Tonic, and so have other folks who have tried it.	Mix up and apply a batch of this Tonic to rid your lawn of gophers and moles.
2 tbsp. of castor oil 2 tbsp. of liquid dish soap 2 tbsp. of urine	1 cup of liquid dish soap 1 cup of castor oil 2 tbsp. of alum (dissolved in hot water)
Combine these ingredients in half a cup of warm water, and then stir the mixture into 2 gallons of warm water. Pour it over the infested areas.	Use your 20 gallon hose-end sprayer to apply the Tonic to the point of saturation.

Gopher Architecture

To successfully get rid of gophers by placing fish heads or other substances in a gopher burrow, you need to know something of the ways of gopher home building.

Whatever you use to deter gophers, you need to place it in the main tunnel. Each burrow network is a series of lateral tunnels that are short and gently sloping. These lead to the main burrow. Lateral tunnels usually have piles of earth around them. The main tunnel has no dirt around it but instead is marked by well-trimmed plants. At least they're neat and clean about something!

A Mole's Toll

Moles are often confused with gophers, but they are entirely different critters. Moles are smaller and have a pointed snout and large, clawed front paws that are well suited for intense digging. You rarely see them, but you sure know they're there!

They Love to Eat!

Moles love to eat underground insects, grubs, and worms, and can, in fact, burrow up to 200 feet in one night! The tasty grubs tumble into the mole's tunnels as they dig their way along. But in their quest for food, these energetic earth movers leave endless raised ridges in the lawn around their burrows, as well as those huge mounds of dirt that they call "Home, Sweet Home."

Some folks deter moles by gassing them, poisoning them, or putting out wind toys to spook them. The moles often leave, but, unfortunately, they don't always stay away. The best thing to do is to eliminate their food source: the insects, grubs, and worms that live in the soil and that moles just love!

Mole-Chasing Strategies

Because moles are such dastardly little critters, you need to arm yourself with an arsenal of weapons. Use several in conjunction with each other to assure complete control. Fight back with these tried-and-true homemade mole repellents.

- **Leave the burrows raised** and add mothballs to the runs every 6 feet or so.

- **Push tiny thorny twigs** (best bets are barberry, raspberry, and rose) down into their runs. Or try broken glass. You may be surprised to learn that moles are incapable of clotting their blood, so even a slight cut can cause them to bleed to death.

- **Sprinkle used kitty litter** into their holes to signal that big, hairy predators are lurking about.

- **Use my Mole Chaser Tonic,** which discourages them fast!

- **Cut Juicy Fruit gum** into small pieces and drop them in runs every foot or so. The moles just *hate* the smell!

- **Apply a commercially available product** like my Liquid Mole Repellent that comes ready to attach to your hose and spray on your lawn. Moles hate the taste of this brew and scurry off in the other direction wherever it's applied.

- **Trap 'em in a Choker Loop** or Harpoon Mole Trap. Both are easy-to-use traps that you put right into the moles' tunnels — out of reach of children and pets.

- **Go "green" high-tech** and use a Natural Mole Chaser, which uses nature's breezes to power a small, quiet windmill that creates underground vibrations and rattles in mole holes.

Gargantuan Appetite

Moles have appetites that are equivalent to that of elephants — they can eat *half* their body weight in food every day. No wonder moles hide underground most of the time. They lack a flattering figure!

Mole Chaser Tonic

In a medium-size container, mix these ingredients.

2 tbsp. of hot sauce
1 tsp. of chili powder
1 tbsp. of liquid dish soap
1 qt. of water

Pour a little in the mole runways to make them run away!

All-Purpose Pest Prevention Potion

This Tonic repels most critters, including gophers and moles. To make it, mix:

1 cup of ammonia
½ cup of liquid dish soap
½ cup of urine
¼ cup of castor oil

Combine in a 20 gallon hose-end sprayer and thoroughly saturate animal runs and burrows.

The Restaurant's Closed!

The first step in battling moles, armadillos, raccoons, and skunks is to stop letting your lawn serve their favorite meal: grubs. To get rid of grubs, treat your lawn with milky spore disease *(Bacillus popilliae)*, predatory nematodes, neem, or, as a last resort, Merit Grub Control.

Insecticides are most effective in controlling grubs if they're applied when grubs are small and feeding near the surface of the soil, usually in late summer. At other times (like spring and fall), it's best to call in a pro.

Jerry Baker Says

"Armadillos, raccoons, and skunks like earthworms, too, so getting rid of grubs is only part of the battle. If you've got an overabundance of earthworms, use my Worms Away Tonic (for recipe, see page 250).

The Other Turf Diggers: Armadillos, Raccoons, and Skunks

The holes dug in your yard may be caused not by gophers or moles but by armadillos, raccoons, or skunks, depending on where you live. As you might expect, armadillos tend to hang out in the warmest regions (from North Carolina to New Mexico). Raccoons and skunks appear from coast to coast. Party time for these critters is early in the morning and late in the evening. If you spot any of them hanging around, try these tactics:

- **Spray my All-Purpose Varmint Repellent** liberally anywhere you want to keep unwelcome critters away.

- **Secure all garbage can lids** to keep these critters from rifling through your trash and spreading it around.

- **Dab nylon stockings with perfume** and hang them up.

- **Sprinkle the area with blood meal,** fox scent, or coyote urine (available at garden centers or from mail-order suppliers).

- **Sprinkle mothballs in and around the areas** where critters like to hang out.

- **Rattle pie tins, streamers, and other noisemakers.**

All-Purpose Varmint Repellent

This Tonic will get rid of just about anything, including your wife and kids. So be forewarned. Mix these ingredients.

½ cup of Murphy's Oil Soap
½ cup of lemon-scented dish soap
½ cup of castor oil
½ cup of lemon-scented ammonia
½ cup of hot, hot, hot sauce
½ cup of urine

Combine in a 20 gallon hose-end sprayer. Apply this Tonic to the point of run-off to any areas that need protection. It is especially effective against animals with a keen sense of smell, like dogs, cats, and deer.

Dodge the Ducks

If you're lucky enough to live on a lake or golf course, then you know that the biggest irritation with ducks and geese is not their noisy cackling but the messy droppings they leave on your lawn. You slip and fall in the smelly goo, plus it kills patches of grass. Well, you don't need to take this sitting down (especially if you've just slipped). Fight back with these strategies:

- **Place stakes in random patterns** along your shoreline, then stretch wire or string in between stakes and flag the string. This fouls up their takeoffs and landings so that the fowl will go elsewhere.

- **Bully them with noise.** Buy a cheap timer and audiotape of loud, barking dogs or a loud horn; have it sound each time they land, and soon, they won't be landing no mo'.

- **Apply a commercial goose repellent** to the areas where geese gather. It tastes truly terrible — enough to make them head for the nearest body of water for a drink.

Ask Jerry

Q I've just been adopted by a new puppy. Is there any grass that will stand up to his frequent bathroom breaks?

A Pups will be pups. But the answer is, yes — fescue and perennial ryegrass are both resistant to damage caused by dog urine. Whatever you do, steer clear of Bermuda grass and Kentucky bluegrass. Your puppy's spraying will do them in quicker than you can say "101 Dalmations."

Regardless of what kind of grass you have, anytime young Fido does what comes naturally, spray the scene of the action with my **Doggie Damage Repair Tonic** (page 330). It'll help keep your lawn green and springy.

Q What's the best way to keep my neighbor's cats off my lawn?

A Simple! Just spray the perimeter of your lawn with my **Meow-a-lous Tonics** (page 334). Those frisky felines will take one whiff and without hesitation head elsewhere — pronto.

Q I've tried shoving every repellent I've heard of down the gopher holes in my yard, but nothing has worked. How come?

A It sounds like you've been getting at their network of lateral tunnels but missing the main one — and that's where you need to concentrate your efforts. Lateral tunnels have dirt piled around the outside. You can spot the main tunnel because its entrance has no dirt piled around it; instead, it's surrounded by well-trimmed plants. Just pour my **Gopher-Go Tonic** (page 331) around that spot and watch those buck-toothed bandits head for the hills!

Q The moles in my lawn are driving me crazy! Every time I think I've gotten rid of them for good, they come charging back again. Is there any hope?

A Sure there is! Pour a dose of my **Mole Chaser Tonic** (page 335) into their little runways. They'll soon beat a trail to who-knows-where.

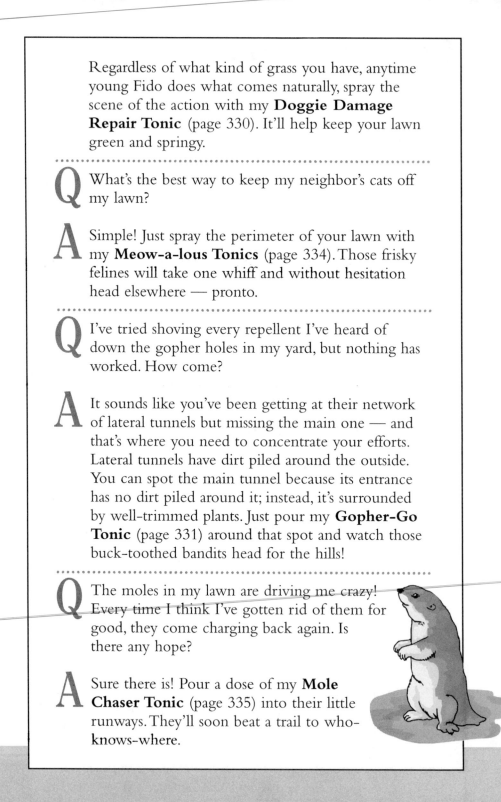

☆ ☆ ☆

As you can see, protecting your lawn from critters means that sometimes you need to use a little extra care with chemicals, and sometimes you'll be waging war against enemies who somehow seem a whole lot smarter than you are! The important thing is to be vigilant, act quickly before your problem multiplies, and remember three of the four Ps of lawn care I outlined in Chapter 1: patience, persistence, and if all else falls, plenty of prayer!

CHAPTER 10

Those Wicked Weeds

Wouldn't you love to just wiggle your nose and wish all your weeds away? Truth be told, you'll never totally win the war on weeds. Even the most pristine lawn in America sports a few weeds here and there. (*Pssst* — the secret is out: Weeds even reside at 1600 Pennsylvania Avenue, home of the President.) But don't get the wrong idea: I'm not suggesting that you throw in the towel and let weeds run wild all over your beloved lawn. Far from it! In this chapter, I'll arm you with knowledge so that you have the upper hand against weeds season after season, year after year. You'll learn how to control 'em so they never show their ugly little mugs in your corner of the world again!

They're Not All Alike

A weed is a weed is a weed, right? Wrong! Weeds are only weeds in the eyes of the beholder. What you regard as an eyesore, a neighbor or someone three states over might see as a beautiful wildflower. It all depends on your perspective.

Just like us, weeds come in all shapes and have their own likes and dislikes. Most weeds love the same soil conditions that healthy grass does, but hardy weeds can live in any lawn, even those with poor soil. Other types of weeds are more selective about where they take root. Some like wet areas; others are happier in dry conditions. Some thrive in acidic soil; others prefer alkaline.

Know Your Enemy

Knowing that different weeds exist is the first step toward eliminating those you don't want in your lawn. If you're not sure of what you've got, take a specimen (roots and all) to your local nursery or County Extension office to determine its identity. Or pick up a good book or scan the Internet for photos until you make a positive ID of your unwanted weed.

Although there are lots of weeds out there, they fall into one of two main groupings, depending on what their leaves look like.

Narrowleaf weeds. These weeds generally have long, grasslike leaves and always have parallel veins. They include crabgrass, quack grass, sedges, and rushes. Some lawn grasses can be weeds if they grow where they aren't wanted. For example, the broad blades of tall fescue can ruin the look of a fine-textured lawn, and the aggressiveness of Bermuda grass can turn a blended turf lawn into a solid mat of Bermuda. There are both annual and perennial narrowleaf weeds.

Jerry Baker Says

"One year's weeds turn into many years' seeds."

Broadleaf weeds. These can have leaves in a variety of shapes, but they are usually wider than those of narrowleaf weeds. The veins in the leaves are netted or weblike. Broadleaf weeds include dandelion, plantain, and chickweed. There are both annual and perennial broadleaf weeds.

The Best Defense:
Healthy, Appropriate Grasses

Practice a little weed psychology. It's easy! When it comes to weeds, the best offense is a good defense. That old adage applies to lawns as well as football teams. Here are some ways to keep weeds from scoring in your yard.

"GOLDEN RULES" OF LAWN CARE

Strong, healthy lawns are able to outmuscle a weed invasion much easier than can weak, neglected lawns; so water, mow, and fertilize properly as we've discussed previously. Regularly apply my All-Season Clean-Up and All-Season Green-Up Tonics (for recipes, see pages 327–28). Aerate to dispatch thatch and compacted soil. For the first cut of the summer, set your mower high so that tall grasses shade weed seeds and prevent them from germinating.

STEP LIGHTLY

Avoid trampling on the lawn when it is wet. The more soles that touch the grass, the greater the risk that soil is compacted and individual grass plants damaged.

KEEP YOUR LAWN THICK

When lawns are lush and thick, there's little wiggle room left for troublesome weeds to take hold. Healthy grass shades out weed seeds and takes advantage of the water and nutrients available.

Methods of Weed Control: From Hand Pulling to Soil Improvement

Unfortunately, none of the natural products that are available can be spread or sprayed over the entire lawn and still be savvy enough to kill *only* weeds. At least not yet! But my research pals at some agriculturally oriented colleges are working on this as we speak. In the meantime, try going *au naturel* with the following chemical-free approaches to weed control. They require a little work but are well worth the effort. And if in spite of all your good deeds and intentions weeds are still a fact of life, stay cool. As they say in Paris: "*C'est la vie.*" Try living in harmony with weeds. If it's green, mow it. You'll be much happier that way.

A Corny Herbicide

Corn gluten is a preemergent (see page 176) herbicide that is a cousin to corn syrup. It tames crabgrass and dandelions easily but takes a little longer to tackle other weeds. On the down side, it's relatively new to the consumer market and not widely available.

Hand-Pulling

Take a hands-on approach. Often, the surest way to get rid of lawn weeds is the old-fashioned way: by hand-to-hand combat. Get down on your hands and knees, grip the wicked weed in your hand, and pull it out, making sure you get the roots and all. Then take on the next weed, and the next. This method works great on young lawns. Just be sure to get the entire weed *before* it flowers and produces seeds.

If getting down and dirty isn't necessarily your cup of tea, there are some ingenious gadgets on the market that make hand weeding a whole lot of fun. Many have a handle attached to an extension that's used to rip the weeds from the ground. Some of these tools really per-form well; others are a waste of money. Before buying any hand weeder, stop in to your local garden center and ask if you can go out back and try out the tool firsthand. Remember, it pays to be a smart shopper!

Stabilize the Soil's pH

Keep your soil's pH between 6.5 and 7.0 for perfect harmony. Most lawn grasses thrive in soils in this pH range, but some weeds are happiest in ranges above or below this. If your soil is below 6.0, add lime to make it more alkaline. If your soil is 7.5 or higher, add sulfur to make it more acidic. (See page 255.)

When All Else Fails

Sometimes you need to call in the heavy artillery to tackle a major weed invasion. That's where chemical her-bicides come in. ("Herbicide" is a fancy term for a chemical weedkiller.)

Wild Weed Wipeout Tonic

If you've got kids or pets running around, and you don't want to expose them to the harsh chemicals that'll kill weeds, here's my healthy solution. Mix:

1 tbsp. of vinegar
1 tbsp. of baby shampoo
1 tbsp. of gin
1 qt. of warm water

Combine ingredients in a bucket, and then pour the mixture into a handheld sprayer. Drench each weed to the point of run-off, taking care not to get any spray on the surrounding plants. For particularly stubborn weeds, you should substitute apple cider vinegar in place of the regular vinegar.

Choose Your Poison

Not all herbicides are alike. Some herbicides kill any plant on contact, others kill broadleaf weeds but leave grass and grasslike plants alone, and still more kill sprouting seedlings. If you choose herbicides to do their dirty deed on weeds, let me offer some advice.

My professional landscape friends give thumbs up to herbicide products containing a mix of at least two of these active ingredients: MCPP (mecoprop), dicamba, and 2,4-D. These chemicals are absorbed into the plant and then move throughout the leaves, stems, and roots, disrupting the plant's normal growth enough to kill the plant. Because grass and grasslike plants grow in a slightly different way than broadleaf plants grow, you can use all these herbicides on established lawns without harming the grass. When you apply herbicides, remember that they work best when plants are actively growing, which is in the middle of the day, especially in spring.

Chemical Killers

• **MCPP and 2, 4–D** kill weeds after they sprout.

• **Dicamba** kills weeds both before and after they sprout.

All three herbicides are available in many forms, including granular, liquid, and ready-to-use. If you don't want to buy these chemical herbicides, try one of my favorite homemade tonics: my Wild Weed Wipeout Tonic.

The Lowdown on Broadleaf Herbicides

Broadleaf herbicides — the kind that get rid of the broadleaf weeds but don't hurt the grass — work best in warm weather, when plants are actively growing. For optimum results, you may need to apply them a couple of times to get rid of all the broadleaf weeds in your lawn. I've found that a 20 gallon hose-end or small tank sprayer works best on almost all but the heaviest infestations.

One other word of advice: Don't spray your whole lawn unless you absolutely have to; spot treat as needed. I'm fond of saying that spraying your whole lawn is like when you were a kid, and your mother gave you castor oil because your brother was sick. That didn't make too much sense then, and it sure as heck doesn't make much sense now, either. The same goes for your lawn.

Herbicides 101

Okay, now, I have to get a little technical here, but what I have to say is pretty important. Herbicides fall into these two main categories:

• Preemergent herbicides

• Postemergent herbicides

"Pre" means before and "post" means after, so that's an easy way to remember what they do. Let me explain.

Preemergent herbicides. These herbicides get rid of your weed problems *before* they start by killing them before or just after they pop up their little noses out of the ground. Because preemergent herbicides don't kill weed seeds, just seedlings, *when* you apply them is important for control.

Apply preemergent herbicides a week or two before the growing season begins, usually from late winter to

THIMK

early spring in most regions. In warm climates, you can apply them in the fall to control winter weeds. You must spring into action when you see signs of weeds cropping up.

After applying any preemergent herbicide, be sure to water the area thoroughly to establish the chemical barrier in the soil. And it's very important not to disturb that chemical barrier for at least a couple of weeks after you put this kind of weedkiller down.

Postemergent herbicides kill already growing and established plants. Use this type when the weeds are present and easy to spot in your lawn.

And Another Thing . . .

Remember that herbicides are classed as either selective or nonselective.

Selective herbicides kill only certain types of weeds. They may kill broadleaf plants, but not harm narrowleaf ones.

Nonselective herbicides, also called broad-spectrum herbicides, kill just about everything they touch. So be careful where you aim! Chemicals that are labeled as broad-spectrum herbicides include glyphosate, diquat dibromide, and pelargonic acid.

Weed-and-feed products do just what their name says: get rid of weeds while feeding your lawn. These products contain both herbicides to kill the weeds as well as nitrogen to green up the lawn. Not all weed-and-feed products are the same, so be sure to read the label to find out just what types of weeds each product controls.

Two Tips for Herbicide Buyers

Tip #1. When you decide to buy a chemical herbicide, don't buy in bulk. Buy the smallest size that'll do the job. You'll save money and avoid having to store a large quantity of poisonous products.

Tip #2. Be sure to select the *right* herbicide for the right job. There's no need to buy unnecessary products and keep them lying around. Remember, safety counts!

Jerry's 10 Herbicide Commandments

No, I'm no Moses, but I do have 10 "Commandments" I want you to follow. First, carefully read the product label. Then practice these safety precautions.

No. 1. Never spray on a breezy day. It will drift into places it doesn't belong.

No. 2. Always apply a warm, soapy water solution (¼ cup liquid soap to 1 quart water) before applying liquid herbicides; the herbicide will adhere better. For larger areas, overspray with my Weed Killer Prep Tonic. And *don't* water the grass for at least 6 hours following the herbicide application.

No. 3. Always keep a separate set of measuring cups, spoons, and sprayers just for herbicide use.

No. 4. Put on a pair of rubber or disposable plastic gloves *each and every* time you handle an herbicide. And wear safety goggles, a long-sleeved shirt, long pants, and work boots.

No. 5. Keep herbicides and pesticides stored out of reach of children, in a ventilated, locked cabinet.

No. 6. Weed killing is not a spectator sport, so keep your lawn off limits to your dog, cat, and kids the day you spray — and for a few days afterward.

No. 7. When spot spraying, keep the sprayer's nozzle close to the weed and shield healthy grass and any nearby trees, shrubs, or other plants with a piece of plastic or cardboard.

No. 8. Avoid pouring granular herbicides into a spreader parked on healthy grass; remember — spills kill!

No. 9. To avoid tramping on the just-sprayed area, start at the far end of your yard and walk back and forth in a zigzag pattern, overlapping the herbicide as you go.

No. 10. Expect to apply herbicides (in diminishing amounts) every few weeks and perhaps even for a few seasons in a row.

Jerry Baker Says

"Don't just win the battle — win the war! Complete victory over weeds takes time, even with herbicides on your side."

Call for Help

For extremely weed-infested lawns, it's best to let your fingers do the walking and call a professional spray company. Don't be shy about asking for credentials. You want to choose a company that's been around long enough to prove they have experience. Be sure they're licensed for the products and techniques they're using. And ask for some references. Play it safe, and you won't be sorry!

Weed Killer Prep Tonic

To really zing a lot of weeds in a large area, overspray it first with a mix of:

1 cup of liquid dish soap
1 cup of ammonia
4 tbsp. of instant tea granules

Combine all of these ingredients in your 20 gallon hose-end sprayer, filling the balance of the sprayer jar with warm water. Apply this Tonic to the point of run-off.

It's Only Neighborly

Unless you live miles away from your nearest neighbor or you're separated by a mountain range, be considerate of your neighbors and let them know a few days ahead of time before you intend to spray any herbicide. That way, if they are concerned about it, they can keep their kids and pets away from your lawn. And I can tell you from years of walking the dog that it's awfully nice to see the little signs near the sidewalk warning that a particular lawn has had chemicals used on it — I make sure that my dog doesn't go anywhere near that lawn!

Boss of Moss

I get loads of questions from people asking how to get rid of moss in the lawn. They say they kill the moss, plant grass over the bare spots, but then, more often than not, the grass fails to grow and the moss returns.

Moss is a low-growing plant that thrives in shady, acidic soil, while grass prefers neutral to slightly alkaline soil. If you kill the moss but don't change the soil pH, the grass, even shade-tolerant grass, won't grow and the moss will return. To get rid of moss once and for all, you have to kill the moss and make the soil a place where grass likes to grow.

Moss Buster Tonic

To get rid of unsightly moss and mold in your lawn, mix:

1 cup of antiseptic mouthwash
1 cup of chamomile tea
1 cup of Murphy's Oil Soap

Combine all ingredients in your 20 gallon hose-end sprayer, and apply to the point of run-off every 2 weeks until the moss is history. For quick results, add 3 ounces of copper sulfate to 5 gallons of water and spray on the moss. After the moss dies, rake away the dead moss and have the soil tested to determine its pH (see page 253). Add ground limestone according to the test recommendations, then reseed.

Jerry Baker Says

"Moss grows where grass won't. To replace your moss with grass, you have to change the conditions from those that favor growing moss to those that favor growing grass."

Try, Try Again

Here are some other terrific toss-the-moss strategies:

- **Aerate the soil.**

- **Improve your soil's drainage.** Most mosses dislike dry ground.

- **Feed your lawn regularly** with my All-Season Green-Up Tonic (for recipe, see page 328).

- **Prune trees to reduce shady spots** on your lawn. Moss is sun shy, so the less shade, the less moss.

- **Spray large patches of moss with a moss killer** containing ferrous sulfate or copper sulfate.

If You Can't Beat 'em . . .

If you've tried everything and you've still got a patch of stubborn moss — make a moss garden! Place some rocks or even driftwood around the moss to define the garden. Avoid rocks (such as limestone) that are alkaline, because moss grows best in acidic environments. Moss grows slowly, so be patient. As the moss grows and becomes even more beautiful, this little garden may become your favorite place in the entire yard. (For more about encouraging moss, see page 229.)

Jerry's Who's Who of Weeds

If this were the wild, wild west, these troublesome weeds would flash their ugly mugs on **WANTED: DEAD OR ALIVE** posters all over the land. Well, here's Marshall Jerry to the rescue with some wonderful ways to corral these culprits.

ANNUAL BLUEGRASS

(Poa annua)

How to Spot It: This weed draws attention with its bright green hue, narrow leaves, and grain-resembling seed heads that speckle the lawn with white dots. Although called an annual, this weed comes in both annual and perennial forms.

How It Harms: This weed infests closely mowed, frequently watered lawns. It can produce seed even when it's closely mowed. It crowds out and kills grass. Perennial types are able to survive long droughts, and annual types produce lots of seeds that can germinate months later.

How to Stop It: Aerate the soil and adjust your mower to a higher setting to shade out seedlings. Hand-pull these shallow-rooted hombres. Water only when your lawn needs it.

This weed is very difficult to control in lawns. Many folks try the opposite approach and make this grass a part and parcel of their lawns. Do this by watering more frequently, mowing closer — about 2½ inches high — and fertilizing heavily in the spring.

BERMUDA GRASS

(Cynodon dactylon)

How to Spot It: No, this grassy weed doesn't wear Bermuda shorts, sippin' a rum and cola on a sandy beach. In fact, this persistent weed comes from Africa, not Bermuda. Unchecked, it spreads quickly in a variety of ways: by seed, stolons, and rhizomes.

How It Harms: So how can a plant that is a great lawn grass also be a nasty weed? Actually, it's pretty simple.

Bermuda grass is a good lawn grass for warm climates, but its wide blades produce a coarse-looking lawn. It is also the bully on the block and can quickly choke out fine-textured grasses. It fades to a dull brown color in the fall when cool-season grasses get their second wind.

How to Stop It: Rake up your clippings after each mowing. Even little pieces can regrow into mature plants (remember the sorcerer's apprentice?). Increase shady areas in your lawn. For chemical control, it is best to call in the pros. If you want to use Bermuda grass in your lawn, be sure to choose hybrid Bermuda grass varieties. Hybrid Bermuda grass does not set seed and has a finer texture than regular Bermuda grass.

BROADLEAF PLANTAIN
(Plantago major)

How to Spot It: This weed displays wide, gray-green, egg-shaped leaves with wavy edges. It looks like miniature rhubarb growing in the lawn.

How It Harms: It spreads by seed and grows easily in moist, compacted soil. It quickly declares bare spots its home and will overrun thin lawns.

Bite Relief!

Plantain has been used since Ancient Greek times to help heal wounds. This common weed has a soothing substance in its leaves and flowering parts. I use it to take away the itch of bug bites and stings. It's easy! Just grab a handful of plantain leaves, crush them up in your fist, and apply the healing juice right on the fast-swelling spot for quick relief! But make sure the lawn you plucked it from is chemical-free.

BURCLOVER

(Medicago lupulina)

How to Spot It: It shouldn't surprise you to learn that this light green weed comes with telltale cloverlike leaves; yellow flowers; and a small, burlike fruit.

How It Harms: Burclover loves dry, infertile soils and just adds to your lawn's misery. It can take over a lawn in the spring and fall during its growth spurts.

How to Stop It: The best way to banish burclover is to take good care of your lawn. Aerate the soil, water when necessary, regularly apply my All-Season Clean-Up and Green-Up tonics (for recipes, see pages 327–28), and follow a good, regular maintenance program. If herbicides are necessary, use a postemergent product containing MCPP, dicamba, or 2,4-D, or use a pre-emergent product in the spring.

White Clover — From Hero to Zero

Long ago, back in my Grandma Putt's younger days, folks referred to clover as the "summer savior" of green lawns when the Kentucky bluegrass fell prey to diseases like mildew or to weeds like crabgrass. But people came to dislike clover because it stains clothing and it's very slippery when wet. So it's no longer deemed acceptable in most grass-seed mixtures.

But Grandma Putt taught me the true beauty and worth of clover in a lawn. Among its many pluses, clover:

+ Fights off chinch-bug invasions naturally and safely.
+ Is so tasty, it draws rabbits away from munching on your vegetable garden.
+ Attracts beautiful, lawn-friendly butterflies to your yard.
+ Adds much-needed nitrogen to the soil.
+ Makes a dandy and very resilient ground cover — *and* you just might find a lucky four-leafer!

COMMON CHICKWEED
(*Stellaria media*)

How to Spot It: No, you won't wake up one morning and find cute little yellow chicks prancing on your lawn. Chickweed is a broadleaf annual that prefers cool, moist weather and shade. It loves slightly acidic soils.

How It Harms: It suffocates your lawn grass by forming a dense mat on top of it.

How to Stop It: The best defense against this challenging weed is a postemergent herbicide, such as dicamba.

Chicken Salad

This is another "if-you-can't-beat-'em, eat 'em" weed. Toss some raw chickweed into salads or, if you have lots of it, steam it. The taste is a lot like spinach. But do not eat any chickweed that has been sprayed with pesticides.

CRABGRASS
(*Digitaria*)

How to Spot It: Nope, this grassy weed isn't a sourpuss. It gets its name because the leaves form a crab-shaped rosette. Seed heads show up in the summer and fall, and stems will continue to spread unless they're stopped. This annual has shallow, but mighty, roots.

How It Harms: It targets close-cropped lawns, bare spots, and thinning lawns. By fall, it leaves your lawn looking a sick, brownish red color. Crabgrass is far and away the no. 1 weed problem of homeowners coast to coast.

How to Stop It: You need to take care of crabgrass before it takes care of you. Go on the offensive by treating your lawn with a preemergent herbicide in the spring. Do this before the temperature gets above 60°F, because warm weather allows the crabgrass to germinate and spread like wildfire. If you didn't get to the crabgrass before the warm weather sets in, it's better to wait until next spring. Otherwise, you're just throwing hard-earned money down the drain.

In the meantime, mow higher, fertilize, and water appropriately for your conditions. Try to grow a thick, lush lawn — crabgrass hates a challenge from a healthy lawn because its seed needs light to germinate. Thick turf shades the seeds, preventing them from sprouting. Water deeply and allow the topsoil to dry out.

Kill two birds with one stone by using a weed-and-feed product formulated to fertilize your lawn and get rid of crabgrass at the same time. Many types of weed-and-feed products are available so read labels carefully and use one that controls crabgrass.

CREEPING BENT GRASS
(Agrostis stolonifera)

How to Spot It: This fine-bladed, shallow-rooted, grassy perennial grows horizontally. For folks in the snow belt, creeping bent grass often appears after the snow melts as a flat, dead-looking spot on the lawn. In the fall, you'll know whether you have creeping bent grass if you pull up long runners in your rake.

How It Harms: It will quickly conquer a lawn mowed too short or watered too much.

How to Stop It: Keeping the soil surface dry the majority of the time should keep creeping bent grass

A Seedy Character

Did you know that one crabgrass plant that makes it to autumn is capable of giving off 100,000 crabgrass seeds the following spring? *Amazing,* but true! That's even more motivation to get rid of this rapidly reproducing weed in your lawn.

at a distance. Regularly rake to prevent it from sprawling sideways. If the infestation is limited to a small area, dig out the turf and resod or reseed the area.

CREEPING CHARLIE:
See GROUND IVY on page 190

CURLY DOCK
(Rumex crispus)

How to Spot It: This broadleaf perennial runs rampant throughout the United States and southern Canada. It features bright, vivid green, lance-shaped leaves. By midsummer, those leaves turn to a reddish purple. Mature plants sport small, greenish flowers on tall, skinny spikes.

How It Harms: Curly dock only adds to the woes of grass suffering from the stress of hot, dry weather. It sticks out like a sore thumb in what is an otherwise grassy lawn.

How to Stop It: Hand-pull or use a small spade to dig it up. Be careful to get the entire root, because even a little left behind will resprout. Postemergent selective herbicides are good to control heavy infestations.

Talk about Prolific!

Just one healthy curly dock plant can produce 40,000 seeds — and that's enough to cover a lot of lawns!

DALLIS GRASS
(Paspalum dilatatum)

How to Spot It: Some folks know these light green perennials by their wide-bladed leaves. Dallis grass features seed heads that resemble the trembling tail of a rattlesnake.

How It Harms: Dallis grass grows by spreading clumps of green, grassy leaves throughout your lawn, especially during the summer and in low, wet spots. This weed spreads by both seeds and rhizomes.

How to Stop It:
Make sure wet areas dry out completely between waterings, and aerate the soil to enhance drainage. Dig out the rhizomes and follow up with a weed-and-feed product.

How to Spot It: The dandelion's yellow flowers and white, puffy seedheads are hard to miss in your otherwise green lawn. Dandelion is a perennial broadleaf weed.

A Dandy Drink

Folks have known for many years that dandelions make a delightful wine, but that's not the only beverage it can boast about. No sir, dandelion roots can also be dried, roasted, and ground into a smooth-tasting, noncaffeinated coffee substitute.

Dig the roots in the fall and scrub them well. (Don't choose any plants that have been sprayed.) Slice them in half lengthwise, and lay them out in a warm, dry spot until they're dry — about 2 weeks. Next, roast them in the oven at 250°F for 4 hours. Cool completely, then store in a glass jar.

When you're ready to brew your dandelion coffee, chop the roots into inch-long pieces, then coarsely grind them in a coffee grinder or food processor. Place 1 heaping teaspoon in a cup of water and simmer, covered, for about 10 minutes. Strain, add cream and sugar or honey and milk, if you want, and enjoy!

How It Harms: Dandelions are thick rooted and will quickly drain the energy from neglected, thinning lawns. The airborne seeds land on the soil and germinate easily, making it possible for a few seed heads to produce enough dandelions to eventually cover your entire lawn.

How to Stop It: Devote an afternoon to hand pulling each and every dandelion in your yard — it will be worth the effort. Cutting off flowers before they form seeds will prevent their dispersal. You can also spot-spray nonselective herbicides, such as glyphosate, directly on individual plants. To control dandelions over a large area, apply a selective broadleaf herbicide containing 2,4-D, MCPP, or dicamba in late summer or early fall. Be sure to apply before plants stop growing.

Problem Solver

Problem: My lawn looks like the local dandelions are holding a convention in my yard. They're everywhere!

Name That Culprit: Actually, this caper may involve two lawn enemies: weed-filled grass seed and unhealthy grass that isn't strong enough to crowd out the dandelion weeds.

Solution: Be choosy as to what type of grass seed you buy and where you buy it. Read labels and select only the bags that clearly state the type of seeds included. Buy your grass seeds from reputable dealers who "weed out" the weed-filled, cheap stuff.

SALAD DAYS

Young dandelion leaves (free of any chemicals, of course) are edible and tasty. So pluck them by the roots and turn your lawn headache into a delicious, fresh garden salad! My herbalist friends tell me that the ingredients in dandelion leaves actually help you digest food. (Be sure to use only dandelions from unsprayed lawns.)

ENGLISH DAISY

(Bellis perennis)

How to Spot It:
Actually, this is a delightful-looking plant. A broad-leaf perennial, it features beautiful, daisylike flowers with white, rose, or red petals on 6-inch-tall stalks. English daisy prefers areas with mild winters and dislikes hot, dry climates.

How It Harms: Because the leaves of English daisy don't look like grass, they give the lawn a rough texture.

How to Stop It: Let 'em be. Your friends and neighbors might just be envious of the flower garden within your lawn. Or pluck them out and treat your lawn with a weed-and-feed product. You can also spot-treat with a postemergent herbicide.

Which Witch?

Ground ivy comes with a lot of folklore. Historically, it's been used for everything from curing heart disease to warning you that witches are nearby. Crush the leaves and inhale them to soothe a headache. The crushed leaves may also relieve bruises or skin inflammations. Do not, however, use it internally; the leaves contain volatile oils that can be toxic.

GROUND IVY

(Glechoma hederacea)

How to Spot It: This one goes by many names: creeping Charlie, creeping Jenny, creeping ivy, or (my favorite) gill-over-the-ground. It's related to mint, which gives you an idea of just how aggressive it can be! Spring is the best time to identify this creeping weed because that's when it produces small, purplish flowers. Its leaves are scalloped and dark green, and the stems are square.

How It Harms: This creeping, spreading broadleaf perennial covers the lawn like a thick blanket, draining it of any nutrients and shading out turf grass. It loves damp soils and poorly drained areas and thrives in both sunny and shady spots.

How to Stop It: Take a multi-pronged approach by hand pulling weeds, spot-treating small infestations with a broadleaf herbicide, and applying a weed-and-feed product. My tonic made by dissolving 5 tbsp. of 20 Mule Team Borax in a gallon of warm water also does the trick. Just sprinkle it over the area. One good reason not to get rid of this plant: If you have a big bare spot under a walnut tree, ground ivy is one of the few plants not affected by walnut toxicity.

HENBIT
(Lamium amplexicaule)

How to Spot It: No, this weed doesn't cluck or lay eggs on your lawn. Henbit is an annual broadleaf weed featuring scalloped leaves and hairy, square stems. During spring and fall, it produces pinkish purple flowers. Some folks call it bee nettle or dead nettle.

How It Harms: Henbit thrives in cool climates and wet, fertile soils. It loves to spread itself all over your lawn and is more common in warm-season grasses than in cool-season turf.

How to Stop It: Mow on schedule and at the appropriate height for your grass. Pull out the eyesores and treat your lawn with a weed-and-feed product.

MALLOW

(Malva neglecta)

How to Spot It: This broadleaf annual-sometimes-perennial weed looks older than it is, with its crinkled, wrinkled leaves that are darkish green and round.

How It Harms: Mallow refuses to go away, especially in new or thin lawns. It can be a menace for the entire season.

A Cheesy Weed

You can eat unripe mallow seedpods — they're crisp and sweet. When they mature, they shrivel and break into segments that look a lot like wheels of cheese, scored with wedges. That's why some folks call this plant "cheeseweed."

How to Stop It: In young lawns, hand pulling works; in established lawns, however, you will need to apply an herbicide labeled to control mallow. Look for products containing the active ingredient dicamba, MCPP, or 2,4-D. Some weed-and-feed products control mallow and fertilize your lawn at the same time.

OXALIS

(Oxalis stricta)

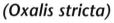

How to Spot It: Petite yellow flowers and shamrocklike leaves are sure signs that your lawn has been visited by this broadleaf perennial weed, which may act like an annual in cool climates. As a kid, I loved chewing on its lemony leaves. Oxalis is also known as yellow wood sorrel.

How It Harms: During the cool spring and fall, oxalis unleashes its creeping stems and seeds all over your lawn, crowding out grass plants. It prefers fertile soils but will grow just about anywhere.

How to Stop It: This is a very stubborn weed. Aerate your soil to make it less compacted. You may also need the bolstered strength of herbicides. Try spot treating the bad places first with herbicides. In spring, apply a pre-emergent herbicide containing oxadiazon. Another option: a weed-and-feed product (you may need to apply it a couple of times to do the trick).

PROSTRATE KNOTWEED

(Polygonum aviculare)

How to Spot It: This creeping, annual broadleaf weed features tiny, pointed, bluish green leaves. In summer and fall, very small yellow or white flowers sprout on the stems. Knotweed favors areas of compacted soil and places where the grass is thin.

How It Harms: Prostrate knotweed ties your lawn into knots by creating a wiry carpet in and out of the grass. Sunlight and water are blocked out, and your lawn grasses choke and slowly die.

How to Stop It: When hand pulling, take your time and be sure to get the crown and roots. Aerate the soil and use a product with the active ingredient dicamba or 2,4-D that is labeled to control prostrate knotweed. Some weed-and-feed products are also labeled to control prostrate knotweed.

PURSLANE

(Portulaca oleracea)

How to Spot It: This annual broadleaf weed displays thick, sprawling, fleshy stems and rubbery-looking leaves. When it's sunny, little, five-petaled, yellow flowers open. This weed shows up anywhere in the United States, but it is

Come and Get Your Vitamins

Crispy young purslane is delicious in salads, and it's loaded with vitamins A, C, and E.

especially fond of states east of the Mississippi. It is most common in newly seeded lawns and in turf near vegetable and flower gardens.

How It Harms: Purslane spreads and spreads, quickly choking thin lawns or preventing new lawns from seeding in the summer.

How to Stop It: Hand-pull or use a small trowel to dig up these weeds. Spot spraying with a postemergent herbicide will help.

SPOTTED SPURGE

(Euphorbia maculata)

How to Spot It: Spotted spurge's attributes include itty-bitty green leaves that are adorned with maroon-red spots.

How It Harms: This broadleaf annual basks when it's hot, hot, hot. It covers the ground with a circular mat and self-seeds prolifically. It can handle fertile and infertile soils with no sweat.

How to Stop It: Play by the rules. Mow at the right height when you should, pluck out individual weeds when you see them, and use the right weed-and-feed product for your lawn type.

TALL FESCUE

(Festuca elatior or F. arundinacea)

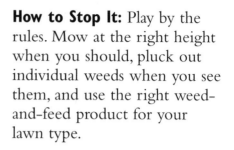

How to Spot It: This coarse perennial plant has two identities. Some folks value it as a grass for their lawns; others scorn it as a weed. Whichever role it takes on, it does it with gusto.

How It Harms: Tall fescue tends to grow in clumps, and by sending up tufts of leaves, it makes your lawn lose its manicured look.

How to Stop It: Practice good lawn maintenance and keep your lawn grass growing thick. As soon as you spot tall fescue, grab a hand trowel or weeding tool and dig it right up. Then sprinkle seed or place sod on the bare spot. If you've been neglectful (or on a month-long vacation), take a flat shovel and slice into the heart of the clump in hopes of weakening it and causing it to die a natural death. This is one grassy weed that rebuffs most herbicides. Reduced watering in summer is sometimes effective.

YELLOW NUTSEDGE

(Cyperus esculentus)

How to Spot It: This wicked weed features three-sided stems and yellow-green, grassy leaves. In summer, it presents a lanky, yellow-tan flower spike.

How It Harms: Yellow nutsedge keeps adding to its family tree by spreading seeds and forming small nutlets on its roots.

How to Stop It: A nice, thick lawn will get the best of yellow nutsedge every time. Make this stubborn weed retreat by aerating to improve drainage and yanking out the young ones by hand.

Ask Jerry

Q Help! After months of digging, I've finally got the dandelions out of my lawn. How can I keep them from coming back without resorting to chemical herbicides?

A Treat your lawn to a dose of corn gluten. It's a natural, preemergent herbicide that'll wipe out dandelion seeds pronto — and then go on to polish off unsuspecting crabgrass seeds. Best of all, because corn gluten is a kissin' cousin to corn syrup, it's safe to use, even with kids and pets on the scene. Before sending those yellow-blossomed nuisances packing, though, treat yourself to a few mugs of my dandelion coffee (page 188).

Q Does it matter what time of day you apply weed-killer? And when's the best time of year to hit 'em?

A Time your assault on existing weeds for the middle of the day — that's when plants are actively growing and most susceptible to being spray-gunned down. When you're using a preemergent to head 'em off at the pass, apply it a week or two before your growing season begins.

Q I killed the moss on my lawn and replaced it (I thought) with grass. But the moss came back — and the grass seed never even germinated! What went wrong?

A In a word (more or less): pH. Moss thrives in shady spots with acidic soil. Grass likes neutral to slightly alkaline soil. To grow a good crop of turfgrass in moss-pleasing territory, you need to change the soil's pH — otherwise, not even a shade-tolerant grass will grow. Get rid of your moss by spraying it with a good dose of my **Moss Buster Tonic** (page 335), then go to work on that pH.

☆ ☆ ☆

So you thought this chapter was just going to be about ridding your yard of those ugly, stubborn plants that are useless to all — an eyesore at their very best. Not on your life! Since I always try to work *with* nature rather than against it, I thought you should know that "weeds" can be beautiful, useful, and well, in some cases, . . . even nutritious! And with some of them, you can even learn to live in peace.

CHAPTER II

Bugs, Slugs, and . . .

Good bugs. Bad bugs. Ugly bugs. There are hundreds and hundreds of different kinds of creatures living in and around your yard. So how can you tell an insect pal from a pestering pest? Unfortunately, good bugs don't wear white hats, and the bad bugs don't wear black hats. Nor do they come up and introduce themselves in a friendly way. The good news is that most lawn insects do little or no damage; in fact, no lawn can thrive without quite a number of 'em. The minority of bad bugs, on the other hand, can destroy all of your hard work before you realize what's going on. In this chapter, we'll sort out which bug is which and discuss some surefire strategies and remedies for dealing with the buggy crowd.

I Dare You to Prove It!

If you suspect that bugs are at the root of your lawn problem, then you need physical proof. Some insects blatantly do their dirty deeds right before your eyes, as if they're daring you to try to stop 'em. Others hide just below the soil surface, thinking that out of sight is out of mind. You'll have to find them before you can identify them and fight them. For some, you're going to need to flood part of the lawn with a good soapy water solution to make them show themselves to you. Other bugs are nocturnal, so you'll have to search for them with a flashlight at night.

The Good . . .

Lawn-friendly insects naturally aerate the soil by making thousands of itty-bitty tunnels in the ground. Other critters feast on bad bugs to keep their numbers down — well below the level at which you need to become concerned about your bad-bug population — and some are important food for other creatures, such as birds, that most of us like to attract to our yards. And, of course, there are those insects that pollinate plants, ensuring that the life cycles keep going.

The Bad . . .

Now, the bad bugs attack nonstop, all season long, or just for intermittent periods when the time and conditions are right. They can live in the soil or be airborne, flitting here and there until they find a place to call home. There are those that create damage anywhere and everywhere. Some stick to the South; others stay in the North. These bugs may target specific types of grass or destroy every blade in their path. In other words, you may be constantly at war!

First Strike

Bugs usually strike first at the edge of the lawn, in shady areas, or in wet spots. But they are hardly systematic in their attacks. That's why, no matter what you do, you may suddenly notice discolored spots sporadically in and around your lawn. The key is to be vigilant and take action. That's why I never, ever wait. First thing in the spring, I get right out and spray down everything in my yard, especially my lawn, with my Rise-'n'-Shine Clean-Up Tonic.

Rise-'n'-Shine Clean-Up Tonic

This Tonic will roust your yard out of its slumber in spring, nailing any wayward bugs that were overwintering in the comfortable confines of your lawn.

1 cup of Murphy's Oil Soap
1 cup of Tobacco Tea★

1 cup of antiseptic mouthwash
4 oz. of hot sauce

Mix these ingredients in your 20 gallon hose-end sprayer and apply to your lawn to the point of run-off.

★ For recipe, see page 326.

Let's See Some ID!

You can see that it's pretty important to know whether the insects you find in your yard are the good ones or the bad ones. The right ID is also necessary so you know how to treat the bad ones with the right tonics to keep them from taking over your turf.

So what do you do? Collect a few specimens and study them closely! If you still can't figure out what they are, put some in a glass jar, seal the lid tightly, and take them to your local County Extension agent or a garden center. These folks should be able to provide you with the true identity of your lawn squatters.

Methods of Control: Organic vs. Chemical

If you've identified bad bugs in your yard, don't panic! I want you to think before you immediately plan an all-out assault with chemical pesticides. First, take a deep breath and step back. Once you've collected your thoughts, then it's time to spring into action.

Jerry Baker Says

"I know I've said this many times, but it bears repeating: Healthy, happy lawns don't attract many bad bugs. Mowing, watering, and fertilizing your lawn properly goes a long way toward preventing an insect invasion."

Bug-Off Tactics

There are a number of easy ways to keep insects in your yard from becoming dangerous pests. Often, all that's needed to keep insect pests from destroying your lawn is to simply change how you *care* for it. Consider trying these simple bug-off tactics:

- **Merely adjusting the amount of water or fertilizer** you give your lawn can send some pests packing. Chinch bugs love to munch on underwatered lawns, and the tender shoots of over-fertilized grass invite lots of insect pests.

- **Use higher mower settings.** This helps keep your grass healthier, plus, you won't be providing a four-star motel for pests.

- **Clear your lawn of insect-friendly thatch.** They love to call it home, so the sooner you get rid of it, the better off you'll be.

- **Time your retaliation tactics** for the most vulnerable phase of the pest's life cycle. Familiarize yourself with its lifecycle and habits so you can strike when it's weakest.

(For information about specific pests, see pages 206–17 in this chapter.)

Jerry's Rules of Insect Engagement

Here are some more of my tried-and-true insect control methods for you to let loose:

SELECT ANTI-INSECT GRASSES

If you notice that the same types of bad bugs pay a visit to your lawn year after year, chances are good that you have the wrong type of grass for your soil and climate conditions. (For example, Japanese beetles prefer Kentucky bluegrass, ryegrasses, and fine fescues.) It may be worth your while to replace your grass type with a higher quality of grass that is strong enough to withstand pesky bugs.

RECRUIT BIOLOGICAL BUDDIES

Let Mother Nature help you deter bad bugs. Most biological fighters attack the larval stage of insects to keep them from repopulating. My favorites are beneficial nematodes, endophytes (see page 205), *Bacillus thuringiensis* (a bacterium nicknamed *Bt* that duels with sod webworms and moth and butterfly larvae), and *Bacillus popilliae,* commonly known as milky spore disease, which is particularly effective against Japanese beetles.

Beneficial Nematodes

These microscopic worms do a powerful lot of good, in spite of their tiny size. They destroy some of the most common and destructive lawn pests, including cutworms, Japanese beetles, mole crickets, and sod webworms. Purchase them from garden product suppliers and apply them to your lawn through your 20 gallon hose-end sprayer. They really work wonders!

WASH 'EM AWAY

Plain and simple, bugs hate soap. It messes up their ability to reproduce, among other thing. Clean grass plants are healthy plants, so discourage insects and disease by bathing your lawn every 2 weeks, right after you mow with my All-Season Clean-Up Tonic (for recipe, see page 202). In addition, insecticidal soaps made from the salts of fatty acids and mixed with warm water work quickly to eradicate chinch bugs, grubs, and sod webworms.

USE BOTANICAL INSECTICIDES

Botanical insecticides are made from plants. While some botanical insecticides, like synthetic chemicals, can do environmental damage, botanicals do not build up in the environment and they break down quickly in the presence of sunlight and air. The latest magic bullet of botanical pesticides is neem. Neem comes from the neem tree and is used to control a wide range of pests including caterpillars, aphids, and beetles. The chemical seems to be very safe to people, pets, and the environment; it works by interrupting the pest's growth cycle.

Caution!

Even though botanical insecticides are relatively safe, you must remember to handle them with as much care and caution as you do synthetic insecticides.

All-Season Clean-Up Tonic

This is the one Tonic that you *absolutely* need to use religiously throughout the season. The secret behind it is that the mouthwash kills bad bacteria and discourages insects from coming around; the dish soap cleans the plants, helps the other controls stick better, and upsets the bugs' tummies; and the Tobacco Tea contains nicotine, which is a mild contact poison that it isn't very good to ingest. To make the Tonic, mix:

1 cup of liquid dish soap
1 cup of antiseptic mouthwash
1 cup of Tobacco Tea★

in a 20 gallon hose-end sprayer, filling the balance of the sprayer jar with warm water. Soak your entire yard (lawn, trees, shrubs, and everything in between) to the point of run-off. Apply it every 2 weeks in the early evening during the entire growing season, and you'll have the healthiest yard in town!

★For recipe, see page 326.

Send in the Marines!

If these natural methods don't put a lid on your bug population, it may be time to take more aggressive measures. Introduce stronger tactics gradually, starting with my Squeaky Clean Tonic, and turn to pesticides only when it's clear that the safer alternatives aren't working.

Squeaky Clean Tonic

This is a more powerful version of my All-Season Clean-Up Tonic, and it really zaps the bad boys in their tracks. Bugs just can't stand the citrusy odor of the dish soap, but if they do come near, the Murphy's Oil Soap suffocates them on contact. Mix:

1 cup of antiseptic mouthwash
1 cup of Tobacco Tea★
1 cup of chamomile tea
1 cup of urine
½ cup of Murphy's Oil Soap
½ cup of lemon-scented dish soap

Combine ingredients in a large bucket and apply with your 20 gallon hose-end sprayer to the point of run-off.

★For recipe, see page 326.

Bring on the Chemical Insecticides

When all else fails, and nothing seems to work against a major bug invasion, then it's time for the commercial products. For grubs, you need a commercial control with the active ingredient imidocloprid. For most others, it's either carbaryl or pyrethroids, which are synthetic versions of the substance derived from several species of chrysanthemum. (The natural version is *pyrethrin*.)

But be careful! Improper use of any of these can harm you, your pets, and your lawn. Follow the instructions on the label. Commercial insecticides work swiftly and powerfully, but they also kill beneficial organisms and bugs.

Different Strokes for Different Folks

Some insects, such as chinch bugs, leafhoppers, clover mites, and billbugs, enjoy dining on grass blades. Others, such as cutworms, armyworms, and sod webworm larvae, go after grass-plant crowns. And white grubs, mole crickets, wireworms, and ground pearls prefer munching on grass roots.

Pesticide Precautions

Always think safety first when using pesticides in your yard. Be sure to follow these safety tips:

- **Select products** that specifically list on the label the particular pest you are trying to control.

- **Choose the least toxic product** capable of doing the job. Look for code words on the label that read CAUTION (slightly toxic), WARNING (moderately toxic), and DANGER (most toxic).

- **Buy only what you need** and use only what you have to.

- **Pick a nice calm day** so that insecticide doesn't blow into places it doesn't belong — like your vegetable garden.

- **Wait for a dry day**. Don't apply a chemical control if rain is in the forecast. Too much water causes chemicals to run off or leach into nearby streams, lakes, or ponds before they get a chance to do their stuff.

- **Avoid inhaling anything** you're spraying. Just to be on the safe side, wear a face mask.

- **Always wear rubber gloves and safety goggles** when mixing and spraying insecticides to prevent them from seeping through your skin or into your eyes.

- **Keep insecticides *far* out of reach of children.** Store them on the top shelf of a cabinet or in a locked storage container. As a general rule, don't keep pesticides for any more than 1 year.

- **Dispose of empty insecticide containers** properly. The label should tell you the safest way to get rid of the container, but if not, ask your local waste disposal company.

Fore!

The once popular insecticide diazinon is now off-limits on golf courses because folks figured out that it is highly toxic to birds. After all, what would a golf course be without birdies?

What Are Endophytic Grasses?

I'm happy to inform you that lawn scientists have cultivated many varieties of grasses known as endophytic grasses, which have itty-bitty fungi (the endophytes) growing inside their leaf stalks and blades. Why should you be interested in these? Because these fungi are poisonous to armyworms, billbugs, chinch bugs, sod webworms, and a whole slew of other lawn pests. This treated grass delivers a clear message: *No bad bugs welcome here.* So, if you're having pest problems, consider planting these types of grasses in your yard.

Meet the Endophytic Clan

Varieties of endophytic grasses include perennial ryegrass (*Lolium perenne*), fine fescue (*Festuca arundinacea*), and tall fescue *(F. rubra)*.

GRASS TYPE	CHARACTERISTICS	RECOMMENDED CULTIVARS
Perennial ryegrass	Shiny, light green grass Shallow roots Often mixed with other grasses Ideal for high-traffic areas Good in cool climates	Palmer II Yorktown III Prelude II Repel II
Fine fescue	Thin blades Slow grower Shallow roots Handles drought, shade, and heat well	Jamestown II Chewings Reliant hard fescue
Tall fescue	Thick blades Tough and durable, often planted on sports fields	Tribute

Jerry's Who's Who of Insect Pests:

Now it's time to introduce you to the sinister lawn predators and some quick and easy ways to repel them.

ATTACK FIRE ANTS

What They Look Like: Fire ants, as their name implies, are reddish brown. They are ¼ inch long, give or take ¹⁄₁₆ inch. (Most other lawn ants are larger.)

Favorite Targets: You — so be careful! These ants may be small, but anyone living in Florida will warn you of these aggressive biters. I even have a couple of friends who've had to go to the hospital after a severe allergic reaction to a fire-ant sting. Fire ants thrive in clay soils and sunny sites from North Carolina to Florida and west to Texas and Oklahoma, as well as in a small section of southern California.

How They Harm Your Lawn: These fast-multiplying ants destroy lawns by building large mounds of soft soil, 1 to 2 feet in diameter and up to 1 foot high. Infested areas can have as many as 150 or more mounds per acre, supporting anywhere from 7 million to nearly 30 million ants. Each colony has at least one queen, lots of workers, and a number of winged males and females. In spring and fall, the winged ants fly off to make new colonies. If you stumble into a mound while you're mowing, they quickly swarm onto your ankles and legs and wreak revenge with painful stings. Nobody wants fire ants in their yard, but even they have a good side. Fire ants eat ticks and actually help control populations of this nasty pest.

¼ inch

How to Stop 'em: Baits seem to work best; those using the active ingredient hydramethylnon or fenoxycarb are the most effective. They lure the ants in. Once inside, they feast on their "last supper" — a deadly meal for sure! Treat your lawn in the fall, around September, for best control.

ANNIHILATE APHIDS

What They Look Like: Aphids, also known in some parts as greenbugs and plant lice, are small bugs with pear-shaped bodies and long legs. Adults are not bigger than 1/16 inch long.

Favorite Targets: Aphids particularly like to attack northern lawns and, specifically, shady places during the heat of summer. Kentucky bluegrass is their top choice for meals.

How They Harm Your Lawn: Aphids suck the life out of the grass blade. In various stages of infestation, the blade turns yellow, then orange, and, finally, dead brown.

How to Stop 'em: Lacewings and ladybugs are your ideal natural allies; neither harms your lawn or shoos away good lawn critters. To attract more of these good guys to your yard, plant ornamental grasses, prairie wildflowers such as black-eyed Susan and echinacea, and sunflowers. You can also go after aphids by spraying your entire lawn with either my All-Season Clean-Up Tonic (for recipe, see page 327) or insecticidal soap.

1/16 inch
H

Aphid Antidote

To keep aphids and other pests out of your yard, mix up a batch of this amazing antidote.

1 small onion (finely chopped)
2 medium cloves of garlic (finely chopped)
1 tbsp. of liquid dish soap
2 cups of water

Put all the ingredients in a blender, blend on high, and then strain out the pulp. Pour the liquid into a handheld mist sprayer and apply liberally to all areas at the first sign of any aphid activity.

ARMYWORMS: MISSING IN ACTION

What They Look Like: Uncle Sam definitely doesn't want to recruit these bugs. Armyworms are greasy-looking moth larvae. Up close, they have three light green stripes that run down their backs and sides. You'll need a flashlight to find them because they usually don't show themselves until after dark. Armyworms can grow up to 1½ inches long.

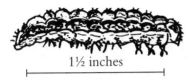

1½ inches

Favorite Targets: Armyworms generally appear during cool, wet springs, and then make a return engagement in the fall. They will strike lawns all over the country but prefer hot, warm, or mildly cold regions.

How They Harm Your Lawn: Armyworms regard your lawn as an all-you-can-eat smorgasbord. They tend to dine more on overcast days and at night. You know you have them by the various sized irregular or circular dead-spot patterns that appear on the lawn. They hide just below the surface by day and can be spotted above ground at night with a flashlight outside.

How to Stop 'em: First, try soaping them out. If that doesn't work, spray your lawn with pyrethrum, reseed with endophytic grasses, or increase the population of armyworm-eating nematodes by buying them at your local garden center. If necessary, treat the lawn with chemical insecticides that specifically control armyworms.

Hup-Two-Three!

Believe it or not, a platoon of armyworms can clear a lawn of foliage in just a few days!

Jerry's Who's Who of Insect Pests

BANISH BILLBUGS

What They Look Like: In the larval stage, a billbug resembles a tiny piece of white goo with a burnt-orange head. Adult billbugs are ¼ to ¾ inch long, are brownish black, and feature a long snout.

¾ inch

Favorite Targets: The east and west coasts of the United States, especially in the South, are the places these bugs like best. Their favorite meals are Bermuda grass and zoysia grass.

How They Harm Your Lawn: Billbug larvae attack your lawn, causing it to wilt and eventually die. Adult billbugs leave medium-sized, irregular-shaped dead spots throughout the lawn that give the impression that the area was killed by spilled fertilizer. In both stages, billbugs are capable of drying out the entire lawn.

How to Stop 'em: Routine aeration and periodic reseeding of your yard with grass varieties high in endophytes will make your lawn strong enough to repel billbugs. Once they've invaded, try introducing beneficial nematodes. Another way to combat billbugs is to attract birds to your yard. Many types of birds like to dine on billbugs, as well as other nasty pests. Billbugs seem to prefer poorly drained areas of the lawn — one more reason to repair that wet spot.

Jerry Baker Says

"Stop billbugs in their tracks ASAP. The larval stage is the most destructive to your lawn, so go after 'em when they're young."

CORRAL CHINCH BUGS

What They Look Like: Chinch bugs are a nearly invisible menace to a lawn. Barely ¼ inch as full grown adults, they are often overlooked. Under a microscope, chinch bugs are red when young and black as adults. Look for a telltale white spot on the back.

Favorite Targets: Chinch bugs aren't fussy. They are capable of damaging any grass type in any climate. Certain varieties of St. Augustine and Kentucky bluegrasses, however, seem to be especially vulnerable.

How They Harm Your Lawn:

Think of a chinch bug as the lawn's equivalent of a vampire. It sucks the nourishing juice from grass blades, causing them to wither and die. What's left are scattered patches of yellowish or brownish dead spots, which is sometimes mistakenly thought to be caused by drought stress.

¹⁄₁₆ inch

How to Stop 'em: Control thatch (see Chapter 6), because chinch bugs seem to thrive in poorly maintained lawns. Once you've cleared your lawn of thatch, reseed the bald spots with endophytic grass varieties. Other control options include diatomaceous earth, insecticidal soaps, and chemical insecticides that contain diazinon.

Problem Solver

Problem: My lawn is full of chewed up blades of grass, damaged crowns, loose sod, and patches of brown sod.

Name That Culprit: If you guessed an insect invasion — specifically chinch bugs and grubs — you're right on the money!

Just to be sure, take a large metal coffee can and remove the top and bottom lids. Stick this open can shell down into the soil 3 to 4 inches deep. Fill the can with water and watch for signs of insects floating to the surface. This'll help you make a positive ID.

COFFEE

Jerry's Who's Who of Insect Pests

Chinch Bug Tonic

This homemade brew is a "cinch" to make.

1 cup of liquid dish soap
3 cups of warm water

Combine these ingredients in a 20 gallon hose-end sprayer, then saturate your lawn with it. For a real "kick," substitute Murphy's Oil Soap in place of the dish soap. After your lawn dries, apply gypsum to the area at the recommended rate.

SEVER CUTWORMS

What They Look Like: Often confused with armyworms, cutworms are greasy-feeling moth larvae. When you find cutworms, chances are these fat, brownish black, striped bugs have curled their 2-inch-long bodies into a ball.

Favorite Targets: Cutworms love new lawns in all but the very coldest climates. They also believe in eating a balanced diet, so you'll want to protect your young flower and vegetable seedlings, too.

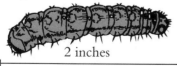

2 inches

How They Harm Your Lawn: Unchecked, cutworms can systematically munch on grass blades and leave circular or irregular-shaped dead patches in your lawn.

How to Stop 'em: Stock your lawn with nematodes or apply a pyrethrum spray. *Bacillus thuringiensis* (the *Bt* bacterium) and endophytic grass seeds also work. A last-ditch option: chemical insecticides that clearly indicate on the label that they control cutworms.

Winterizing Tonic

Give your lawn and garden a heavy soaking in the fall to zap cutworms and other bugs before winter with this Tonic:

1 cup of Murphy's Oil Soap
1 cup of Tobacco Tea★
1 cup of antiseptic mouthwash

Mix all of the ingredients in a 20 gallon hose-end sprayer, filling the balance of the sprayer jar with warm water. Saturate your lawn, and then follow it up with an application of a pyrethrum-based insecticide for total control.

★For recipe, see page 326.

SCRUB THE GRUBS

What They Look Like: Grubs are the larvae of various types of beetles, including June beetles (also called May beetles) and Japanese beetles. All grubs look much alike, with cream-colored bodies, brown heads, three sets of legs, and a tendency to curl into a C-shape.

Favorite Targets: Grubs tend to attack the yard in the late spring and early fall. If you're not watching, they will expand their range to include trees, shrubs, and other plants.

1½ inches

How They Harm Your Lawn: Grubs do their dirty work below the soil surface. They feast on grass roots, leaving a surefire clue that they have invaded: Dead clumps of grass pull up like pieces of carpet — there are no roots left to hold down the turf anymore.

How to Stop 'em: Time your counterattack by striking with beneficial nematodes when the grubs are in the larval stage. Use milky spore for Japanese beetles. Commercial insecticides containing pyrethrum will also wipe out grub larvae. And if moles or skunks have been a nuisance, here's a bonus: Once grubs are gone, moles and skunks leave, too, in search of lawns that have grub chow on the menu.

Got Grubs?

In early spring and late summer, grubs are closer to the soil surface than at any other time of year. To see if you've got grubs, try this: Cut the top and bottom off a soup can, and sink the can into your lawn almost up to its rim. Then fill it close to the top with water. Do this in several places around your yard, spaced about 10 feet apart. Count the grubs that come to each watering hole. If you've got 8 to 10 grubs in each can, that's about how many you've got per square foot of lawn. That's not bad, but more than 30 grubs per square foot, look out and take action!

Jerry's Who's Who of Insect Pests

LASSO LEAFHOPPERS

What They Look Like: These yellow, brown, or green, wedge-shaped insects are usually no bigger than ¼ inch long. As you approach, they tend to fly or hop away. Young leafhoppers are wingless and hide in a white, frothy spittle that clings to stems and leaf blades.

¼ inch

Favorite Targets: They can be found anywhere attacking any type of grass. In northern states, only one generation appears each year. On the other hand, up to three generations may be born in southern states.

How They Harm Your Lawn: Leafhoppers suck the juice from grass, causing the lawn to turn white, yellow, and finally brown. Look closely and you will see small, white spots on individual blades of grass. Leafhoppers can also cause grass to thin and become stunted.

How to Stop 'em: Apply my All-Season Clean-Up Tonic (for recipe, see page 327) or Lawn Pest Control Tonic at the first sign of yellowing, white-spotted grass blades.

Lawn Pest Control Tonic

1 cup of Murphy's Oil Soap
1 cup of Tobacco Tea★

Mix these ingredients in a 20 gallon hose-end sprayer and apply to the point of run-off.

★For recipe, see page 326.

MANHANDLE MOLE CRICKETS

What They Look Like: Mole crickets are brownish insects about 1½ inches long. They look a lot like the common cricket, with the notable exception of having a larger head and shorter front legs.

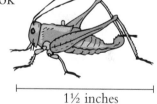

1½ inches

Favorite Targets: This lawn thug does the most damage in the southeast Atlantic and Gulf Coast states, probably because of their moist, warm climate.

Jerry's Who's Who of Insect Pests

How They Harm Your Lawn:
Mole crickets cut off underground stems and roots and tunnel beneath the turf, actually pushing grass plants out of the soil. They can tunnel as far down as 8 inches per day, causing the soil to dry out beneath the lawn and the grass to show up as dry, yellow patches.

How to Stop 'em: Predatory nematodes repel mole crickets. Also try cricket baits containing neem in the spring about a week after spotting tell-tale dry patches.

LAY LOW MOSQUITOES

What They Look Like: You know them all too well. And you also know that high-pitched hum that signals a soft landing on its next tasty meal — *you!*

Favorite Targets: These bugs may not bother the lawn, but they sure can make life miserable for the lawn keeper.

How They Harm:
These nuisances not only leave us with itchy bites, but nowadays they can also carry some pretty nasty diseases, including encephalitis and West Nile fever.

Buzz Buster Tonic

Who wants to be swatting at mosquitoes when they should be relaxing in their favorite patio chair? Keep those blood-suckers away from you on those warm summer nights with this Tonic:

1 cup of lemon-scented ammonia
1 cup of lemon-scented dish soap

Pour into your 20 gallon hose-end sprayer, filling the balance of the sprayer jar with warm water. In the early morning or late evening, thoroughly soak any places around your yard where mosquitoes tend to gather. Repeat this process three times each week, and it will keep the little buggers away. This Tonic also works nicely for the rest of the yard, too.

Jerry's Who's Who of Insect Pests

How to Stop 'em: Mosquitoes like to set up housekeeping in areas of stagnant water, like puddles. Getting to work improving any drainage troubles will go a long way toward eliminating mosquitoes from your yard. (See pages 242–46.) Add fish to your water garden to gobble up the mosquito larvae before they turn into biting adults. You can also purchase mosquito dunks, tablets that contain the natural pesticide Bti *(Baccillus thuringinesis israelensis)* that kills the young mosquitoes in the water. For good measure, mix up a batch of my Buzz Buster Tonic and spray the area liberally.

SLUG OUT SLUGS

What They Look Like:

Slugs are mollusks (not insects) that look like snails without the shell, which means they're pretty ugly. There are many types of slugs, from small ones about an inch long to big ones nearly 4 inches long. Slugs can be gray, brown, or even yellow, but all are slimy and love to munch on your (and their) favorite plants.

Favorite Targets: Slugs like many of the same plants that we do, from flowering perennials to lawn grass. If they don't seem too picky about what they eat, they do show some distinction about when they eat it. Slugs prefer the most tender parts of plants, and that means the newly emerging leaves. One slug can munch down a growing grass plant in no time flat.

1 inch

How They Harm Your Lawn: Slugs damage your lawn by eating the part of the grass plant that produces more grass, the crown. After a slug has nibbled on your grass, the blades that do emerge are often chewed with ragged-edged holes all over them. Severe infestations can kill many grass plants, leaving the lawn thin and giving it a brownish cast.

How to Stop 'em: Slugs do most of their dirty work at nighttime when they crawl out from their hiding places and feast on your lawn and garden. Fortunately, they aren't real smart and can be controlled in a number of ingenious ways. There are lots of baits to try, including iron phosphate baits that are much safer for pets and wildlife than many other baits. Slug traps are inexpensive and work quite well. All you do is sink the trap into the ground, add a little beer or fruit juice for bait, and the slugs will come flocking to the bar.

STOP SOD WEBWORMS

What They Look Like: In the larval stage, sod webworms are grayish or tan caterpillars with black spots on their back. In the adult stage, they are night-flying moths known to fly helter-skelter over your lawn in a zigzag pattern in front of your mower. You won't find the caterpillars during the day because they hide in tunnels. You'll need to dig up the thatch layer to discover

1⅛ inch

Super Slug Spray

For slugs that are too small to hand-pick or be lured into traps, try my Super Slug Spray.

1½ cups of ammonia
1 tbsp. of Murphy's Oil Soap
1½ cups of water

Mix all of the ingredients in a hand-held mist sprayer bottle and overspray any areas where you see the telltale signs of slug activity.

Slug It Out Tonic

Let slugs drink themselves to death with this powerful concoction.

1 can of beer
1 tbsp. of sugar
1 tsp. of baker's yeast

Combine all of the ingredients in a large bowl and let it sit uncovered for a few days. Then, pour the mixture into shallow, disposable containers. Set the containers below ground level in various areas around your yard and bid bye-bye to your slug problem.

their silken tunnels or spotlight the flying moths or creeping caterpillars with a flashlight at night. If you're mowing at dusk, you may spot them then because that's when they become active; they sleep during the day.

Favorite Targets: Sod webworms will harm any type of grass, but they are particularly fond of Kentucky bluegrass and bent grass. These lawn pests seem to strike predominantly in America's heartland.

How They Harm Your Lawn: The night-flying moth varieties lay their eggs on lawns. Within 2 weeks, the eggs hatch into lawn-munching worms. At first, they just eat the grass blades, but as they get bigger, they start in on the stems and even the crowns of the grass plants. All of this feasting creates small, irregular dead patches of grass that slowly get larger. They're usually concentrated in heavily thatched or dry areas of the lawn. The worms feed only at night; during the day, they rest in their silk-lined tunnels. What a life!

Jerry Baker Says

"One clue that you've got sod webworms is if you see flocks of birds feeding on your lawn. They can't resist these tasty treats!"

How to Stop 'em: Prevent their arrival by regularly aerating your lawn to remove thatch and improve water penetration. Once you know you've got 'em, try treating 'em naturally with *Bacillus thuringiensis* var. *kurstaki (Btk),* nematodes, my All-Season Clean-Up Tonic (for recipe, see page 327), insecticidal soaps, or a pyrethrum-based insecticide. For extreme cases, don't pull any punches: Fight back by reseeding the lawn with endophytic lawn seed, or about 10 days after you notice the infestation of moths, spray with chemical insecticides containing diazinon. Communities of webworms get increasingly larger as the summer wears on, so be prepared to apply whatever treatment you choose every 2 months, beginning in late spring.

Ask Jerry

Q My lawn has suddenly developed irregular-shaped bald spots that are all over the place. I know the problem can't be lack of water — we had the coolest, wettest spring I can remember. What gives?

A From the sound of it, your lawn has been invaded by armyworms, my friend! These guys usually go on maneuvers during cool, wet springs, and if you don't hop to it, they'll wipe out your grass in no time flat. To find out for sure if armyworms are the culprits, take a flashlight outside tonight and look around — nighttime is when they do their dirty work. Once you've made a positive ID, let 'em have it with my **All-Season Clean-Up Tonic** (page 327). It'll send 'em AWOL in a hurry!

Q How can I get rid of the grubs in my yard? They've already eaten my lawn. Now they're moving into the flower beds.

A The best time to go gunning for grubs is early spring or late summer, and the best ammo to use depends on the kind you've got: Grubs are the larvae of various kinds of beetles, including Japanese beetles. If you see these guys around, let 'em have it with milky spore — one of my favorite biological controls. To eliminate the offspring of these and other beetles as well, release a hoard of beneficial nematodes (see page 201).

Q My lawn here in Des Moines has got little dead patches everywhere. I don't have a clue what's causing them. Every time I look out the window, there are flocks of birds walking around, but I can't believe their footsteps are killing the grass! What's causing my lawn to go bald?

A No, the birds aren't stomping your lawn to bits — they're eating dinner. And that — along with your Corn Belt address — is an almost surefire indication that sod webworms are hard at work. (The Midwest is their prime stomping ground, and no bird worth his feathers can pass up a yard full of these guys!) Send the worms slithering off into the prairie sunset with my **All-Season Clean-Up Tonic** (page 327).

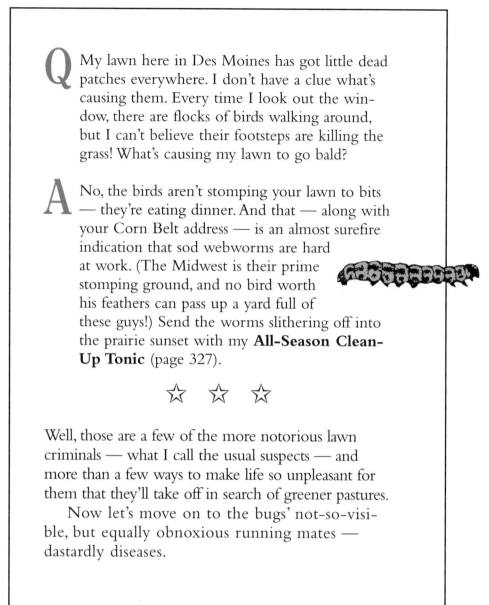

☆　☆　☆

Well, those are a few of the more notorious lawn criminals — what I call the usual suspects — and more than a few ways to make life so unpleasant for them that they'll take off in search of greener pastures.

Now let's move on to the bugs' not-so-visible, but equally obnoxious running mates — dastardly diseases.

CHAPTER 12

Dastardly Diseases

No part of the country is safe from turf troublemakers. From
Portland, Maine, to Portland, Oregon, and all parts in between,
lawn disease can pay an unscheduled visit to any yard. A disease
that suddenly appears in your backyard is a clear indicator of
poor lawn and soil conditions. And, in general, poor lawn housekeeping. In this chapter, we're going to get up close and personal
with some of the most common types of lawn diseases, and look
at the best ways to control them.

Know Thy Lawn Enemy

When it comes to defeating lawn diseases, half the battle is knowing what you're dealing with. Unfortunately, lawn diseases usually don't arrive packing little identification cards, so figuring out what they are can be kind of tricky. Sometimes the real culprit is an insect invasion, and sometimes it is fertilizer or lawn mower burn. But when you know what to look for, you'll recognize some clues. And once you know what you've got, you'll be able to fight back.

Fitness for Your Lawn

Don't let lawn disease take away your yard's good health! Ideally, the best defense against the menacing spread of lawn disease is a great offense. Treat your lawn the same way you treat your body. You know that eating healthy foods, working out with regular exercise, and getting plenty of rest will keep you fit as a fiddle. Well, your lawn, too, will benefit from the good, regular care and maintenance program we talk about in this book.

Not Veggies Again!

No, I'm not suggesting you feed your lawn steamed asparagus or make it do push-ups! Rather, you've got to realize that under that green carpet of grass is living, breathing soil. With the right amount of water, fertilizer, and care, your lawn and soil will be stocked with enough microbes and nutrients to take on any disease that dares to trespass. As I've said before, regular use of my All-Season Clean-Up and All-Season Green-Up tonics will go a long way to preventing lawn disease problems.

Water Wisdom

Good water habits are the key to preventing lawn disease — over-watering and watering at night invite disease. A damp lawn is a welcome mat for the fungus among us, making disease feel right at home! This simple fact explains why arid regions of the country are less prone to lawn diseases.

Watch the Clock!

If you follow these timely tips, you'll reduce your risk of lawn disease because your grass will remain strong and healthy:

Tip #1. Always wear your golf shoes whenever you're working in your yard.

Tip #2. Apply my All-Season Clean-Up Tonic (for recipe, see page 327) every 2 weeks in early evening to control insects and disease.

Tip #3. Water early in the morning, preferably between 5:00 and 8:00 A.M., but always well before noon. *Never water at night.*

Tip #4. Pick up all grass clippings and add them to your compost pile or use them as mulch.

Tip #5. Apply weed controls between 1:00 and 3:00 P.M. on a bright, sunny day. Prep the area by applying my Weed Killer Prep Tonic (see page 340), followed by a good application of a liquid or dry weed control.

Tip #6. Apply any disease controls after 7:00 P.M.

Tip #7. Mow your lawn *after* 6:00 P.M. If you mow during the heat of the day, you may burn newly cropped grass blades.

Tip #8. Apply my All-Season Green-Up Tonic every 3 weeks during the growing season (for recipe, see page 328). Also do this *before* noon to give the grass plants adequate time to digest the food before nightfall.

Disease-Control Choices

It's time to take a closer look at the two primary methods of disease control: choice A, organic methods, and choice B, synthetic fungicides. You make the call.

Choice A: Organic Methods

My first choice in combating disease is to rely on natural products and preventive care. Here are some simple, natural ways to maintain a healthy lawn:

- **Aerate your lawn**, remove thatch, and let the drying air reach down into the soil.

- **Keep dense shrub and tree growth** properly pruned. This helps maintain a free flow of air over the grass.

- **Plant a mixture of grasses** instead of just one type. A team of different grasses will be more resistant to disease than a single type of grass can be.

- **Mow at the proper height**. A buzz cut leaves the grass plants too weak to fend off disease.

KEEP IT CLEAN

Soap helps remove dust, dirt, and pollution on plants so that they can take in the sunlight more readily. Clean plants are healthier plants, which helps them stand up to disease!

The Poop Scoop

Doggie-doo-doo damage is often mistaken for soil disease. But here's the real scoop: Besides the smell and unpleasant sight, fecal matter often contains microscopic parasites that can be harmful to people if their hands or feet touch the contaminated soil. So remove dog waste as soon as possible; don't let it linger around for somebody to step (or worse, fall) in.

Most Common Fungicides

Before using any of these, refer to product label for directions and other important information.

Here are some of the active ingredients you'll find on labels:

Benomyl
Mancozeb
Maneb
Thiophanate-
   methyl
Thiram
Tridimefon
PCNB
   (Quintozene)
Etridiazole

Choice B: Synthetic Fungicides

I'm not a big fan of dousing my lawn with chemicals if I don't have to. In fact, I strongly caution you to spot-treat only the problem areas, not the whole yard. Chemicals are mighty powerful products that sometimes claim innocent victims — like otherwise healthy grass blades. I regard them as the last resort to stop stubborn, spreading diseases. If you're not careful when using synthetic fungicides, you'll harm beneficial plants, insects, birds, and other lawn allies — not to mention what toxic chemicals can do to you, your kids, or your pets!

Choosing the right fungicide can be a tricky — and risky — business. If you choose wrong, you could do further harm to your yard. So pay attention!

My advice? If natural alternatives don't stop the spread of disease, have a professional lawn company do the chemical spraying. They generally have the equipment and know-how to make the right diagnosis and restore your yard to good health in the safest possible manner.

Lawn Diseases: How to Fight Back

The green in your grass has turned a sickly brown. What do you do? First off, don't fret! Grit your teeth, get in there, and fight back before the intruder completely takes over your lawn.

Once you've looked at all the possibilities and are sure you've identified the problem as a particular disease, the first step when disease strikes is to rake out the affected grass so that you can reseed. Then prep the new seed with my special Seed Starter Tonic (for recipe, see page 336).

Jerry's Who's Who of Plant Diseases

Different diseases strike different places and in different ways. So, of course, you need different solutions. I've waged many a war against many a lawn disease; I lost a few, but then again, I've also won more than my fair share of battles. So, here are the villains that I think of as the 10 most troublesome lawn diseases, and how to stop, cure, or avoid them.

Lawn Public Enemy Top 10 List

- Brown patch
- Dollar spot
- Fairy ring
- Leaf spot
- Phythium blight
- Powdery mildew
- Red thread
- Rust
- Snow molds
- Summer patch

BROWN PATCH

How to Spot It: Brown patch ranks high on my Lawn Public Enemy Top 10 List. Be on the lookout for:

- Irregular circles of brownish discoloration on the lawn.
- Grayish color on grass at the outer edge of a brown patch.
- Filmy, white tufts covering the grass during the morning dew.

Favorite Targets: This fungus-among-us infects practically all kinds of grasses. Bent grasses, centipede grass, fescues, Kentucky bluegrass, ryegrass, and St. Augustine grass are favorites.

How It Harms: It tends to create the most damage during warm, wet weather and when a home-owner goes overboard in applying fertilizer that is high in nitrogen. So go easy! Brown patch usually kills the blades of grass, but not the roots. It's sneaky, so be careful! New infections of brown patch occur when this fungus spreads on grass clippings, mowing equipment, and yes, even on your shoes!

How to Stop It:

- Follow the label directions on your lawn fertilizer bag and avoid excessive applications. That's one of the reasons why I recommend only two dry feedings a year. Remember, a little is good, but more is not necessarily better! And don't forget to flip back to Chapter 2 for my great lawn feeding tips, tricks, and tonics.
- Rake up grass clippings and put them on your compost pile.
- Always water your lawn in the morning to give the grass plants ample time to dry off completely before nighttime.
- If brown patch appears, apply my Lawn Fungus Fighter Tonic. If it persists, treat it with a fungicide such as chlorothalonil. (Don't water within 48 hours of applying this chemical.) Repeat this treatment three times at weekly intervals. Remember to wear your golf shoes in your yard, so you can aerate your lawn while you're treating it. That should do the trick!

Lawn Fungus Fighter Tonic

If your lawn develops brown or yellow patches that eventually die out, fight back with this fix-it formula.

1 tbsp. of baking soda
1 tbsp. of instant tea granules
1 tbsp. of horticultural or dormant oil
1 gal. of warm water

Mix all of the ingredients together in a large bucket, then apply with a handheld sprayer by lightly spraying the turf. Do not drench or apply to the point of run-off. Repeat in 2 to 3 weeks, if necessary.

DOLLAR SPOT

How to Spot It: This lawn disease cashes in on grasses that are deficient in nitrogen.

How can you be absolutely positive that your lawn has dollar spot? No, dollar signs don't show up in your yard *(that would be nice!)*, but these telltale clues do:

- Tan spots the size of silver dollars start to form.

- The grass dies, leaving the turf dotted with tan freckles.
- Irregular tan-colored patches may appear.
- A cobwebby, fine, white fungus is seen with morning dew.

Favorite Targets: It can infect just about any grass, but it's especially menacing to bent grasses and lawns in the humid northern regions of the United States during May and June and again in September and October. However, if you live in the South, don't breathe a sigh of relief. Dollar spot has even invaded turf south of the Mason-Dixon Line on occasion.

How to Stop It: Don't let dollar spot bankrupt you! At the first sign of trouble, treat it with my Anti-Summer-Patch Tonic (for recipe, see page 328). Also, a good maintenance program goes a long way: Water deeply but infrequently. Give your grass ample time to dry out before the next watering. Aerate to remove any thatch (which only makes matters worse) and mow at the right height (no close cuts).

FAIRY RING

How to Spot It: Mushrooms (toadstools) will sometimes appear in the grass in circular arrangements called fairy rings. Folklore holds that these fungi rings come from elves, leprechauns, and fairies dancing and prancing on the lawn at night. In the early stages, the grass inside the ring darkens. Later, as the fungus depletes the soil of nutrients, the ring turns pale green. Rings appear in the same spot year after year, but each year they are bigger in diameter than the last time.

Favorite Targets: Fairy rings commonly appear in soils that contain woody organic matter, such as dead tree roots. Sometimes, a fairy ring appears without mushrooms. All grasses are potential targets.

How to Stop It: The best prevention is to apply an adequate amount of nitrogen fertilizer on the lawn. Fairy rings are often triggered by nitrogen deficiency, so flip back to Chapter 2 for information on how to ensure that your lawn gets enough nitrogen. If you've got it, pluck and discard mushrooms as soon as you spot them. Next, puncture the turf with your golf shoes or aerating lawn sandals, and sprinkle 1 cup of dry laundry soap over the area. Then apply my Fairy Ring Fighter Tonic.

Fairy Ring Fighter Tonic

1 cup of baby shampoo
1 cup of antiseptic mouthwash
1 cup of ammonia

Mix all these ingredients in your 20 gallon hose-end sprayer and apply to the point of run-off *after* you've sprinkled dry laundry soap over the area.

LEAF SPOT

How to Spot It: This lawn disease, known as "melting out" in some parts of the world, appears in cool weather. Leaf spot shows up on grass blades as elongated, circular, brown spots with a purplish edge to them. After a while, the blades turn completely brown, and your entire yard starts to "melt out" or fade away.

Favorite Targets: Be especially on guard if you have Kentucky bluegrass and you live in a cool, wet climate.

How to Stop It: Avoid leaf spot by adjusting your mowing height upward during the spring. Also, go easy on the nitrogen fertilizer. Get rid of thatch and aerate to enhance water penetration. My County Extension friends tell me that some of the newer Kentucky bluegrasses are not bugged by leaf spot, so give this grass serious consideration if you're looking to replace or repair your lawn.

Jerry's Who's Who of Plant Diseases

POWDERY MILDEW

How to Spot It: This is one shady character because it absolutely loves the shade.

- First, tiny, superficial patches of white to light gray fungus show up on leaves.
- If ignored, these patches get bigger and become powdery as spores are produced.
- In advanced cases, the leaf tissues turn yellow, tan, then brown before dying.

Favorite Targets: It generally infects grasses (especially blue-grasses) in shaded and protected areas (like on the north and east sides of your house, garage, and other buildings). This fungus stalls or halts the growth of leaves, roots, and rhizomes, creating dead spots in the lawn.

How to Stop It: Let the sun shine in! Prune or remove shrubs and trees that shade or border turf areas. Also, fertilize your lawn regularly (see Chapter 2), but don't go overboard. Water when it's dry, mow at the right height for your grass, and rake up clippings after each trimming. When you see trouble, retaliate with my Mildew Relief Tonic (see next page).

Fight Mildew Loss with Moss

If you have so much shade that no matter what you do, you can't grow a decent lawn free of powdery mildew, consider simply giving up on grass and growing a moss lawn. Some folks think of moss as an eyesore, but in the right place, it can be a resilient, soft, low-maintenance substitute for unhealthy grass. And it's green all year-long, too!

I've found that moss grows best if you sour the soil a bit to bring the pH to a level of 5.5 or so. Do this by adding sulfur or aluminum sulfate at the rate recommended on the package, which will kill the grass and encourage the moss to grow. If need be, transplant small pieces of moss to the area, pressing them firmly into the soil. Lightly mist-spray them for the first 3 weeks. When it comes to quelling persistent diseases in shady areas, moss is boss!

Mildew Relief Tonic

1 cup of baby shampoo
1 cup of hydrogen peroxide
4 tablespoons of instant tea

Pour this mixture into a 20 gallon hose-end sprayer, filling the balance of the sprayer jar with water. Every week to 10 days, spray the affected area of lawn, and your lawn will soon be in the thick of things again.

PYTHIUM BLIGHT

How to Spot It: Summertime is when this blight comes to light. The first signs of trouble are irregular patches of slimy and soft grass. The grass blades begin to wither and fade, turning straw or reddish brown in color.

Favorite Targets: You'll find pythium blight in areas with moist soils, hot days, and warm, humid nights. Among grasses, its prime targets are bent grass, Bermuda grass, tall fescue, Kentucky bluegrass, and annual ryegrass.

Problem Solver

Problem: My lawn has puzzling brown spots scattered here and there.
Clues:
• Do you see circles of green grass growing in the middle of these brown spots?
• If you stand back and look at your lawn, does it look like a bunch of frog eyes?

Name That Culprit: Looks like your lawn has been invaded by fusarium blight, also known as frog's eye.

Blight Solution: Fusarium blight is most common on lawns of Kentucky bluegrass that have developed thick thatch. Set your mower to 3 inches high, water deeply and infrequently, and aerate to reduce the thatch. Restore the green by applying my Blight Buster Tonic.

Overly alkaline soil is more prone to pythium blight, so check your pH. For information on how, see page 251.

Jerry's Who's Who of Plant Diseases

How to Stop It: Reduce your risk by not going hog wild with your watering. Also, make sure your lawn has good drainage to keep water from building up (especially when those heavy summer showers strike). If pythium blight becomes a persistent problem, call a lawn professional to help out.

Blight Buster Tonic

To fight fusarium blight, which is also known as frog's eye, apply this Tonic at the first signs of trouble.

1 cup of baby shampoo
1 cup of Tobacco Tea★
1 cup of antiseptic mouthwash
½ cup of ammonia
8 tbsp. of rose/vegetable dust
3 tbsp. of saltpeter

Combine ingredients in a 20 gallon hose-end sprayer. Apply it early in the morning to the point of run-off.

★For recipe, see page 326.

RED THREAD

How to Spot It: Red thread first surfaces as pink or red areas on grass blades. The grass then looks greasy before the spots dry and the blades fade to a tan color.

Favorite Targets: Mark your calendar to be on the look-out when fall arrives, especially if your lawn is made of bent grass, red fescue, Kentucky bluegrass, or ryegrass, and you live in an area with lots of humidity.

How to Stop It:
- Regularly feed your lawn my All-Season Green-Up Tonic (for recipe, see page 328) and follow my spring and fall feeding routines (see Chapter 2).
- Maintain the right amount of nitrogen in your soil (see Chapter 2 for details).
- Water only in the morning and never at night.
- Maintain a soil pH between 6.5 and 7.0 (learn more about soil tests in Chapter 13).
- Mow at the right height.
- Don't let thatch build up and take over your turf.

Jerry's Who's Who of Plant Diseases

RUST

How to Spot It: Yes, believe it or not, rust is a living lawn disease. Besides the red hue, look for another sign that rust has infected your lawn — dustlike spores that form elongated and circular shapes on the grass blades. It can even get so bad that it turns your lawn mower and catcher bag yellowish orange.

Favorite Targets: Midsummer to fall in warm, moist weather, rust can turn your green lawn into a redhead. Rust affects most grasses in any zip code, but it especially seems to like to traumatize Kentucky bluegrass.

How to Stop It: How can you bust rust? Mow every 4 or 5 days and regularly feed your lawn as I outlined in Chapter 2. The main ingredient your soil needs to fight rust is nitrogen, but a balanced fertilizer will keep your lawn in healthy, fighting trim. For stubborn rust problems, bathe your lawn every 2 weeks with my All-Season Clean-Up Tonic (for recipe, see page 327). Then apply chlorothalonil fungicide four times — in early spring, around May 1, July 1, and, finally, September 1. For long-range improvement, overseed with a rust-resistant grass, such as 'Cherokee' and 'Oration' perennial rye and 'Geronimo' and 'Parade' Kentucky bluegrass.

SNOW MOLDS

Also called winter scald, snow mold is usually divided into gray snow mold and pink snow mold. It got its name because it strikes when snow covers the grass for a long time — like during some of those Minnesota winters! You know snow mold has arrived when:
• You see a thin layer of nearly translucent, gray to pink, cottony growth on the grass leaves.
• As leaves die, they turn tan and clump together in an ugly mat.
• Diseased spots tend to range from 1 to 12 inches in diameter.

Jerry's Who's Who of Plant Diseases

Favorite Targets: This abominable snow menace first takes hold when snow falls on unfrozen ground. Cool air temperatures and humid conditions in the early spring seem to kick it into high gear. By the way, you don't need snow to have snow mold — the disease can also attack grass under unraked leaves.

How to Stop It: Now, you can't control Mother Nature, but you *can* fight back. Here are some tricks that have worked for me:

- The most important step is to prep your lawn in the fall for the upcoming cold winter months. The best way I've found is to avoid applying high nitrogen fertilizers late in the fall, because they often will spur tender new grass growth, which isn't tough enough to stand up to winter cold.
- Keep cutting your grass until it stops growing in the fall.

- Avoid compacting or trampling down any snow on the lawn.
- If you have had significant problems with snow mold in the past, try applying neem to the lawn before the snowflakes begin to fall.
- A late-season application of WeatherProof will also go a long way toward preventing this problem.
- If your lawn gets socked with snow molds, give it a good raking ASAP to reduce thatch and enhance the soil's ability to absorb water.
- Try to reduce shady areas by pruning trees and shrubs to let in more sunshine.
- As a last resort, fungicides containing benomyl, iprodione, or methyl thiophanate (that's a mouthful to say!) are effective. You'll need to repeat the application in another 10 to 14 days.
- Don't make yourself crazy trying to get rid of snow mold. Remember: It usually affects only the blades and not the crown of the grass plants, and when the warm, sunny weather arrives, the grass quickly turns green and lush again.

SUMMER PATCH

How to Spot It: This turf disease is caused by a fungus that aggressively attacks grass during periods of wet, warm weather, from late spring to late summer. Acting as your lawn's doctor, let me help you identify its symptoms.

- Look for small, scattered, dark green, wilted patches of turf that turn tan in color. The patches are usually elongated in shape and typically less than 12 inches across, sometimes with a small green spot in the center.
- Grass blades die back from the tip.

Favorite Targets: Summer patch strikes heat-stressed grass that is mowed too short and/or that is growing in compacted soils. Too much nitrogen, humidity, and temperatures consistently above 78°F will spur the spread of summer patch.

How to Stop It:
- First, let your grass grow, but don't let it get out of hand.
- Second, aerate compacted soil and remove the thatch.
- Third, hold off on mowing when the grass is wet, and use a slow-release, nitrogen fertilizer when fertilizing.
- Overseed with grasses that are resistant to the disease, such as the Kentucky bluegrass varieties 'Bristol', 'Rugby', and 'Wabash'.
- Now for the final, vital step: Apply my Anti–Summer-Patch Tonic every 3 weeks.

Jerry's Anti–Summer–Patch Tonic

1 cup of liquid dish soap
1 cup of Tobacco Tea★
1 cup of antiseptic mouthwash
1 cup of ammonia
3 tablespoons of saltpeter

Combine all ingredients in a large bucket and pour into your 20 gallon hose-end sprayer. Apply to your lawn to the point of run-off every 3 weeks.

★For recipe, see page 326.

Going Into Action

Now that you've got the lowdown on these lowlife diseases, here's some advice on choosing commercial fungicides that will go to work getting rid of them. This chart lists the active ingredient to look for on the label of common fungicides. Be sure to use only products labeled for use with the disease you've identified, and follow the label directions for amounts and timing of applications.

JERRY'S MOST USEFUL FUNGICIDES DISEASE BY DISEASE

DISEASE	FUNGICIDE (ACTIVE INGREDIENT)
Brown patch	Benomyl
	Mancozeb
	Maneb
	Thiophanate-methyl
	Thiram
	Triadimefon
Dollar spot	Benomyl
	PCNB (Quintozene)
	Thiram
	Triadimefon
Fairy ring	Fungicides usually not recommended
Leaf spot	Maneb + zinc
Pink snow mold	Benomyl
	Mancozeb
	PCNB (Quintozene)
	Thiram
	Triadimefon
Powdery mildew	Triadimefon
Pythium	Etridiazole
	Mancozeb
Red thread	Maneb
Rust	Mancozeb
	Maneb
	PCNB (Quintozene)
	Triadimefon
Summer patch	Benomyl
	Triadimefon

Ask Jerry

Q We have a lovely lawn that's made of mostly fescues. This spring was cool and wet, and we noticed pinkish spots in the lawn. It looked like snow mold, but there wasn't any snow. What is this stuff, and how do we get rid of it?

A The spots you saw in the lawn were pink snow mold. I know: There wasn't any snow. But snow mold can show up during cool, wet weather, snow or no snow. This year, spray your lawn with my **Lawn Fungus Fighter Tonic** (see page 334), and say so-long to the snow mold shenanigans.

....

Q We have a Kentucky bluegrass lawn, and it's beautiful every summer. The trouble is, each spring it takes forever to green up. Does it have a disease of some kind, and what can I do to make it look better faster?

A Your lawn doesn't have a disease problem — in fact, it's probably as healthy as a Kentucky Thoroughbred horse. Kentucky bluegrass just naturally gets off to a slow start in spring compared to many other grasses. This year, overseed the lawn with perennial ryegrass to help the scene green up faster.

☆ ☆ ☆

So, are you "sick" of hearing about lawn diseases? Well, fine then — you've learned about all of the things that can go wrong with your lawn. Now it's time to move on and talk about how to get a new lawn started — or redo an old one so that it looks like new. Ready? Let's grow!

Part III

New Lawns to No Lawns . . . and Everything in Between!

CHAPTER 13

Soil Savvy

Congratulations! You've just bought yourself a brand-new home. You can smell the fresh paint on the walls, wiggle your toes in the newly installed carpet, and marvel at the shiny kitchen appliances. Outside, though, it's an entirely different matter. Chances are, you've got only the bare essentials (not to mention some construction-site leftovers like nails and chunks of wallboard). That grassless area around your new home needs some major sprucing up. And you're eager to throw down some sod or sprinkle some seeds and have a lawn full of thick-growing grass — right now! Here's what you should do.

Whoa, Pardner!

First thing — put on the brakes! There's a lot more to growing grass than just slapping down some sod. In fact, there are plenty of steps you must take before you even begin to consider the type of sod or grass seed you want on your new lawn.

In this chapter, I'll guide you every step of the way to prepare your new homestead for its new lawn. You can also use the same techniques if your old lawn is in such bad shape that you decide it's beyond repair. A neglected lawn can be a major eyesore. Its soil condition can be so poor that it may be best to just rip out the turf and start over. You'll need to rent some heavy-duty equipment to rip out an existing lawn. You'll also need to wipe out the weeds. (See Chapter 10.) But by following these guidelines, you'll be able to steer clear of a mess of costly problems that the uneducated homeowner faces down the road.

Keep a Scrapbook

To keep you encouraged and inspired, I want you to get out your camera. Take some photos *before* you start this landscaping project, being sure to capture the front, back, and side yards on film. Don't forget to date the photos. You may want to take shots at other times of year, as well.

Don't forget to take photos as you prep the site and also at the end, when you've christened your healthy, gorgeous green grass with a can of cold beer (more on that later). Put all of these photos in a lawn scrapbook in chronological order. Then the next time you think you're facing an impossible task at home or at work, just pull out the old scrapbook, flip through the pages, and remind yourself of your past accomplishment. Believe you me, it'll motivate you for future projects!

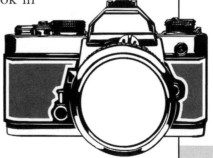

Tools of the Terrain

You're going to need plenty of help in the form of must-have tools to get your yard in tip-top shape and ready for planting a healthy, new lawn.

Some tools you'll want to have because they're basic garden and landscaping tools that you'll use over and over for a variety of chores. Others, because of their cost or because it's unlikely you'll need them often, you can rent.

Tiller. For small or medium yards, a tiller is a great choice. It digs out weeds that need to go, plus, it helps revive ailing grass. I like to rent a rear-tined rotary tiller; it handles a whole lot easier than a front-tined tiller.

Also, plan on double tilling. First, till the soil to 8 inches deep, rake out the unloosened weeds and grass, and then till again. Finally, hose down the yard, wait a few dry days, and then till again.

Bulldozer. You need this major piece of earth-moving equipment only if you have a doozy of a yard. Small, wheeled bulldozers, known in the lawn biz as skiploaders, can quickly scrape off layers of grass.

Plow. For big yards, attach a metal plow to the front end of a riding lawn mower or full-size farm tractor. In no time at all, the plow blade scoops out the top 6 to 8 inches of soil. Your mower or tractor must have enough horsepower to power the plow.

Sod cutter. This is definitely a tool to rent rather than buy. A sod cutter bores down through grass and weeds at just below soil level.

Rake. For grading or tilling tasks, use a long-handled rake with a steel head — the wider, the better.

Shovel. For easier sod removal, use a long-handled shovel with a squared-off blade. It's much kinder to your back than is a short-handled shovel.

Jerry Baker Says

"Let the mound of discarded old lawn sod break down naturally in a compost pile. In time, you'll have a home supply of valuable nutrients to add to your soil."

Fork. Use this to open new ground, dig up old grass plants, and turn cultivated soil. I like a fork with a waist-high, D-grip handle.

Water-filled roller. Fill the big, porous cylinder halfway with water before rolling it up and down your yard after laying sod or sowing seed.

Seed spreader. Choose among a drop spreader, broadcast spreader, and hand-held spreader. Each features settings that adjust the desired rate of seed dispersal.

(See pages 60–61 for more info.)

Hose. Rubber hoses are heavier than reinforced vinyl. Both have advantages. Be sure to buy a hose with at least a ⅝-inch diameter, brass couplings, and a psi (pounds per square inch) minimum rating of 500.

Wheelbarrow. For carting soil, compost, and other heavy lawn materials, it's unbeatable. I prefer models with extra-deep trays and inflatable tires.

The Lay of the Land

Walk across the street from your homestead and take a careful look at the contours of your property. Does it lean one way or the other? Are there mounds, hills, or dips? Or does it appear to be as level as a tabletop?

Next, I want you to take a piece of paper and map out the general lay of the land. Jot down wet spots, dry spots, slopes, shady areas, and possible dead-air pockets caused by trees and buildings.

Knowing the lay of your land helps immensely. From the information you've collected, you'll be better informed if some — or all — of the soil needs to be graded, or if there are some potential trouble spots that must be corrected *before* you get too far along.

Down the Drain

Poorly draining yards can be easy and cheap to fix — or they can be a money pit. It all depends on what type of soil you have, but before you rush out and call the nearest drainage contractor, here are a couple of nifty ways you can test just how well your yard drains water.

Drains like a Sieve?

Test 1. Grab your shovel and dig a few 1-foot-deep, 1-foot-wide holes in different spots in your yard. Empty a gallon bucket of water into each hole. Let it drain, then fill each hole with water again. On the second round, the water should percolate gradually and completely into the surrounding soil in 6 to 8 hours. If it doesn't, then you've got problems.

Test 2. Take a garden hose to a selected area and give it a thorough soaking. Wait for a couple of days and then dig a 6-inch-deep hole at that spot. If the bottom of that hole is bone dry, your soil is letting water escape too rapidly for good grass growth.

Test 3. After a heavy rainfall, time how long it takes for the water to drain from the lawn near your house. If it takes longer than 3 hours, chances are pretty good that you need an underground drainage system. But don't fret! The solution is easier than you may think. You can opt for a gravel-filled trench drainage system or rely on flexible drainpipes to take excess water away from around the foundation and into a gutter, a nearby ditch, a sump, a dry well, or a stream.

Jerry Baker Says

"Consult a home improvement reference or hire a landscape contractor for advice. This is one problem you want to fix right the *first* time, to avoid damage to both your plants and your home."

Making the Grade

Yes, you can make sure your lawn earns all A's when it comes to being properly graded. If you're fortunate to live in some flat area of the country, like Sioux City, Iowa, grading can be an easy but muscle-taxing, do-it-yourself task. However, if you happen to live on uneven, sloping turf — near Bethlehem, Pennsylvania, for example — you'll most likely need to shell out some dough for professional landscapers with earth-moving equipment to do the deed right.

$$$$$

Before you do anything, let your fingers do the walking: Call around and get bids from a few professionals. Make sure they give free estimates, and contact several of their "satisfied" customers before making your selection.

Away from the House

Let's back up to the beginning and explain why level ground is so important. You never, ever want a slope to move gradually toward the house foundation. Each time it rains, the water will flow toward the house, saturate the foundation walls, and seep into the basement or wooden floor joists. What's at stake is your home's basic structure, and you don't want to mess with that!

Aim for a gradual slope that moves *away* from the foundation. The general rule of thumb is 6 inches for every 25 feet. What this means is that if you're 100 feet from your house, the ground you're standing on should be 2 feet lower than it is at the base of the house.

Determining the Slope

How do you measure the slope? Glad you asked! You can eyeball it, or you can be more precise by using some string or twine, stakes, and a string level.

Set stakes. Take one 3-foot wooden stake, and hammer it down into the soil at the base of your home. Use a tape measure to find a distance 25 feet from this base. Then, take a second stake, and pound it into the ground.

Run a level string. Now, attach a string, right at ground level, to the stake close to the house. Pull the string taut, and take it to the second stake. Place a string level on the string. Now, raise or lower the string until the bubble within the carpenter's level appears within the grooves. Keep the string at the level and attach it to the second stake.

The moment of truth. Measure the distance between where the string attaches and the ground. If the drop measures 3 inches or more, you've got plenty of slope and don't need to worry about grading. But if it's anything less than 3 inches — or you can't even find the level because the ground actually slopes *toward* the house — you'll have to regrade.

Grade-Aider Tool Kit

Spade
Large wheel-
  barrow
Long-handled,
  steel-headed
  rake (wider
  than a regular
  garden rake)
8-foot-long,
  2- by 4-inch
  piece of wood
Carpenter's level

Do-It-Yourself Grading

If your ground is only slightly off-kilter based on the string-and-stake measurements, you'll save a lot of money by grading the lawn yourself. Start out by gathering the grade-aider tools listed at left. Once you have these together, the first step, even with new lawns, is to make sure you've cleared away all weeds or leftover clumps of grass. Then you can dig in.

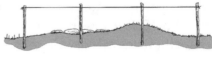

Call Before You Dig

Make sure you know what's buried underground before you make any grading adjustments. Be sure that digging won't interfere with underground power lines, cable television lines, water lines, or sewer lines. If you're not sure of their location, contact your local utility company: A representative will be more than glad to come over and mark the lines for you.

You folks with a septic system and an in-ground well should also know where your well, its water line, and your septic tank and drain field are located. All this is usually marked on your surveyor's map. If you can't find your map, there should be copies at the local municipal building department.

Now Move That Dirt!

Pick a day when the soil is moist — not dry, but not saturated. (Lightly moist soil is the easiest to work with.) Use the shovel to dig up dirt from higher spots and move it to lower areas with the wheelbarrow. In some cases, you may have to haul in new topsoil to level the area.

Once you've relocated the dirt, use the rake to make the ground level and free of dirt clods.

Put It to the Test

To test your efforts, place the piece of wood on the ground and lay the carpenter's level on top of it to make sure you're getting the desired gradual slope away from the foundation of your house.

Steer the Water Clear

More serious drainage problems may call for installing drainage pipes or gravel-filled trenches to funnel away the excess water. Either collects the runoff, steers it from the wet area, then spreads the water over a better-drained area where it is absorbed.

Option 1: Drainage pipes. Dig a trench with a very slight grade away from the wet area, beginning about a foot deep and about 3 inches wider than the pipe. Fill the bottom of the trench with 2 inches of coarse stone, and place the drainage pipe on top. Cover the pipe with stone to a depth of about 2 inches, then fill the trench with the excavated soil.

Option 2: Drainage trench. Dig a trench about a foot deep and 3 inches wide; it should have a slight grade away from the wet area. Fill the trench with coarse stone to about 3 or 4 inches from the top, then finish filling with soil. Rake the area and plant grass seed.

Or Make the Hire

Large areas or yards that need major corrections may be too difficult to fix on your own, so you'll need some professional help. Sure, it will cost you some money, but you'll have the peace of mind of knowing that a tricky problem has been solved. Be choosy about whom you pick — a bad grading job can cause many years of woe.

After getting three estimates, select the licensed landscaper who will guarantee to:

✔ Grade without damaging tree roots.
✔ Provide topsoil that is free of rocks, weed seeds, debris, and toxic waste.
✔ Incorporate compost into the topsoil for better grass growth.

Working around Existing Elements

In addition to drainage, you may also find trees, shrubs, or man-made objects in the middle of your lawn project. Ever try to move a 40-year-old maple tree? It's worse than trying to move an elephant! For major immovable yard obstacles like trees, buildings, sidewalks, driveways, and paths, take my advice: Work around them.

If you need to strip off weeds or field grasses, exercise plenty of caution when using heavy-duty, lawn-chewing equipment, especially around established trees. Sure, you can spot the roots that poke out above the ground, but the roots travel much farther than that, and you don't want to injure them.

"WHAT A DRIP!"

My Grandma Putt taught me all about the *drip line*. She explained that a tree's roots usually extend at least as far as the leaves do on the ends of the tree's branches. So use that as your guide when plowing up the ground around trees. You don't want to slice 'n' dice the tree roots, because it will damage or even kill the tree.

Is Your Lawn Made in the Shade?

A major factor in the health of any lawn is how much sun reaches — or doesn't reach — down to the roots. A lot of that depends on how many trees you have, as well as their size. Also, if your property is adjacent to tall structures that block out sunlight, your grass's health is likely to be adversely affected.

I'm an old tree hugger from way back. There's nothing like a tree to block harsh winds, muffle traffic noise, and provide shade. Unless their roots are tearing up your driveway or muscling into your water or sewage lines, I say keep your trees and grow shade-tolerant grasses.

Know Your Soil

Before you toil, get to know your soil. By definition, soil is made up of organic matter, air pockets, and mineral particles. You know these mineral particles better as sand, silt, and clay, the same elements found in your prized flower beds and vegetable garden. I like to view my lawn as a garden of grass containing thousands upon thousands of itty-bitty plants.

The Deep-Down Search: What Kind of Soil Do You Have?

The soil is the heart and blood of any lawn. Good soil keeps the roots anchored and the grass blades strong and sturdy. That's why it's so doggone important to first test for the *type* of soil you have, so you'll know how to best pamper it and keep it growing strong! Allow me to introduce you to the three basic types:

Sandy soil. Everything drains quickly through this loosely composed type of soil, especially water and nutrients. The best way to care for sandy soil is to give it lighter, more frequent helpings of water and fertilizer.

Clay soil. This soil is h-e-a-v-y. When wet, it packs onto your shoes and tools. When dry, it cracks. It takes a mighty long time for water to enter and exit clay soils. On the upside, clay soils tend to retain moisture and nutrients for a long time.

Loamy soil. The most desirable soil, loam drains easily, is well aerated, and is loaded with nutrients. It is the cream of the lawn crop, so to speak. It contains a blend of about 40 percent silt, 40 percent sand, and 20 percent clay.

So What's Silt?

Silt is a soil type with particles smaller than sand but larger than clay.

THE MASON JAR SOIL-TEXTURE TEST

- Collect several teaspoon-size samples from the top 6 inches of your soil at various locations around your yard.

- Dry these samples out.

- Mash the dried soil into a fine powder with a rolling pin, and pour a 1-inch layer into a clean, glass jar.

- Fill the jar two-thirds of the way with water, and add 1 teaspoon of liquid dish soap.

- Screw a lid on the jar; shake it vigorously for 15 to 20 seconds.

- As the soil particles settle, mark the layers of sand, silt, and clay with grease pencil. It takes about an hour for sand particles to settle, a few hours for silt particles, and a couple of days for clay particles. After a few days, you'll see the approximate percentages of sand, silt, and clay. The one that's more than half the total is your dominant soil texture.

Worms Away Tonic

Here's some advice about worms from my Grandma Putt. She knew that worms are valuable because they break down decomposable matter into fine humus and help aerate the soil. But, too many can render a fine lawn unsightly, plus all kinds of pests may join them. Grandma Putt used this recipe to take care of the problem.

2 lbs. of mustard
1 tub of water

Pour the mustard into a coarse canvas bag, cheesecloth, or old pantyhose, and soak it in the water. Then, drain off the mustard water and sprinkle it over the lawn. This will bring worms to the surface, where you can easily gather them up for your compost pile — or use them for some mighty good fishin'!

Soil Tests — the Inside Story

Want to get the "inside dirt" on the type of soil you anchoring your grass? Well, you're in luck! I've got safe tests to offer you.

If you just want a ballpark idea of your soil type its texture, I can suggest two informal tests. Among eran lawn tenders, the tests are known as the Legend Blue-Ribbon Test and the Old Reliable Mason Jar Te

LEGENDARY BLUE-RIBBON TEST

This is the quick-and-easy way to figure out whether you've got sandy, clay, or silt soil. Now, this test isn't scientifically precise, but it'll give you a good idea of what you've got. And besides, it's fun.

- Go to an out-of-the-way area of your lawn. Take a trowel and plunge it into the lawn 6 to 8 inches deep. Carefully lift up the grassy turf and gather a handful of soil from underneath it.

- Lightly mist this soil sample with a spray bottle. Not too much — you don't want to saturate it.

- Grab a handful of moist soil and squeeze it so that it's the size of a tennis ball. Roll the dampened soil between your open palms to form a ribbon.

How the soil takes shape clues you in on its type. For instance, if the soil feels sticky and holds tightly together, it's a sure bet that the soil is made mostly of clay. If it feels silky smooth and forms a temporary ribbon shape before breaking apart, the soil is high in silt. If you can't get the soil to form a ribbon and it feels gritty, you've got a whole lot of sand on your hands. If it forms into a ribbon almost effortlessly, you're in luck — you've got loam.

250

Soil Tests — the Inside Story

Want to get the "inside dirt" on the type of soil you have anchoring your grass? Well, you're in luck! I've got a few fail-safe tests to offer you.

If you just want a ballpark idea of your soil type based on its texture, I can suggest two informal tests. Among us veteran lawn tenders, the tests are known as the Legendary Blue-Ribbon Test and the Old Reliable Mason Jar Test.

LEGENDARY BLUE-RIBBON TEST

This is the quick-and-easy way to figure out whether you've got sandy, clay, or silt soil. Now, this test isn't scientifically precise, but it'll give you a good idea of what you've got. And besides, it's fun.

• Go to an out-of-the-way area of your lawn. Take a trowel and plunge it into the lawn 6 to 8 inches deep. Carefully lift up the grassy turf and gather a handful of soil from underneath it.

• Lightly mist this soil sample with a spray bottle. Not too much — you don't want to saturate it.

• Grab a handful of moist soil and squeeze it so that it's the size of a tennis ball. Roll the dampened soil between your open palms to form a ribbon.

How the soil takes shape clues you in on its type. For instance, if the soil feels sticky and holds tightly together, it's a sure bet that the soil is made mostly of clay. If it feels silky smooth and forms a temporary ribbon shape before breaking apart, the soil is high in silt. If you can't get the soil to form a ribbon and it feels gritty, you've got a whole lot of sand on your hands. If it forms into a ribbon almost effortlessly, you're in luck — you've got loam.

Jerry Baker Says

"This type of soil test reminds me of my childhood days when I made mud pies and mud snakes with my Grandma Putt! Little did I know what she was trying to teach me!"

THE MASON JAR SOIL-TEXTURE TEST

- Collect several teaspoon-size samples from the top 6 inches of your soil at various locations around your yard.

- Dry these samples out.

- Mash the dried soil into a fine powder with a rolling pin, and pour a 1-inch layer into a clean, glass jar.

- Fill the jar two-thirds of the way with water, and add 1 teaspoon of liquid dish soap.

- Screw a lid on the jar; shake it vigorously for 15 to 20 seconds.

- As the soil particles settle, mark the layers of sand, silt, and clay with grease pencil. It takes about an hour for sand particles to settle, a few hours for silt particles, and a couple of days for clay particles. After a few days, you'll see the approximate percentages of sand, silt, and clay. The one that's more than half the total is your dominant soil texture.

Worms Away Tonic

Here's some advice about worms from my Grandma Putt. She knew that worms are valuable because they break down decomposable matter into fine humus and help aerate the soil. But, too many can render a fine lawn unsightly, plus all kinds of pests may join them. Grandma Putt used this recipe to take care of the problem.

2 lbs. of mustard
1 tub of water

Pour the mustard into a coarse canvas bag, cheesecloth, or old pantyhose, and soak it in the water. Then, drain off the mustard water and sprinkle it over the lawn. This will bring worms to the surface, where you can easily gather them up for your compost pile — or use them for some mighty good fishin'!

Your Nose Knows!

Tap your sense of smell to gauge the health of your soil. Just grab a loose handful of soil and rub it between your palms. Then take a big whiff. A rich, earthy aroma is a good sign — it usually indicates that the soil contains lots of organic humus. Now, if the soil smells sour or vinegary, then the pH may need some adjusting.

Go with a Pro

In addition to determining your soil's texture, you also need to know how acidic or alkaline it is (its pH) and what chemical elements it contains or lacks. You can eliminate any guesswork right off the bat by getting your soil professionally tested. You'll learn all about your soil's nutrient content, the pH level, the amount of organic matter, and whether any harmful salts or other chemicals are present.

The most reliable method involves taking soil samples to your County Extension office, a private lab, or, in some areas, a local university (especially if it is a land-grant college offering degrees in agriculture or landscaping).

For a small fee (there's no such thing as a free lawn!), the lab analysts will tell you your soil's pH level and its nutrient content. Both help you determine how much of which fertilizer will work best for your soil conditions.

If you're going to do this, expect to bring the lab up to a dozen soil samples from different locations in your yard, because the levels of acidity and alkalinity can vary from location to location. The test results will also provide a breakdown of the amount of nitrogen, phosphorus, and potassium in your soil. They will tell you what essential nutrients your lawn lacks and whether you need to add lime (which raises the pH) or sulfur (which lowers the pH) to bring it into balance (more on that later).

Jerry Baker Says

"Call ahead to the soil testing lab for instructions and ask whether they have a handy information kit they can send to you."

Do It Right

Although each testing lab's requirements may differ slightly, here are the basic steps you must follow to collect your soil sample:

Step 1. Use a hand trowel and scrape away any litter, gravel, and vegetation from the soil site you've chosen.

Step 2. Remove a thin slice of soil about 6 inches deep.

Step 3. Collect 2 to 3 tablespoons of soil from a dozen different places in the yard.

Step 4. Pour all of the soil samples into a big bowl and stir it up until they are well blended.

Step 5. Scoop out 1 to 2 cups of soil and pour it into a bag or box provided by the testing service.

Step 6. Label the sample with your name, address, phone number, and the date the soil sample was collected.

Testing Tip

You must follow the home-kit instructions "to the T." Too much or too little soil can throw off the results drastically, and your efforts will be all for naught.

Turn Your Lawn into a Home-Grown Lab

If you want to save a few bucks and you have the time, test the contents of your soil by using a do-it-yourself kit, available from garden stores and supply catalogs.

These kits are not as accurate as the professional lab tests, of course, but they are ideal if you don't suspect a major problem with your soil. They'll give you a pretty good idea of the pH and sometimes the N-P-K (nitrogen, phosphorus, potassium) levels.

pH Preferences

The acidity of soil is measured by its pH (the abbreviation for "potential of hydrogen"). The pH is calculated on a scale of 0.0 to 14.0, with 7.0 being the midpoint. That means a soil pH of 7.0 is neither acid nor alkaline — it's neutral. Any measurement above 7.0 pH means that you have "sweet," or alkaline, soil. Any measurement of pH that falls below 7.0 shows that you have "sour," or acidic, soil.

Most lawn grasses grow best when the pH is between 6.0 and 7.0. In this range, grass plants get the most benefit from whatever organic matter and nutrients are present. Even so, different lawn grasses have different pH preferences. Here's a chart that shows the best pH level for *your* grass.

The pH Fizz Test

Want a fast and fizzy way to tell whether your lawn is top-heavy with acidity or alkalinity? Put a couple of spoonfuls of dry soil in a glass jar and add an equal amount of white vinegar. Tighten the lid, shake the jar vigorously, remove the lid, and hold the jar close to your ear. If you hear a loud, fizzing sound, your soil is very alkaline.

pH RANGE FOR POPULAR LAWN GRASSES

NAME	pH RANGE	NAME	pH RANGE
Bent grass	5.5–6.5	Clover, white	5.5–7.0
Bermuda grass	5.0–7.0	Fescue, chewings	5.5–7.5
Bluegrass, annual	5.0–7.5	Fescue, creeping red	5.5–7.5
Bluegrass, Canada	5.5–7.5	Fescue, tall	5.5–7.5
Bluegrass, Kentucky	6.0–7.5	Gramma grass	6.0–8.5
Bluegrass, rough stock	5.5–7.5	Redtop grass	5.0–7.5
		Ryegrass	5.5–8.0
Buffalo grass	6.0–8.5	St. Augustine grass	6.0–8.0
Carpet grass	4.5–7.0	Wheat grass	6.0–8.5
Centipede grass	4.0–6.0	Zoysia grass	4.5–7.5

What's Next?

You may decide that you need to raise or lower your soil's pH so that you can grow the grass that's best for your climate or other needs. Many labs will work with you to help select the appropriate supplement needed to elevate or lower your soil pH. Let's look at both cases.

Raise the pH. When your soil's pH is lower than 6.0, it's lime time! Add lime to your soil in the spring or fall. Avoid adding it in the summer or within 2 weeks of applying any type of fertilizer. If your turf needs 50 pounds of lime per 1,000 square feet, add the first half in the spring and the other half in the fall. Your lawn will be able to "digest" it better in two smaller "servings."

Other soil sweeteners you can use for soil that's too acidic are wood ashes from the fireplace, bonemeal, and crushed eggshells. If you live near the ocean, you have access to other good sources of lime: ground oyster shells, clam shells, and other seashells.

Lower the pH. When your soil's pH registers above 7.5, that's a clear signal that your soil is too sweet and the pH needs to be lowered. One of the best materials to use to lower the soil pH is elemental sulfur — in pellet form. Use your handheld, broadcast spreader; the soil test will tell you how much elemental sulfur you'll need for your lawn size. Add sulfur only during the spring or fall. And to prevent turf burn, make sure you water it in thoroughly.

Other options for soils that are too sweet include adding fresh beech or oak sawdust, peat moss, cottonseed meal, and pine needles to the soil. All of these will boost the acid levels in your soil.

Material Used to Correct pH

To Raise pH
- Lime
- Wood ashes
- Bonemeal
- Eggshells
- Oyster or clam shells

To Lower pH
- Elemental sulfur
- Beech or oak sawdust
- Peat moss
- Cottonseed meal
- Pine needles

PEAT MOSS

ADJUSTING SOIL pH

Here's my handy reference guide for how much lime you'll need to raise your lawn's pH or how much sulfur you'll need to lower it.

RAISING pH BY ADDING LIMESTONE
(POUNDS PER 1,000 SQUARE FEET)

pH CHANGE REQUIRED	SANDY SOIL	LOAMY SOIL	CLAY SOIL
4.0–6.5	60	161	230
4.5–6.5	51	133	193
5.0–6.5	41	106	152
5.5–6.5	28	78	106
6.0–6.5	14	41	55

LOWERING pH BY ADDING SULFUR
(POUNDS PER 1,000 SQUARE FEET)

pH CHANGE REQUIRED	SANDY SOIL	LOAMY SOIL	CLAY SOIL
8.5–6.5	46	57	69
8.0–6.5	28	34	46
7.5–6.5	11	18	23
7.0–6.5	2	4	7

DON'T GET MOWED OVER!

Be cautious if you're using aluminum sulfate or ferrous sulfate to make your soil more acidic. Ferrous sulfate contains iron and sulfur; aluminum sulfate contains aluminum and sulfur. To avoid burning those poor little blades of grass with these products, follow directions on the bag precisely.

Soil Tests for Existing Lawns

Even a healthy-looking lawn can benefit from regular checkups. Just as you and I make a habit of seeing our doctors for annual physicals, you need to take on the role of "lawn doctor" and make a house call to your soil. So, test your soil's pH at least every 3 to 5 years.

What the Tests Say about Fertility

Here'a a brushup on the basic three elements that soil needs.

- **Nitrogen** is the most important nutrient for the green parts of grass; it helps grass grow strong, with dark green leaves.
- **Phosphorus** assists roots below ground as they grow.
- **Potassium** boosts the growth and health of the entire grass plant, from top to bottom.

The three hyphenated numbers on fertilizer bags (for instance 10-10-10) tell you what percentage of nitrogen, phosphorus, and potassium the bag contains. In Chapter 2, you'll find lots of good advice on fertilizing existing lawns. In this section, I'm going to tell you how I want you to use fertilizer when you're starting with a clean slate — a bare seedbed.

Starter Fertilizer

You first need to use *starter fertilizer* just before you plant or sow grass. When you buy it, make sure it contains about equal amounts of nitrogen, phosphorus, and potassium. This type of fertilizer helps new grass grow stronger, faster. If you had your soil tested by a lab, they may advise you on the amount and specific type of fertilizer, as well as adding other materials to improve the soil, including Epsom salts or gypsum; or follow my recommendations in the chart on page 32.

Apply whatever fertilizer you use 2 or 3 days before seeding, then follow that up with a good dose of my Soil Prep Tonic (for recipe, see page 337).

The Magic, All-Purpose Soil Conditioner

Organic matter, in the form of compost, ground bark, composted tree leaves, and even composted sawdust, is truly a wonder conditioner, whatever your soil problems may be. These organic materials make your soil more loamy and nutrient rich. They help sandy soils retain water and nutrients and assist clay soils in becoming looser and better aerated.

Here's the best part about organic matter: It acts like a military recruiter, enlisting the aid of many lawn-friendly allies, such as earthworms, fungi, and other top-notch microorganisms.

Of all organic matter, compost ranks at the top of the heap in my book. Compost converts yard waste and food scraps into an excellent soil amendment. You can make it yourself by heaping this stuff in a pile in the back of your yard or buy it by the bag or truckload. (See page 86 for more details.) For new lawns, you may want to order a load from a local nursery. In some areas, local waste-disposal companies make compost and you may be able to buy it fairly cheaply.

Computing Compost

When you're starting a new lawn, you should figure on providing a 1-inch to 2-inch layer of compost over the entire area. Compost is sold by the cubic yard. So, to determine just how much you'll need, remember this equation:

3 cubic yards of compost = 1-inch layer of compost per 1000 square feet

FOR CLAY OR SAND

My "Computing Compost" formula applies to loam soil. If clay or sand rules your soil, go with a 2-inch layer for added conditioning.

Top It with Topsoil

Topsoil, by its very name, sounds high class, like an "upper-crust" type of soil. If your soil tests showed that your soil is poor, you may want to order enough topsoil to spread a 2- or 3-inch layer over your lawn-to-be. If you have a brand-new home, this is especially important because chances are that much of the good topsoil was removed during construction.

But be careful! Ask a lot of questions about the origin of the topsoil you're about to buy. You certainly don't want topsoil from any site that has been soaked in toxic chemicals. You want your lawn to be green, not to glow in the dark!

Also look closely at the topsoil. Steer clear of any that's riddled with weed seeds or full of rocks and other litter. Before you order topsoil, discuss these concerns *in writing* with the supplier.

Topsoil Checklist

✔ Clean
✔ Weed-free
✔ No debris
✔ Nontoxic
✔ Get it *in writing*

A Word of Advice

Not every new yard needs topsoil. Save your money if your yard scores high in loam. Some folks also save on the expense of buying topsoil by adding the right amount of lime or sulfur, compost, and fertilizer to fortify the soil they have.

But remember, don't cut corners! Proper preparation is key to planting a new lawn on old or new turf. It'll save you a ton of time, money, and effort in the long run!

One final note: Timing is crucial. You must allow 4 to 6 weeks for prep work before you plant grass seed. If you're going to undertake this effort, get a big calendar, hang it in your garage or shed, and mark up a work schedule to help you remember to do everything in its proper sequence.

Make a Clean Sweep

You're almost there! There's just one last step before laying sod or sowing seed. Before preparing the soil, you've got to remove debris, especially if you're working on a new construction site. Debris in soil could eventually kill your grass or damage your equipment, and you don't want that!

So get out your work gloves and a sturdy wheelbarrow, and walk slowly up and down and then side to side around your yard. Carefully search for any signs of leftover construction debris that's littering your new yard. Get rid of nails, wooden stubs, chunks of cement, pieces of wallboard, or anything else hiding on or just beneath the surface.

Step-by-Step Soil Prep

Step 1. Loosen the soil with a rototiller.

Step 2. Remove all debris: stones, roots, wallboard, etc.

Step 3. Comb through the yard with a rake, breaking up any dirt clods.

Step 4. Apply appropriate starter fertilizer, organic matter, pH adjusters, and topsoil, as needed.

Step 5. Grade the yard using an old tire, box spring, or piece of chain-link fence. (Attach whatever you've got to a piece of sturdy rope and pull it over the whole yard a few times, removing the collected debris as you go.)

Step 6. Retill, rake, and grade 3 weeks *after* the first tilling to aerate the soil and remove any weeds.

Step 7. Overspray the soil with my Soil Prep Tonic (for recipe, see page 337) to activate the nutrients that'll soon be feeding your newly planted grass.

Ask Jerry

Q I just bought a new house with no lawn and a yard that's as flat as a pancake. I've heard that I have to grade it before I sow seed. What does that mean?

A Simply put, grade is slope, and, yes, you do need to ensure that your yard has a modest slope (about 6 inches for every 25 feet). Make sure that the slope goes away from your house. If you don't get the proper grade, you're likely to end up with water in your basement or soggy spots in the lawn that will cause problems later on, like making it difficult to mow or making it an easier target for diseases.

Q I'm about to dig up my old lawn and put in a new one, but I've got a couple of beautiful old sugar maple trees in my yard. Do I need to worry about them when I work?

A If you love those maples, you do! When you dig around these — or any other — trees, take care not to injure their roots, at least as far out from their trunks as the spread of their branches above. When you redo the yard, be sure to choose a shade-loving seed mixture for under the trees. Use my **Seed Starter Tonic** (page 336) to get your seeds off and growing.

Q I've heard that blueberries and pine trees both grow best in acidic soil. I've got lots of both around my property. Does this mean that I've got acidic soil and I don't need to test it?

A I wouldn't count on it. Even though these plants perform their best in acidic soil, the pH isn't all they care about. Your home turf may have other things these plants thrive in, such as sandy soil texture or a high elevation. Do the test — it's not hard and it can really pay off in the long run!

Q We're turning a section of our vegetable garden into lawn. As we get older, it's a lot easier to mow a little more lawn than take care of vegetables. Does grass grow well in soil that grew great vegetables?

A You bet! Most vegetables prefer the same type of soil that grass prefers, so you should have a wonderful new lawn that grows like crazy and is as green as the Emerald Isle. Before you sow the grass seed be sure to spray the area with my **Soil Prep Tonic** (page 337) to get your new lawn off to a great start.

Q I don't even need to do a test to see what kind of soil I've got. My yard — and all my neighbors' yards — are cursed with soil that's pretty close to solid clay. I've heard that adding a truckload of sand might help. Shall I try it?

A Hold on before you fool around with sand — unless you're looking to mix up some concrete! The best way to improve clay soil is to work in as much organic matter as you can. Compost is great, or better still, dig in chopped up yard waste that hasn't completely decomposed yet. One of the disadvantages of clay soil is the way it compacts, and the chunky organic matter provides some aeration along with its other benefits. My **Aeration Tonic** (page 327) is a good choice to help curb against compaction; apply monthly.

Q I live on the seashore and along with a beautiful view of the ocean, I've got sand for soil in my front yard. Do I have to give up on having grass?

A My Grandma Putt taught me never to give up! Believe it or not, the best treatment is the same one I recommend for clay soils: lots of organic material. Let me give you a couple of other pieces of advice as well: When you fertilize, go easy on the dosage. Lawns in sandy soils do better if you give them smaller amounts of fertilizer more frequently throughout the season. Next, because water drains away from sandy soils so quickly, you'll have to water more frequently than if you had loam or clay soil. You may want to seriously consider installing an automatic watering system to give you a hand with this important chore. And be sure to choose a lawn grass that puts up with sandy soils. Some good choices are Bermuda grass, blue gramma grass, Buffalo grass, and zoysia grass. And finally, use my **Drought-Buster Tonic** (page 330) weekly during the growing season to minimize any damage caused by your dry conditions.

☆   ☆   ☆

Now step back and survey the results! You should have a fairly smooth yard, sloping away from your house. The soil not only should be free of construction and other debris, but also should be fortified with nutrients and other soil amendments — ready and waiting for those tiny little grass seeds to germinate and grow into a big, beautiful, green lawn! Now, let's take a look at what kind of grass to grow and how to get it off to a great start.

CHAPTER 14

From Seed to Sod

Now that you've successfully prepped your yard by following my advice and timely tips in the last chapter, you're ready to frame your homestead with that all-important, eye-catching color — green. Just make sure it's in the form of grass, not money! Starting a lawn from scratch is ideal in many ways. You aren't stuck with mistakes from the past — like the wrong grass, runaway weeds, pesky pests, or the former owner's bad maintenance habits. So take advantage of this opportunity to do it right, and that way you'll end up with a lawn that's thick, green, and healthy. You have three main methods of creating a lawn from scratch: seed, sod, and plugs and sprigs. In this chapter, I'll explain how each one works. Ready? Let's get started!

Starting a Lawn from Seed

This is the one and only time you should accept some "seedy" advice. I'm no shady character, but I *am* here to help you select the right seeds at the right time that will grow in sun, shade, and everything in-between.

The Pros and Cons of Seed

So why rely on seeds to grow your lawn? Glad you asked! The biggest advantage is cost. Starting a lawn from seed takes less of a bite out of your wallet than does starting a lawn with sod or plugs. Why, the money you save could be used toward a chaise lounge or maybe a new grill. With seed, you can be lean with the greenbacks and still cultivate plenty of green, green grass!

Beyond price savings, sowing seeds brings out the maternal/paternal nature in many homeowners. I know it does in me. There is something nurturing about sprinkling life-bearing seeds onto raked dirt, watering them, and watching them transform themselves into a lush green lawn.

On the flip side, seeds are fragile. They are susceptible to hungry birds, too much water, too little water, and an invasion of bullies, including weeds. And seeds can be tricky to plant on slopes — if you're not careful, they'll wash away with the rain!

You also need to stay put until the seeds turn into healthy grass plants. Just like little babies, your seeds need you! So if you plan on sowing seeds, don't book a 2-week exotic vacation any time soon.

You're the Wrong Type for Me!

Dash any dreams of sowing your lawn with St. Augustine, zoysia, or hybrid Bermuda grass seeds. These types of grass produce better lawns from sod or plugs.

Best Grasses to Sow

Let me play lawn-seed matchmaker and assist you in selecting the best seed for your yard. At last check, there were more than 300 varieties of grasses to choose from. That can make finding the perfect match for your lawn quite a challenge! But don't you worry, here's what you need to know to make an informed decision.

Ask Questions First

Before you rush out and buy bags of seed or truckloads of sod, sit down and run through this checklist of questions.

✔ Is the grass variety suited to your soil type?

✔ Is it adapted to your climate?

✔ If you have a lot of big, shady trees on your property, is the grass a shade-tolerant variety?

✔ Can the grass type withstand occasional weather extremes, such as freeze or drought?

✔ Will the variety you're considering be best suited for the soil and climate conditions of your area?

✔ Will it suit the purpose of your lawn? For instance, will it have to survive lots of rough play or heavy foot traffic?

By answering each of these questions, you will narrow down your selection list to appropriate grasses for your particular lawn and its intended use.

Kentucky's in *Asia?*

Even though we call it *Kentucky* bluegrass, explorers brought this European and Asian native grass seed to North America several hundred years ago — long before Kentucky was even a state! But these days, the best Kentucky bluegrass seed *does* come from Kentucky and surrounding Midwestern states.

Seed Label Reading 101

All the information on a seed bag may appear overwhelming and confusing at first glance. It's enough information to fill a yard! But pause, take a deep breath, and exhale slowly. Then give the label a careful read. Here are the key phrases you need to know and understand to make the best buy for your lawn — and your wallet.

Type of grass. In big letters, the label should clearly tell you whether you're holding a bag of tall fescue, Kentucky bluegrass, or a blend, for example.

Variety. By definition, varieties are usually much better than generic types. If you see these listed on the label, it's a sign of quality.

Origin. The state or country of seed origin must be declared when seed quantities represent more than 5 percent of the mixture. Traditionally, some areas produce better grass seed than others. Also, seed from certain locations may be more free of disease than is seed from another location.

Germination percentage. This tells you the percentage of seed that germinates under optimal conditions. *Tip:* Never buy seed that predicts less than 70 percent germination.

Pure seed percentages. The percentages reveal the proportion of grass by weight, not by seed count. Thus, 58 percent on the label means that 58 percent of the weight of the contents of the bag is grass seed. The rest is "inert matter" (see next page).

Other crop seed. A good lawn mix does not contain any "other crop seed." If it does, keep right on walkin'.

Weed seed. Nobody's perfect, not even lawn-seed growers. But stick with any bag that contains less than 1 percent of weed seed.

Noxious weeds. They are as bad as their name implies. By law, manufacturers must declare per ounce the names and number of seeds of bothersome weeds such as field bindweed. A quality bag of seed is free and clear of noxious weeds.

Inert matter. This covers the amount of dirt, chaff, and miscellaneous materials in the seed bag. Don't worry about knowing too much about inert matter. When it comes to that stuff, what *really* matters is that you don't buy a bag that contains more than 4 percent of it.

Test date. Just as you read the date on your carton of milk, check out the dates on bags of seed. Stick with bags that list a date no older than 1 year. Fresh is best — this is not wine. The seeds won't improve with age!

The Law's on Your Side

Since 1939 (when the Federal Seed Act of 1939 was adopted), all grass seed sold in the United States must have certain items listed on the label, including the percentage of each type or variety of grass inside, its birth-place, approximately how many seeds will sprout, and its expiration date.

Whale-Watchers

Most grass seed produced in the United States hails from the Pacific Northwest — specifically, the great state of Oregon. For some reason, most of our nation's grass-seed companies opted to set up headquarters there. They must know something we don't!

Hmmm . . . maybe the CEOs like to watch the migrating whales along the Pacific coast-line or love to get their special brew from the drive-through coffee shops in the Beaver State. I'm just grateful they grow such terrific grass seed!

Climate Cues

Need more tips? Read on! Climate-wise, the lawns of America belong in one of two camps:

- **Cool-season grasses**
- **Warm-season grasses**

Cool It

Cool-season grass varieties are cold hardy and don't like hot weather. So for you folks living in the cool climates, where temperatures dip below 40°F and snowfall is a common sight, this is the type of grass for you. The best choices are:

- Bent grass
- Blue gramma grass
- Buffalo grass
- Fescues (all)
- Kentucky bluegrass
- Ryegrasses (all)

All of these grasses follow a predictable pattern. They grow easily during cool weather but slow down in the heat of summer. In places with snow, they hibernate but wake up rarin' to grow come spring.

Warm Up

Warm-season grasses, sometimes known as subtropical grasses, hate the cold and love the heat. These strangers to Jack Frost grow aggressively in the warm months of summer and then go dormant during cooler times. Some warm-season varieties may turn yellow or brown during this dormancy.

Good choices for the mild to warm parts of the country include:

- Bahia grass
- Bermuda grass
- Centipede grass
- St. Augustine grass
- Zoysia grass

If you live in a tropical area like Miami, give carpet grass a strong consideration.

Hone in on Your Zone

I divide the continental U.S.A. into six major grass zones, based on things like how much it rains, how hot it gets in summer, and how cold it gets in winter. Check out my maps to see where you fit in, then read on to learn the best kinds of grasses to grow there.

ZONE 1

Location: Northeast Atlantic Coast from southern Maine to Middle Atlantic states and Pacific Northwest Coast from Washington to Northern California

Grass Class: Mostly cool-season and some hardy warm-season grasses

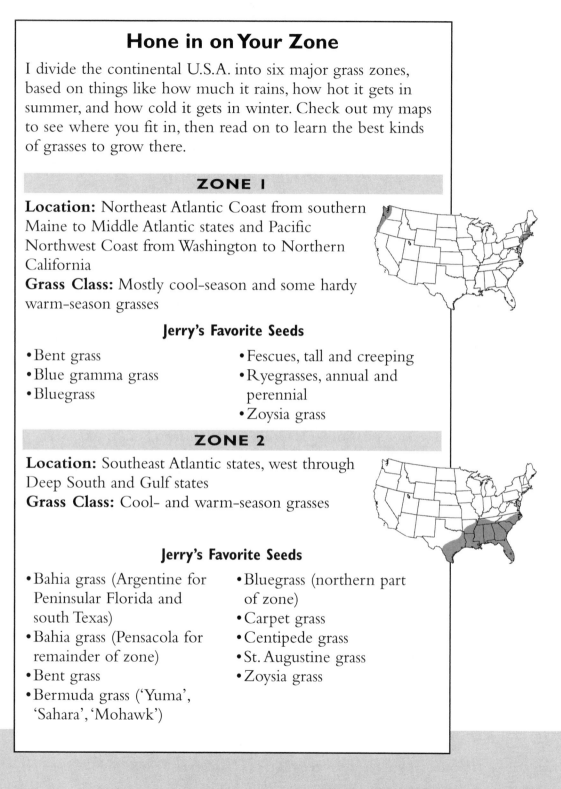

Jerry's Favorite Seeds

- Bent grass
- Blue gramma grass
- Bluegrass
- Fescues, tall and creeping
- Ryegrasses, annual and perennial
- Zoysia grass

ZONE 2

Location: Southeast Atlantic states, west through Deep South and Gulf states

Grass Class: Cool- and warm-season grasses

Jerry's Favorite Seeds

- Bahia grass (Argentine for Peninsular Florida and south Texas)
- Bahia grass (Pensacola for remainder of zone)
- Bent grass
- Bermuda grass ('Yuma', 'Sahara', 'Mohawk')
- Bluegrass (northern part of zone)
- Carpet grass
- Centipede grass
- St. Augustine grass
- Zoysia grass

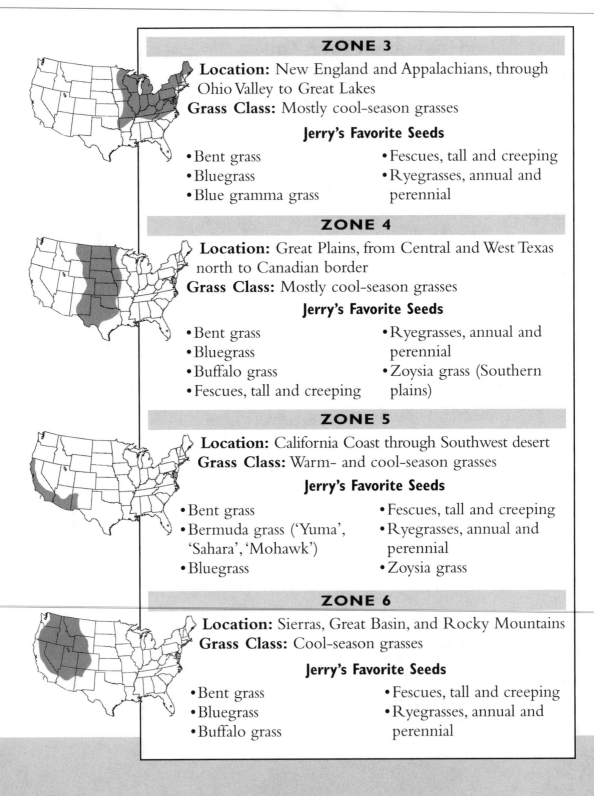

ZONE 3

Location: New England and Appalachians, through Ohio Valley to Great Lakes

Grass Class: Mostly cool-season grasses

Jerry's Favorite Seeds

- Bent grass
- Bluegrass
- Blue gramma grass
- Fescues, tall and creeping
- Ryegrasses, annual and perennial

ZONE 4

Location: Great Plains, from Central and West Texas north to Canadian border

Grass Class: Mostly cool-season grasses

Jerry's Favorite Seeds

- Bent grass
- Bluegrass
- Buffalo grass
- Fescues, tall and creeping
- Ryegrasses, annual and perennial
- Zoysia grass (Southern plains)

ZONE 5

Location: California Coast through Southwest desert

Grass Class: Warm- and cool-season grasses

Jerry's Favorite Seeds

- Bent grass
- Bermuda grass ('Yuma', 'Sahara', 'Mohawk')
- Bluegrass
- Fescues, tall and creeping
- Ryegrasses, annual and perennial
- Zoysia grass

ZONE 6

Location: Sierras, Great Basin, and Rocky Mountains

Grass Class: Cool-season grasses

Jerry's Favorite Seeds

- Bent grass
- Bluegrass
- Buffalo grass
- Fescues, tall and creeping
- Ryegrasses, annual and perennial

HOW TO CALCULATE THE CORRECT AMOUNT OF LAWN SEED

When you're ready to buy seed, don't just pick up any old amount. Waste not, want not, so buy only what you need, plus a little extra in case you have to overseed any sparse area. To figure out how much seed to spread on your lawn you don't need a working knowledge of calculus or even a calculator. Here's my handy guide for some of the more popular types of grasses.

GRASS TYPE	LBS. OF SEED PER 1,000 SQUARE FEET	DAYS TO GERMINATE	COMMENTS
Bahia grass	5–6	18–28	Wears well, drought tolerant
Bent grass	1–2	4–12	Cold tolerant, looks good, high maintenance
Bermuda grass	1–2	10–30	Wears well, drought tolerant
Blue gramma grass	1–3	15–30	Drought tolerant
Buffalo grass	2	14–30	Very drought tolerant
Centipede grass	1–2	14–30	Heat tolerant, good in poor soils
Fescues, creeping	4–5	7–14	Cold and shade tolerant
Fescues, tall	6–10	7–12	Great for high-traffic lawns
Kentucky bluegrass	2–4	14–30	Cold tolerant, wears well
Ryegrass, annual	6–8	5–10	Temporary lawns and in mixtures
Ryegrass, perennial	6–8	5–10	Excellent just about anywhere

Want to have the best of both worlds between annual and perennial ryegrasses? The varieties 'Agree' and 'Oregreen' are hybrids of both that germinate quickly, like annual rye, and hold up to the weather, like its perennial cousin.

Mix-and-Match Seeds

I like to blend several compatible grass varieties, because they not only give a terrific-looking lawn, but they're also healthier and hardier! Here are three of my favorite "lawn recipes."

Cool-Climate Premium Mix

40% Kentucky bluegrass
40% Perennial ryegrass
20% Creeping red fescue

Warm-Climate Premium Mix

40% Bermuda grass
30% Carpet grass
30% Bahia grass

In-Between Premium Mix

25% Bermuda grass
25% Buffalo grass
25% Kentucky bluegrass
25% Perennial ryegrass

Time It Right

Time your sow-to-grow day just before the grass type's season kicks into its fastest growth spurt.

For warm-season grasses, time to sow is late spring when the temperatures are consistently about 75 to 80°F or more during the day. The weather is typically mild enough to accommodate them, and you're on the brink of the warm to hot weather that plants need to keep growing once they've sprouted.

If you live in cool-season-grass country, sow seeds during the late summer or early fall after the heat of summer has passed. The ground is still warm enough to speed germination, but the weather is cool, which is the cue for cool-season grasses to grow like wildfire.

Wind and Rain, Go Away!

If you want to breeze through the task of sowing seeds, don't pick a breezy day! The seeds will just blow this way and that way; any way but the right way. Also, rule out a day of heavy rain, when only ducks are out "quacking" smiles.

Checkerboard Sowing

When you're ready to sow your seed, picture your yard as one giant checkerboard. Why? To get uniform coverage, of course! Lots of crisscrossing is needed to make sure the seeds get in every little nook and cranny. Once you've determined how much seed you need for the size of your yard (see chart on page 271), divide the amount into two equal parts. Then follow my seven steps to easy sowing (page 274) so you can be darn sure you get the right coverage.

Jerry Baker Says

"If you cool-season folks miss sowing your grass seed at just the right time, don't worry: Here's Plan B. Sow your seed in early spring. It's not as mistake-proof as sowing in the late summer/early fall, but the seeds still have a good chance of getting established and growing strong enough before the dog days of summer."

Seed-Starter Alert!

Just a friendly reminder to use two of my surefire tonics to get your lawn off to the best start possible:

- Energize your grass seed so that it'll get up and grow with my surefire Seed Starter Tonic (for recipe, see page 336). Use this tonic and you'll speed up seed germination by about 75 percent! *Amazing,* but true!

- Prepare your soil several days before you sow by spraying it with my Soil Prep Tonic (for recipe, see page 337). Your seed will get established better — and faster!

Seven Steps to Easy Sowing

Step 1. Divide your seed in half and sow one half of it across the prepared area in rows. If you've got an itty-bitty place, do this using a handheld spreader. If you've got a bigger area, distribute the seeds with a broadcast or drop spreader.

Step 2. For the critical second batch, sow the other half in rows at right angles to the first half of seeds. You'll be creating a crisscross pattern — like a checkerboard. This is the very best way to sow and grow!

Step 3. Last but not least, lightly rake the entire area to make sure there is ample contact between seed and soil. Don't be too aggressive with the rake, or you'll end up burying some seed too deep, which will create bare spots in your lawn.

Step 4. Go over your newly seeded yard with a water-filled roller. If you don't own one, rent one. It's worth the investment and will speed up germination.

Step 5. When all the seeds are sown, spray the whole area with a light misting of my Spot Seed Tonic (for recipe, see page 337).

Step 6. Apply a thin layer of mulch — about ¼ inch thick. Mulch is your seeds' best friend. It keeps the soil moist and boosts the germination rate.

Step 7. Last but not least is the H_2O. Get out the hose or turn on the sprinkler system, and turn the nozzle to fine spray or mist. Give the newly seeded soil a complete soaking. Water until there is a 6-inch depth of moist soil (at this point, don't guess — rely on a ruler).

Keep Hay at Bay!

Please don't confuse straw with hay. It's a horse of a different color! Hay contains lots of weed seeds, so keep the hay where it belongs — in the barn!

Mulching Magic

Mulch is food for your hungry seeds to grow on. It also protects the young, frail seeds from drying up in the hot sun and, to some extent, from weeds and bugs. Here are some of the best mulches to use.

Peat moss. Peat moss lightly spread on top of the soil makes an ideal mulch because it's pure organic matter. A little goes a long way, so only put down a ¼-inch layer. For you math buffs, that computes to 1 cubic foot of peat moss for every 50 square feet of yard.

Shredded bark, sawdust, or compost. Other good mulches are extrafine shredded bark, old sawdust, or screened compost from your backyard pile. As with peat moss, spread only about a ¼-inch layer.

Straw. Shake the straw out thoroughly and spread it evenly. The rule of thumb is 1 bale of straw per 1,000 square feet of yard, light enough to eliminate the need to remove the straw once the seeds have germinated.

Week One after Sowing

You must treat your lawn like a newborn baby — so give it plenty of pampering. (Luckily, you won't have to change any diapers!) During the time between when you sow and when the seeds sprout, make your number one priority to ensure that the new lawn doesn't dry out. Spray the lawn lightly three or four times a day without fail until the grass starts growing and becomes established.

When you water, try not to do a lot of tromping and stomping on your fragile, young lawn. Instead, stand on the edge of the seedbed and lightly pull the hose to drag the sprinkler from place to place until you've covered the entire yard.

Jerry Baker Says

"If you live on a ranch-size spread with more than 1 acre of land, you'll need to seed in sections. Buy what you think you'll need and then go step by step. Be patient and soon you'll have a yard full of strong, healthy grass!"

The Catch behind Using Rye

When your lawn needs a quick fix, consider using annual ryegrass. First things first, though: Don't confuse *annual* ryegrass with *perennial* ryegrass. They're like distant cousins, and they lead very different lives.

Annual ryegrass *(Lolium multiflorum)* is less prestigious than its stellar cousin, perennial ryegrass *(Lolium perenne)*. From its very name — annual — you realize that this type of grass lasts only one season. So now you may be asking yourself, Why bother with annual ryegrass at all?
That's a good question.

Why Annual Rye?

1. Annual rye serves as an inexpensive, temporary remedy for brownish-looking lawns.

2. It germinates and grows very quickly.

3. It's ideal for those times when you need a temporary lawn until you can plant a more permanent grass type.

4. It's blessed with nurturing qualities: It anchors soil and protects young seedlings from the big, bad sun until tender new grasses are big enough to fight their own battles.

5. It stays green through the winter on lawns in the South and West when warm-season grasses are dormant.

Now I need to fill you in on some of the drawbacks of annual ryegrass: It can be a bit pushy — literally. It may shove out perennial grass from your lawn and then double your woes by dying on you. And annual ryegrass doesn't handle temperature extremes, droughts, or shady spots very well. So you are forewarned!

The Family Star

Perennial ryegrass got most of the looks and talent in the family. This attractive, deep green, premium lawn grass mixes well with Kentucky bluegrass and fine fescues. It handles heavy traffic loads, resists a whole slew of diseases, and stays green through winter.

Know When to Mow

I have one word for you before you crank up your mower: Whoa! Give your new lawn ample time to reach the maximum height in inches for the specific type of grass you selected *before* you give it its first haircut. Otherwise, you run the risk of killing the grass because its root system hasn't had a chance to develop.

Also, the first mowing may shock young grass plants. It can slow the rate of root growth and, depending on where you live and how much Mr. Sun shines, you may unintentionally expose and burn the stems to a crisp. So be patient.

When Is the Right Time?

Well, timing *is* everything when it comes to mowing grass, and it depends upon the type of seed you've planted.

• **If you planted a cool-season grass,** like Kentucky bluegrass, wait until the new grass is 2½ inches tall before your first cutting.

• **If you sowed a warm-season grass,** like Bahia grass, keep the mower in the shed until the grass is 3 inches tall.

For the first cut, adjust your mower's deck to a higher-than-normal level. Make sure the blades are sharp for clean cuts. Dull blades make ragged cuts and will damage new grass. For the last cut of the season, set your mower deck a notch lower than normal, so that the grass goes through the winter nice and trim. (See the chart on page 81 for more advice.)

Starting a Lawn from Sod

Want or need an instant lawn? Don't have the time or patience to nurture seeds into grass plants? Instead of starting from seed, you can save yourself some time — but alas, not money — with the instant lawn method: sod. One day the ground is bare, then poof! The next, you've got a carpet of green. Talk about instant gratification!

Sure, sod costs more on the front end, but it has its advantages over seed. Because it has already reached at least its teen years (lawn-wise), it isn't as prone to drying out as young seedlings are. It anchors itself into the soil quickly, so it packs the muscle to smother weed seeds that may pop up. Plus, it's ideal if you want grass on slopes, where seeds can easily wash away during watering or rainstorms. Sodding remains the number one choice for small-to-medium-size lawns.

Nothing's Perfect

Okay, now that I've tooted the sod horn, I have to admit that nothing is perfect. Sod has its downsides, too.

- **You'll pay a lot more** for this speedy convenience than for seeds.

- **There is the risk** that the sod is harboring some bugs, a disease, or weeds.

- **I've had the misfortune** to get sod delivered that is so tightly matted that I've had to aerate it first so water and fertilizer could penetrate the soil to the root system below.

- **You have to weigh speed** against choice. Not all grass types are available as sod. Depending upon where you live, the sod option may not be wise if you can't buy it in the grass type that's best suited to your climate and soil conditions.

The Best Time to Lay Sod

Any time during the growing season is the perfect time to install sod — within reason.

For warm-season grasses, you'll fare far better if you lay the sod during either early spring or early fall.

Cool-season grasses take hold best as sod when planted in mid- to late spring, just before the hot and hazy days of summer arrive.

No matter where you live, aim for a cool, cloudy day. With all the lifting and bending over you'll be doing, *you'll* be happier not working in the heat. More important, if you lay sod on a blazing-hot summer day, you'll need to give the sod *lots* of extra water. Help yourself — and your sod — and try to lay sod right before rain is predicted, so that those clouds will share some of your watering chores.

Keep the Goal in Mind

Regardless of where you live or what type of sod you use, your goal is to get the sod's roots to weave into the soil as quickly as possible once it is in place. Strong, mature roots help keep the sod from drying out and prepare it for the onset of drought or a cold winter. So keep the ground moist to a depth of at least 6 inches to encourage those roots to head downward in search of water!

BEST GRASSES TO GROW FROM SOD BY REGION

The good news is that most grass types are available as sod, especially warm-season grasses.

Cool-season grasses include bent grasses, blue-grasses, and fescues.

Warm-season grasses include Bahia, Bermuda, buffalo, St. Augustine, and zoysia. You can also get sod that's made of a blend of varieties or grass types.

Let's Go Sod Shopping!

Okay, so it's not as exciting as shopping for a new car, but you still need to bring your savvy shopping skills with you when you go sod shopping. Here are some inside pointers:

- **The moisture test.** The sod should be moist but not dripping like a sponge. The roots should be damp.

- **Certified.** When you see the label "certified" sod (required by a few states), you're guaranteed that the sod is composed of certain identified grasses, and that it probably has been treated for diseases and insects.

- **Climate right.** Match the sod with your yard and locale. Bent grass, Kentucky bluegrass, and Merion are premium sods for the North. Zoysia grass, dichondra, and some bent grasses are top-quality sods for the South.

- **The right price.** Get several estimates and make sure the price covers all costs, including delivery.

- **The touch test.** Healthy sod feels cool to the touch. If it is warm or hot, that's a bad sign, so keep right on looking.

- **Age.** Avoid sod that's matted tightly with tall grass blades. This sod has been sittin' around for far too long, and it's too old for your lawn.

- **Thickness.** Choose sod that has roots at least ½ inch long; the total thickness (roots, grass blades, and soil) should be between 1 and 3 inches.

- **Color.** Not just any hue will do. Don't pick sod that is yellowish or brown. You want vibrant green sod.

- **Hidden problems.** Look under the hood. Check the underside of sod for any signs of grubs or other lawn bugs.

Sod Math

Don't worry — this is much easier to master than high school calculus. Each piece of sod is generally 6 to 8 feet long, 2 feet wide, and 1 to 3 inches thick, depending on the type of grass. It's sold by the square foot. When figuring out how much sod to order, here are some tips:

- **For square or rectangular lawns,** it's easy. You just figure length times width. So, if your lawn measures 30 by 40 feet, you'll need 1,200 square feet of sod. Always add another 10 percent as a cushion so you don't run short. In this case, your final total would come to 1,320 (1,200 + 120 = 1,320).

- **Got a weird-shaped lawn?** No problem! Follow my directions on pages 30–31) for figuring your lawn area, and then order 15 to 20 percent *more* than your measurements. It's better to err on the safe side.

Keep Sod Fresh until It's Ready to Plant

Congratulations! The truck with its bed filled to the brim with fresh-cut sod has just pulled into your driveway and tooted its horn. You rush out your front door, feeling a little giddy. Green Day has arrived!

If you're going to lay the sod yourself to save a few dollars or to get a good, sweat-inducing workout, let me give you some helpful advice: Time is not on your side. When it comes to installing sod, wait makes waste. Sod will die quickly unless it is kept watered and fitted into your yard *ASAP*. You have roughly 48 hours to install it before irreversible damage occurs.

If you must wait a day or so, store the sod in a shady place. Unroll it and lay it out on a flat surface. Take the hose to it, set the nozzle to a light mist, and spray the sod a couple of times a day to keep it moist until you can lay it in its new home.

Jerry Baker Says

"Yes, I know you know this: Sod is alive. So don't forget to let it breathe. Never cover it with sheets of plastic, because this will only suffocate it. And then where will you be?"

Tools and Equipment

Here's what you'll need.

✔ An old kitchen knife to cut the sod.

✔ A wheelbarrow. This is not an option; it's a necessity: One piece of sod can weigh as much as 40 pounds! And all that weight soon adds up.

✔ A piece of plywood or sturdy cardboard to kneel on so you don't squish the newly planted sod. You might want to get yourself some knee pads — your knees will be a lot happier if you do.

✔ A steel-headed rake to keep the soil nice and level and to tamp the sod into place.

✔ A water-filled roller to level the lawn after you lay the sod.

✔ A hose or sprinkler system to soak the sod.

Sodding Savvy

Jerry Baker Says

"For those small, odd-shaped spots in your yard, custom-fit the sod by cutting it with a sharp knife."

When you're ready to lay the sod, begin early in the morning on a cool, cloudy, breezeless day, if possible. Recruit lots of friends to help. (Treat them to plenty of cool drinks while they're working and maybe a barbecue once the chore is done.) If you're building a superlarge lawn, you'd better have a lot of friends who owe you a lot of favors! If not, consider having a local landscaper do the job. Folks in this line of work have the manpower and machinery to install the sod quickly and efficiently.

If you decide you can handle the job yourself, impress your friends with my five-step plan of action on the next page.

5-Step Sod Laying

Step 1. Before you unroll your first piece of sod, apply my Soil Prep Tonic along with a starter fertilizer (see page 337). Then water the soil lightly.

Step 2. Work like a bricklayer by laying the sod strips snugly together, with staggered joints like bricks in a wall. Make sure that there are no gaps between the ends. Use a metal rake to pat down the sod to encourage good contact with the soil.

Step 3. After you've laid all of the sod pieces, go back and add a thin topdressing of soil to cracks between the ends and joints.

Step 4. Soak the sod thoroughly to quench its thirst.

Step 5. Roll your lawn with a water-filled roller to even it out.

Post-Sodding Pointers

Once the sod is in place, you can't just forget about it. For the first few weeks or so, water it every morning before the hot sun does its stuff. Apply enough water to soak the soil 6 to 8 inches below the sod. Stick a ruler into the ground to check how far the water has penetrated.

Regular watering keeps the soil moist, which encourages roots to spread and anchor in the soil. Never let sod dry out. If you notice curled edges, bring out the hose — quick! That's the sod's way of complaining.

Even if you've been diligent about watering, please remember that it still needs food to grow. Use my All-Season Green-Up Tonic every three weeks to encourage faster, thicker growth (for recipe, see page 328).

Don't walk on your installed sod any more than is absolutely necessary for the first month or so — or until the grass is 3 to 4 inches tall. Even if you weigh 100 pounds soaking wet, you'll still sink into the sod and damage it.

Don't Jump the Gun!

Bring out your mower for the first cutting of your sod once the blades of grass are at least 3 inches tall, especially if you're growing a bluegrass variety. This is your benchmark, as the height indicates that the roots are in deep and strong.

If you jump the gun and cut too soon, you risk slowing down the root growth or, worse, shortening the life of your sod to one season. Too many of my neighbors have suffered this fate, and that's an awfully expensive lesson. So be patient!

As with lawns started from seed, you need razor-sharp mower blades for clean cuts. So before you mow, check out my mower maintenance tips in Chapter 4.

Plug Your Lawn

By definition, plugs are round patches of turf 2 to 4 inches in diameter — about the size of the pineapple slices you get from a can. Each plug usually contains a couple of inches of soil. Plugs, or biscuits, as some folks have nicknamed them, are cut out of a mature lawn and transplanted into a new yard.

The Pros and Cons

Advantages of plugs. Plugs are ideal when you want to make minor lawn repairs. They cost less than a full yard of sod and grow just as well.

Disadvantages of plugs. The problem with using plugs for the entire lawn is that it takes quite a while (up to a year) for the plants to fill out enough to look like a lawn, not like a bunch of hair plugs on a child's inexpensive doll. While you wait, you have to be very vigilant and keep weeds from popping up between the spaces. Once they gain a toehold, it can be pretty tough to get rid of them.

The Best Times to Plant Plugs

Plugs will thrive if you plant them in late spring or early summer for warm-season grasses. The sooner the better for you and your lawn — the plugs will have more time to anchor their roots into the ground and stretch out on top for a complete green cover.

Whatever you do, don't plant within 2 months of the first scheduled frost date in your area. The poor little plugs may not be able to settle in quickly enough to handle the cold, and they'll either get very sick and not perform well, or die. Then you're back to square one.

Purchasing Plugs

Plugging is a technique that is primarily used in the South, the land of warm-season grasses. In fact, a lot of my friends living in the North have never even heard of plugs. You northern folks will fare much better if you start a new lawn with seed or sod.

I'm going to get a bit technical on you again — stoloniferous and rhizomatous grasses make the best plugs because they are hardy and strong. In some places, zoysia grass is hailed as the "Prince of Plugs" because it generally anchors well in the soil and it spreads quickly throughout the area.

PLUGGING TECHNIQUES

To plug your sorry-looking lawn, first prep the soil for plugs. Follow my advice in Chapter 13 for preparing a yard for seeding or sodding. Rake the area well and get rid of all stones and debris. And do the same for any unwanted weeds.

Plugging is a lot like hemming a pair of pants. You want to plant the plugs in rows, spaced evenly like stitches in a hemline. For my advice on how to plant plugs, just turn the page.

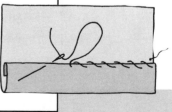

10 Steps to Perfect Plugging

Here's everything you need to know to plant plugs.

Step 1. Rake the ground to make it level. Roll it lightly using a water-filled roller.

Step 2. Apply a starter fertilizer to the soil, along with my Soil Prep Tonic (see page 337).

Step 3. Give the site a good soaking with the hose the day before you plant.

Step 4. Buy plugs in small plastic trays — or cut your own plugs from thick, healthy sod. Make sure that each plug is between 2 and 4 inches in diameter, with plenty of soil on its roots.

Step 5. When you're ready to plant, sprinkle water on the soil to dampen it, but don't give it so much water that it becomes mud.

Step 6. Guarantee military-straight rows by stretching out a long string to keep your plugs in line. Following the string guideline, make 2- to 3-inch-deep furrows about 6 inches apart.

Step 7. Make a hole for each plug using a bulb planter. Place the plug in the hole and pack down the soil around its sides.

Step 8. Plant the plugs 4 to 6 inches apart and stagger them from one row to the next to minimize the bare spots.

Step 9. When the plugs are snugly in place, treat them to my All-Season Green-Up Tonic (for recipe, see page 328).

Step 10. Water thoroughly, and keep them moist.

Gradually, the plugs will grow together, filling in and creating a new lawn.

Best Plugs for Warm Regions

Plugs work best for warm-season regions. Topping the list are:
- Hybrid Bermuda grass
- St. Augustine grass
- Zoysia grass

Watering Tips

For the first month, it must be your sworn duty as the Patroller of the Plugs to keep the soil evenly moist. That gives the roots plenty of time to get settled and anchor themselves in.

I recommend that you water plugs one or two times a day — even more if you haven't seen a rain cloud in weeks. Whatever you do, don't let the plugs get thirsty! If they dry out, you can kiss your plug investment goodbye, and you'll have to start plugging all over again. Believe me, it's not a lot of fun!

Post-Plugging Advice

Weeds. Plugs need a good hoedown. No, I'm not talking about one of those knee-slappin', foot-stompin' country dances. I mean that these newly planted plugs must be kept free and clear of weeds.

Use a hoe on young weeds for the first 6 weeks or so after planting plugs. After that, while you're tending your lawn, hand-pluck any weeds you spot. The last thing you want after doing all of that hard work is for your young plugs to be overpowered by weeds!

Fertilizer. On the day you plant the plugs, skip forward on your calendar and put a big red X on the date that's 5 weeks later. That's the optimal time to apply my Plug Feeding Tonic.

Plug Feeding Tonic

Mix together:

3 lbs. of Epsom Salts
1 bag of lawn food (enough for 2,500 sq. ft.)

Apply at half the recommended rate with your handheld broadcast spreader.

Mowing Time

Ladies and gentlemen of the lawn world, start your mowers! Just wait to tool up to the starting line until 4 to 6 weeks after you've planted the plugs. And set the mowing deck higher than normal. You don't want to accidentally scalp your newly settled grass, do you?

Keep a close eye on the mower wheels, too, and make sure they aren't causing any ruts. If your mower should yank a plug up and out of the ground, don't fret. If the plug's still in good shape, just pop it back into place, water it well, and wait a couple of weeks before you run your mower over that area again.

A Plug Is *Not* a Sprig

Sprigs are individual grass plants or runners that have been dug up from the soil and pulled apart. They are much smaller and skinnier than plugs. Sprigs are definitely best used for small repair jobs, not to start a lawn from scratch.

Why? For 1,000 square feet of lawn, you'd need 5 bushels of sprigs. You'd literally be spending days trying to plant sprigs. Wouldn't you rather be out on the golf course or lying in the hammock watching the grass grow? I know I would!

Ask Jerry

Q I live out west where wildfires are a real hazard. Are any lawn grasses less of a fire hazard in dry weather?

A You bet. Many lawn seed mixes made of native grasses can reduce fire hazard. These are often available at local nurseries, blended for your region.

Many non-native grasses also provide some protection, and they are sometimes easier to find. A nice blend is Canada bluegrass, wheat grass, sheep fescue, and blue gramma grass.

Q I saw some half-priced sod at my garden center, left over from a landscaping job. It's a little pale, but at 50 percent off, it sounds like a good deal. What do you think?

A I think you should say, "Thanks, but no thanks." Sod dies easily, and it's often hard for even the best garden centers to keep it in good shape for more than a few days. After that, the edges often dry out and turn brown, and much of the sod strip starts looking pale. When you're shopping for sod, always ask when it was delivered to the nursery. The less time it has spent in the garden center, the better it is for your lawn.

☆ ☆ ☆

Whether you've seeded or sodded, I guarantee you'll be satisfied with your new lawn if you follow the advice in this chapter to a tee. As my Grandma Putt always said, "Nothin's worth doin', unless you do it right." And nothing's more satisfying than gorgeous green grass nurtured by your own efforts. It sure feels good, doesn't it? So reach around and give yourself a big pat on the back.

CHAPTER 15

A Gallery of Grasses

Yes, the grass can be greener on the other side of the fence —
as well as in your own yard. But you don't have to be green
with envy anymore! What's the secret? Grass selection. Often,
the difference between a great lawn and a not-so-great lawn
boils down to selecting the right type of grass for your particular
kind of soil and climate. And if you're starting a lawn from
scratch, take this golden opportunity to be a turf matchmaker
extraordinaire by making sure the grass you pick suits your
yard's conditions. If you've inherited an established yard, knowing the specific type of grass (or grasses, for that matter) in your
lawn helps you figure out how best to care for it. Here's what
you need to know.

Do Be Choosy

There are numerous types of grasses sprouting up in lawns all across America. Surprisingly, none is named after famous folks like presidents and movie stars. Names tend to be based more on where they grow and what they look like. Names range from St. Augustine (a tough-bladed turf grass that's anything but saintly) to Kentucky blue-grass (even though it is emerald green) to buffalo (which "roams" nicely through parts of Texas).

There are fine-bladed grasses, which tend to be thin and soft to the touch, and coarse-bladed grasses, which are thick and rough. That's the quick overview; now for the details.

How Does Your Grass Grow?

As we discussed in Chapter 1 (see pages 10–11), grasses have four different ways to spread themselves around.

Rhizomes. This growth method involves underground stems that, as they grow away from the original plant, create new plants. Grasses that grow by rhizomes are easy to tend and stand nice and tall.

Seeds. If you allow grasses to "let their hair down" and grow for a while, they will go to seed. These seeds blow about and take root in bare spots in your yard.

Stolons. Grasses that spread this way rely on stems that grow along the ground, root, and produce new plants. This type is often superaggressive and may bully other types of grasses in your lawn into extinction.

Tillers. Grasses that spread this way depend on new shoots being added to the base of the original plant. These are known in some parts of the country as clump grasses.

Hot and Cold

Grasses fall into two major categories: cool season and warm season. Cool-season grasses can handle the moist and cold climates of the North. They enjoy peak growth spurts in spring and fall and slow down during the summer.

Warm-season grasses, on the other hand, thrive in zip codes with palm trees, outdoor swimming pools, and mild winters. They tend to turn brown when the temperature slips consistently below 60°F, and they grow well during the long, hot summer.

For ease of reference, I've divided this chapter into cool-season grasses and warm-season grasses, and I explain the pros and cons of each variety. Refer to the maps on pages 269–70 to find out what grass zone you live in.

Cool-Season Grasses

COLONIAL BENT GRASS (Agrostis tenuis)

Characteristics: Pale green color, fine leaves.
Best lawn zones: 1 to 6.
Soil needs: Ordinary to slightly acidic soil; full sun.
Advantages: Popular choice for golf greens.
Disadvantages: Vulnerable to winter injury, snow molds, and other diseases because of its naturally weak growth.
Mowing height: ½ to 1 inch.
Maintenance: Water often and feed light sprinklings of dry and liquid fertilizers frequently. This grass requires the most care of all the cool-season grasses.
Popular cultivars: Mix and match 'Arlington', 'Bardot', 'Old Orchard', 'Springfield', 'Toronto', and 'Washington'.

KENTUCKY BLUEGRASS *(Poa pratensis)*

Characteristics: Blue-green blades; narrow, upright-growing.

Best lawn zones: 1 and 3 to 6.

Soil needs: Fertile soils.

Advantages: Ideal choice for northern lawns that get lots of sun and water. Looks nicely manicured when mowed.

Disadvantages: Cannot handle a lot of traffic.

Mowing height: 2 to 2½ inches.

Maintenance: Water during dry spells and treat to light fertilizer feedings in late summer to early fall. May need to be dethatched at times.

Popular cultivars: Use a blend of several compatible cultivars for best results. Top choices are 'Adelphi', 'Blacksburg', 'Challenger', 'Classic', 'Columbia', 'Eclipse', 'Glade', 'Julia', 'Midnight', 'Newport'. Be aware that 'Merion' is prone to rust and thatch, and needs lots of fertilizer feedings.

Test Your Lawn IQ

Can you name the most common lawn grass in the United States? If you answered Kentucky bluegrass, congratulations! Mow your friends over with this piece of turf trivia!

FESCUE, CHEWINGS
(Festuca rubra var. commutata)

Characteristics: Dark gray, fine-bladed; stands straight and tall.

Best lawn zones: 1 and 3 to 6.

Soil needs: Sandy, acidic, and infertile soils.

Advantages: Mixes well with other types of grasses. Great choice for shady, low-traffic areas in lawns and parks. Infrequent mowing required.

Disadvantages: Can overtake other grasses in the lawn.

Mowing height: 1½ to 2½ inches.

Maintenance: Keep your mower blades sharp, because rough cuts will leave blade tips shredded and discolored.

Popular cultivars: 'Banner', 'Banner II', 'Bridgeport', 'Jamestown II', 'SR 5000'.

FESCUE, CREEPING RED (*Festuca rubra*)

Characteristics: Don't be fooled by its name. The leaves of this grass are actually deep green — only its base is red. Posture-perfect blades are fine and thin.

Best lawn zones: 1 and 3 to 6.

Soil needs: Mix with perennial ryegrass, as it tends to grow in clumps when planted solo.

Advantages: Your best bet to include in a lawn mixture for challenging turf situations.

Disadvantages: Not mighty enough to handle a lot of heavy traffic.

Mowing height: 2 inches.

Maintenance: Avoid overfeeding. Too many fertilizer nutrients can actually harm this grass. Be stingy with water, too. Too much H_2O opens the door to fungal disease invasion.

Popular cultivars: 'Claudia', 'Ensylva', 'Flyer', 'Marker', 'Medallion', 'Salem', 'Shademaster'.

FESCUE, TALL (*Festuca elatior*)

Characteristics: Tough with sharp-edged, wide blades; prone to form clumps.

Best lawn zones: 1, 3, and 5.

Soil needs: Adaptable to most soils; tolerates salt.

Advantages: Can handle a lot of wear and tear, which is why it's a top choice for playgrounds. Deep roots provide erosion control on banks.

Disadvantages: A bit too coarse for those seeking a manicured lawn. It tends to be aggressive, frequently crowding out other grasses.

Mowing height: 2 to 3 inches.

Maintenance: Needs regular watering in summer to prevent dormancy; does best when mixed in with other types of grasses.

Popular cultivars: New cultivars tend to be nicer looking, more resistant to diseases and bugs, and hardier than older types. Look for 'Falcon', 'Guardian', 'Mustang', 'Olympic', 'Pacer', 'Titan'.

RYEGRASS, ANNUAL (Lolium multiflorum)

Characteristics: Coarse, light green leaves with a tendency to clump.

Best lawn zones: 1 to 6.

Soil Needs: Grows in lots of different soils.

Advantages: Hardy, germinates quickly, grows straight and tall. Keeps its green color and is fairly resistant to drought, insects, and diseases.

Disadvantages: Has short life span. Lasts only one season. Use more as a quick crop until a better grass can be introduced and germinate.

Mowing height: 2 inches.

Maintenance: Keep your mower in tip-top shape because this grass requires frequent haircuts. Be sure to water during dry spells.

Popular cultivars: 'Gulf', 'Tarn'.

RYEGRASS, PERENNIAL (Lolium perenne)

Characteristics: Light green, wide leaves that look coarse. Tends to grow in bunches.

Best lawn zones: 1 and 3 to 6.

Soil Needs: Fairly flexible; grows on a wide range of soils.

Advantages: Sprouts swiftly, controls erosion, is able to handle heavy foot traffic, especially on playing fields. Repels most insects and diseases, especially when endophytes are added.

Disadvantages: Depends on you. Some folks are turned off by its light green hue. Does not fare well in shade, extreme cold, or heat and drought.

Mowing height: 2 to 3 inches.

Maintenance: Easy to care for. Just fertilize sparingly once it is established. Plant in spring or late summer.

Popular cultivars: 'Blazer II', 'Citation II', 'Fiesta', 'Manhattan II', 'Palmer II', 'Pennant', 'Pennfine', 'Regal', 'Repel II'.

Warm-Season Grasses

BAHIA GRASS (*Paspalum notatum*)

Characteristics: Tough, coarse texture, flat blades.

Best lawn zone: 2.

Soil needs: Adapts nicely to a wide range of soil conditions.

Advantages: Spreads slowly by short rhizomes, but once it takes hold, it grows thickly and requires little care. Pushes out weeds without creating thatch.

Disadvantages: Tolerates drought but needs frequent mowing. Prone to mole crickets, dollar spot, and brown patch.

Mowing height: 2 to 3 inches.

Maintenance: Keep lawn mower's blades sharp to avoid uneven, ragged cuts.

Popular cultivars: 'Pensacola', 'Wilmington'.

BERMUDA GRASS (*Cynodon dactylon*)

Characteristics: Deep roots, fine to medium texture; likes to creep all over.

Best lawn zones: 2 and 5.

Soil needs: Grows best in fertile soils but adapts to others.

Advantages: Attractive looking, handles heavy foot traffic well, and repels most diseases. Tolerates drought and heat.

Disadvantages: Invest in a lawn edger, because this grass grows aggressively and will spill over onto your sidewalks and driveways. Prone to thatch and may look dead from winter to spring.

Mowing height: 1 to 2 inches.

Maintenance: Needs regular watering and frequent fertilizer feedings to retain its color.

Popular cultivars: 'Cheyenne', 'Tifdwarf', 'Tifgreen', 'Tiflawn', 'Tifway', 'Turcote'.

BUFFALO GRASS (*Buchloe dactyloides*)

Characteristics: Fine-textured, curling blades that are gray-green during growing seasons and straw-colored in winter.

Best lawn zones: 3, 4, and 6.

Soil needs: Grows best in heavy soil, but can handle finer-textured soils.

Advantages: Requires virtually no irrigation or fertilization. Grows in places that receive only 12 to 25 inches of rain annually.

Disadvantages: Presents a matted look with blades that are an off-green color. Prone to browning during extremely hot or cold weather.

Mowing height: 4 inches.

Maintenance: Requires little tending.

Popular cultivars: 'Bison', 'Buffalawn', 'Cody', 'Tatanka', 'Texoka'.

CARPET GRASS (*Axonopus affinis*)

Characteristics: Smooth, sharp blade tips; creeping grass grows thick and quickly.

Best lawn zone: 2.

Soil Needs: Acidic and sandy soils, with or without fertilizer.

Advantages: Creeping stolons quickly form a dense turf that stands up to heavy foot traffic.

Disadvantages: Won't win any beauty contests and can't handle cold or drought. Must be mowed frequently.

Mowing height: 1 to 2 inches.

Maintenance: Needs regular irrigation in areas with infrequent rainfall.

Popular cultivars: None.

CENTIPEDE GRASS (Eremochloa ophiuroides)

Characteristics: Pale green leaves with coarse texture; spreads very s-l-o-w-l-y.

Best lawn zones: 2 to 6.

Soil needs: Not choosy. Grows well in sandy, clay, even slightly acidic soils.

Advantages: Doesn't need to be mowed very often, maybe every couple of weeks. Repels most insects.

Disadvantages: Vulnerable to chlorosis (yellowing) and can't handle a lot of heavy foot traffic. Its shallow roots won't tolerate moderate droughts or low temperatures.

Mowing height: 1½ to 2 inches.

Maintenance: Nicknamed the "lazy man's grass," it requires only periodic feeding but needs frequent watering because of its shallow roots.

Popular cultivars: 'Centennial' (for alkaline soils), 'Georgia Common' (for acidic soils).

GRAMMA GRASS, BLUE (Bouteloua gracilis)

Characteristics: Narrow, blue-green leaves; tends to form thick clusters.

Best lawn zones: 3, 4, and 6.

Soil needs: Dry soil.

Advantages: Grows in a wide range of climates. Can shoulder a lot of foot traffic and is fairly resistant to most diseases and insects.

Disadvantages: A slow grower; not regarded as the favorite for a classy-looking lawn. Tends to turn brown during hot, dry weather.

Mowing height: 1½ to 2 inches.

Maintenance: Doesn't need to be mowed often; fairly easy to maintain.

Popular cultivars: 'Alamo', 'Hachita', 'Lovington'.

ST. AUGUSTINE GRASS
(Stenotaphrum secundatum)

Characteristics: Very thick-bladed, coarse grass; grows quickly and spreads by aboveground stolons.

Best lawn zone: 2.

Soil needs: Sandy, moist soil, but tolerates the full gamut of southern soil conditions.

Advantages: Can handle intense heat. Turns brownish in winter but stays green longer than Bermuda grass. Squeezes out weeds.

Disadvantages: No match against chinch bugs and warm-weather lawn diseases. Even with the best of care, tends to look coarse and rough.

Mowing height: 2 to 3 inches.

Maintenance: Dethatch regularly and keep mower blades razor sharp to avoid brown tips. Water regularly and plant plugs or sprigs on new lawns when seed is not available. Needs plenty of fertilizer.

Popular cultivars: 'Bitter Blue', 'DelMar', 'Floralawn', 'Floratum', 'Jade', 'Seville', 'Sunclipse'.

ZOYSIA GRASS (Zoysia japonica)

Characteristics: Tough, thick, creeping turf featuring needlelike blades. Spreads slowly by both rhizomes and stolons and digs down deep with its roots.

Best lawn zones: 1 and 2.

Soil needs: Ordinary soil.

Advantages: Tolerates moderate foot traffic; resists drought and most pests and weeds.

Disadvantages: Vulnerable to billbugs; not able to handle cold climates; tends to thatch easily.

Mowing height: ½ to 1 inch.

Maintenance: Requires less-than-average mowing and watering.

Popular cultivars: 'Bel Air', 'El Toro', 'Emerald Jade', 'Meyer', 'Sunburst'.

Oh, Boy — Zoysia!

Until recently, if you wanted a lawn of zoysia grass, you had to purchase plugs. Well, now you have a choice. New varieties of zoysia are available as seed, and that makes installing a zoysia grass lawn easier than ever.

Ask Jerry

Q I need some help, Jerry. My yard is up north where winters are cold. I've got lousy soil and lots of shade, to boot. I've tried every kind of grass I can think of, and nothing seems to grow well. Is there anything that will grow in these conditions and still look good without being pampered?

A Hard fescue is just what you need. This superhardy grass is most often used in conservation mixes to stablize soil. It has a clumpy growth pattern and you'll need to leave it higher than other fescues to have it looking smooth. But it makes a nice lawn where just about nothing else will grow. Be sure to give your hard fescue an easy time by giving it a dose of **Grandma Putt's Homemade Organic Fertilizer** (page 332).

Well, my friends, we're nearly at the end of our long journey through the ins and outs of lawn care. Along the way, you've learned a lot — what makes a lawn healthy and what makes it sick, the differences among fertilizers, all about mowers and mowing — and probably most important, you're now familiar with the grasses themselves, what they like and don't like, and what you will like or not like about them.

So what more could there possibly be? Well, not everyone wants more grass to take care of. If that's you, or you're just curious as to what kind of life there is after lawns, read on and you'll see.

CHAPTER 16

There's More to Life Than Just Lawns

Who says that each and every American yard has to be filled with grasses that constantly demand a mower manicure? To my knowledge, there's no such rule in the homeowner's handbook, and believe you me, I've checked! Yet somehow, back in the early 1950s, Americans fell in love with the idea of a home bordered with white picket fences and framed in green by a healthy-looking lawn. For the most part, this notion has stuck with us for nearly five decades. Until now, when the Baby Boomers have taken over.

New Choices

Welcome to the new millennium! All yards need not be filled from front to back with gorgeous blades of grass. This is the century of choice. In many ways, yards have evolved just like that good ol' cup of Joe. Twenty, even thirty years ago, coffee came in three basic types: black, with cream, or with sugar. Today coffee houses boast menus with dozens of choices, ranging from iced mocha to steaming hot latté with nonfat milk.

Break Out of the Pattern

I want you to apply this same creative thinking to your yard. Unleash yourself from the ordinary, those that's-the-way-we've-always-done-it thoughts, and those frustrating we've-got-to-keep-up-with-the-Joneses ambitions. A postage-stamp-size lawn may be right down your alley!

Honey, I Shrank the Lawn!

Be candid with yourself. Does the thought of pushing a lawn mower back and forth across the yard all summer long hold zero appeal? Don't want to even think about spending hours over the weekend fertilizing, weeding, watering, and mowing? Does your job keep you longer at the office than you'd like? Do you live in an area where growing — and maintaining — a lush, green lawn is more trouble than it's worth because of varmints and pests driving you crazy or you've got too much shade or too much foot traffic? Or are you just plain bored by all those grass blades?

First, let's take a look at some ways to have *less* lawn. Just because you started out with an acre of rolling green doesn't mean that you'd like it to stay that way. You certainly have the power and creativity to make your lawn less of a presence on your property.

Going Grassless

If you're one of those people who never, ever wants to see a lawn mower again, yet you want your home on a nice-looking piece of property, just go completely grassless! In place of grass plants, you have many delightful options, including adding elaborate bedding areas, and building a deck or patio that meets the specific needs of your family. Some of my favorite alternatives to growing grass include:

- Ground covers
- Ornamental grasses
- Meadow plants and grasses
- Rock gardens
- Decks and patios
- Outdoor play areas

Why Go Grassless?

In one single growing season, a half-acre of lawn produces more than 5,500 pounds of grass clippings.

Jerry's How-to-Get-Rid-of-a-Lawn Strategies

When you determine that it's in the best interest of your lawn — and you! — to make it smaller, you'll need to first get rid of the turf you've got. Here's how to do it.

Use herbicides. Apply nonselective glysophate-based herbicides (at the recommended rate) to kill the grass in an unwanted area. A word of caution here, my friends: Many herbicides kill or damage *any* plant they come in contact with. Spray drift or careless application can lead to unintentional damage (and even death) to the lawn you want to *keep*, nearby shrubs, or gardens, SO BE CAREFUL!

Burn it off. Recruit Ol' Sol to burn off all the unwanted turf. In the hottest part of summer, cover the selected area with clear plastic for a few weeks. Step back and let the sun put its magic rays to work. The lawn under the plastic will heat up and be burned to death, roots and all. The result? No more lawn.

Dig it, man. Do it the old-fashioned way — remove the sod manually with a spade. For large areas, I recommend renting a sod stripper. It makes the job go much faster, and it's much easier on your aching back.

More Lawn-Away Strategies

Extra! Extra! Read all about it! Take lots of newspaper and spread it on top of the lawn areas you want to get rid of. Then add layers of shredded bark or other mulch to hold it down and keep it in place. Over the course of a few weeks, the paper and mulch will work together to shade out the unwanted turf, causing it to die.

Shrub it out. Shrubs make terrific lawn shrinkers because they serve so many purposes. They act as natural screens covering eyesores like that big air-conditioning unit. They direct traffic by guiding people on pathways. They decorate space in a prominent spot in your lawn that is simply too small for a tree. And they (if they're low growing) can even act as ground cover.

Replace it. Install a circular driveway or add paths, courtyards, or patios. Keep in mind, however, that if you decide to go this route, you will probably have more trimming to do, even though your lawn-mowing time is decreased.

Honey, I Expanded the Lawn!

Some folks *love* to mow grass. I know I do! We're the ones who love the smell, the look, the feel of grass, and we want as much of it as possible surrounding our homes. So what's the trick to more lawn if you don't have enough?

Lose the losers! I remember one of the first homes I ever lived in. It was a classic fixer-upper with the backyard dominated by a huge, leaky aboveground pool and three trees with roots that were threatening to take over New Jersey. I knew that pool and those trees had to go. Abracadabra! The bare spots that remained after they were gone gave me the chance to expand my lawn quite nicely.

Forget flowers. Other folks who want more lawn choose to replace old flower or vegetable gardens with sod. Or they discover they have a patch of weeds or even poisonous plants thriving on their home turf and yank them out. Powie! Get rid of them and you've got got that much more lawn to enjoy.

Ground Covers

Ground cover is a broad term that describes low, spreading plants that for a number of reasons produce a terrific effect when you allow them to spread and blanket a particular area. Some of the personality traits that qualify a plant to work well as a ground cover are these.

• They never grow taller than about 18 inches.

• They need very little care to survive and look good for most of the year.

• They spread easily and fill in to make a nice, even-looking mass of foliage and color.

Many kinds of plants make great ground covers, including grasses, sedges, creeping perennials, and suckering shrubs.

The Right Ground Cover

Selecting the most appropriate ground cover for your purposes is easier than you may think. When shopping for ground covers, all you need to do is to keep in mind the types of terrain in your yard and the climate in your locale. Then tap into your artistic side. Choose colors and textures that accent the look of your homestead and help convey your personal signature. The result? They can turn a boring lawn into a dramatic landscape full of plants of different sizes, shapes, colors, and foliage.

To find out the top 10 reasons I'm such a great fan of ground covers, please turn the page.

And the Top 10 Reasons to Plant Ground Covers Are . . .

I'm a big fan of ground covers because they offer so many benefits. Here are the top 10:

No. 1. Many ground covers are "wallet allies" — my pet phrase for inexpensive garden plants and tools.

No. 2. Ground covers step in as quick solutions to replace ailing areas (particularly lawns).

No. 3. They are very versatile. In areas that are prone to periodic drought, some ground covers are like tiny camels, able to survive on minimal amounts of water, while in rainy areas, some types of ground covers act like sponges, eagerly soaking up excess water.

No. 4. Terrain-wise, ground covers can rescue steep banks from erosion or may be a low-maintenance lawn substitute for rocky or steeply sloped areas.

No. 5. Many ground covers are quite content when planted in the gaps among paving stones on your walkway or as borders along your paths.

No. 6. Ground covers often eliminate the need for trimming around trees, shrubs, paths, and walkways.

No. 7. They function as yard bullies in stopping weeds dead in their tracks.

No. 8. They reduce the need to mow, a feature you'll especially appreciate if you have terribly tricky terrain.

No. 9. If you live in the land of falling leaves, ground covers can drastically reduce the need for raking because they trap the decomposing leaves.

No. 10. And the *best* reason to plant ground covers is, quite simply, they are wonderful looking! Many offer distinctively shaped and textured foliage as well as eye-catching flowers and berries.

Jerry's Favorite Ground Covers

For Slopes and Rocky Places

- Ajuga *(Ajuga reptans)*
- Common periwinkle *(Vinca minor)*
- Creeping juniper *(Juniperus horizontalis)*
- Crown vetch *(Coronilla varia)*
- English ivy *(Hedera helix)*
- Lace shrub *(Stephanandra incisa* 'Crispa'*)*
- Rugosa rose *(Rosa rugosa)*
- St. John's wort *(Hypericum calycinum)*
- Virginia creeper *(Parthenocissus quinquefolia)*
- Wintercreeper *(Euonymus fortunei)*
- Woolly yarrow *(Achillea tomentosa)*

For Shady Spots

- Ajuga *(Ajuga reptans)*
- American barrenwort *(Vancouveria hexandra)*
- Barren strawberry *(Waldsteinia fragarioides)*
- Common periwinkle *(Vinca minor)*
- Creeping lilyturf *(Liriope spicata)*
- English ivy *(Hedera helix)*
- European ginger *(Asarum europaeum)*
- Pachysandra *(Pachysandra terminalis)*
- Piggyback plant *(Tolmiea menziesii)*
- Sweet woodruff *(Galium odoratum)*
- Wintercreeper *(Euonymus fortunei)*

For Wet Soils

- Creeping Jenny *(Lysimachia nummularia)*
- Japanese primrose *(Primula japonica)*

For Drought-Prone Areas

- Moss pink *(Phlox subulata)*
- Showy sundrop *(Oenothera speciosa)*
- Two-row sedum *(Sedum spurium)*

Ornamental Grasses

Are you into grass but not into the manicured lawn look? Then consider replacing your turf grass with an ornamental grass. Ornamentals are the wild, free-spirited members of the grass clan, while lawns are their conservative, sedate cousins. Ornamental grasses reward you with beauty all season long and beyond. Long after most annuals and perennials have finished blooming, many ornamental grasses still retain their color, shape, and sometimes flower blossoms well into the fall. No wonder there's a bit of jealousy among the roses!

A Diverse Bunch

I want you to be aware that ornamental grasses represent a mighty diverse family. Just to give you an example, those grasses that form 6-inch mounds and others that turn into towering 20-foot screens both belong to the same ornamental grass family!

Here's the textbook definition: Ornamental grasses are any and all grasslike plants deemed to be suitable for inclusion in a yard or garden.

AND THOSE ARE?

Bamboos. These are tropical or semitropical plants with hollow, woodlike canes ranging in height from 1 to 100 feet. They spread quickly and form thick clumps.

Sedges. Although they look like true grasses, sedges have pith-filled stems that are triangle-shaped when cut in cross section. They're perfect candidates for moist and shady to sunny locations where traditional grasses are hard to grow.

Rushes. These plants feature cylindrical, stiff stems that seek moist soil and shade to part sun. They grow quite well in marshes and water gardens or as lawn substitutes in both shade and dappled sun.

Ornamental Grass Care

Overall, ornamentals are a cinch to grow because they are highly adaptable. And the best part is that you need to get your lawn mower out only once a year, usually for a spring haircut.

Give ornamental grasses regular feeding with my All-Season Green-Up Tonic (for recipe, see page 328) and some slow-release, low-nitrogen fertilizer. Then bring out the hose only during dry spells. As a final measure, treat these grasses to an organic mulch, which, in turn, helps suffocate unwanted weeds, holds moisture in the soil, and protects any newly planted roots against winter damage.

Do the Division

Some ornamental grasses can grow for years without much maintenance. But there may come a time when you need to divide your plants. You'll know they're ready for a split when you see discolored, deteriorating leaves — sure signs that there are too many mouths to feed and not enough nutrients to go around. They are literally squeezing one another out. Dividing your grasses every 3 years or so will keep them looking and feeling healthy. The best time to divide is in early spring, just when these grasses start their growth spurt.

Here's how to divide your ornamental grass clumps: With a spade or shovel, dig out a section of the plant. Make sure it contains top sprouts and roots. Then replant this section in a new spot. Water thoroughly for a few weeks so the section can reroot itself and keep on growing. It's as easy as pie!

Jerry's Guide to Ornamental Grasses

There are dozens upon dozens of ornamental grasses. Which type would look best in your yard? First, you need to find grasses that are best suited to your growing conditions. Allow me to introduce you to some of the key members of the ornamental grass gang and provide you with a short bio on each. The zones given here represent the USDA hardiness zones. See page 322 for a map and an explanation of what these zones mean.

Jerry's Top 10 Ornamental Grasses

BIG BLUESTEM

(Andropogon gerardii)

This stately, blueish, sun-seeking, clumping perennial grows best in well-drained, moist soil. It's got terrific purplish flower clusters that bloom on 6-foot stems. This plant curbs erosion on slopes and can be used in borders or in mass plantings. (Zones 4–9)

BLUE LYME GRASS

(Leymus arenarius)

This low-level, spreading, drought-tolerant perennial needs ample drainage. Its metallic blue leaves cascade forward and turn to tan by winter. This grass is a good candidate for containers, borders, and flower beds. (Zones 4–9)

FALSE OAT GRASS

(Arrhenatherum elatius 'Variegatum')

Noted for its blue-green leaves with white stripes and oatlike flower spikes, this grass prefers fertile, well-drained, acidic soil in sun or light shade. Use for edging your flower beds, as a ground cover, or for accenting a rock garden. (Zones 4–9)

FOUNTAIN GRASS

(Pennisetum alopecuroides)

This clumping perennial needs fertile, well-drained, moist soil and lots of sun. Its showy seed heads flow like fountain waters over mounds of shiny, green leaves. Great as an accent plant in borders or as a ground cover, it does especially well in coastal regions. (Zones 5–10)

Jerry's Guide to Ornamental Grasses

INDIAN GRASS

(Sorghastrum nutans)

Once covering the prairies, this clumping perennial thrives in rich, loamy, moist soil and likes lots of sun. Its feathery flower clusters erupt into hues of orange and gold in the fall. Terrific for mass plantings, as well as for stopping erosion on slopes.
(Zones 4–9)

JAPANESE SILVER GRASS

(Miscanthus sinensis)

This clumping perennial grows in moist, humus-rich soil. It's big — up to 8 feet tall and 3 feet wide! Its silvery-toned, sharp-edged leaves vary from green to bronze, and bear white to reddish floral plumes in summer. Good for a hedge, border, or screen.
(Zones 5–9)

JOB'S TEARS

(Coix lacryma-jobi)

Named after that unfortunate Biblical man, this annual is easy to grow anywhere. It sports hard seeds, short gray tassels on its flowers, and coarse leaves.
(Zones 9–10)

QUAKING GRASS

(Briza media)

The heart-shaped, green florets of this clumping perennial shimmer and tremble in the spring breeze. The flowers turn purple and then golden yellow. An ideal ground cover, or rock garden, flower border, and edging plant. (Zones 4 to 10)

SIDE OATS GRAMMA GRASS

(Bouteloua curtipendula)

This clumping perennial has delicate, gray-green leaves that turn purple or red in late summer. Great in well-drained soil. Use as an eyecatching ground cover or for erosion control.
(Zones 4–9)

SWITCH GRASS

(Panicum virgatum)

Switch grass can adapt to many growing conditions. A clumping perennial, it features pinkish clusters of flowers that bloom on tall stems by midsummer. (Zones 5–9)

Meadow Mixes

As a little tyke, didn't you love to run through a meadow on a lazy Sunday afternoon? I sure did! We'd get out of our church clothes, slip on some comfortable overalls, and head for the hills.

Now you can relive the sight, smell, and feel of a meadow right in your own backyard! All you have to do is plant some low-growing, prairie-type wildflowers and native grasses.

As much as I love my lawn, I also have a soft spot in my heart for meadows. Meadows are open places with lots of sunshine and blue sky, just like lawns. But meadows don't require a lot of attention to look great. All through the growing season, a meadow holds pleasant surprises, like wildflowers in bloom and butterflies floating by. And meadows have a practical side as well. Did you know that they actually help your lawn and garden because many common meadow plants attract beneficial insects, like honeybees and ladybugs, to your yard?

Wildflowers of the Continent

Black-eyed Susan, purple coneflower, scarlet sage, and butterfly weed headline the list of some of my all-time favorite meadow plants. Here are some wildflowers that grow in every part of the United States.

Annual phlox *(Phlox drummondii)*

Baby blue-eyes *(Nemophila menziesii)*

Black-eyed Susan *(Rudbeckia hirta)*

Blanketflower *(Gaillardia aristata)*

Blue flax *(Linum perenne* ssp. *Lewisii)*

Butterfly weed *(Asclepias tuberosa)*

Cosmos *(Cosmos bipinnatus)*

The Three Main Types

1. Native grasses. This type is superadaptive and prides itself on being low maintenance. As the name implies, these are grasses that feel right at home because the good ol' USA is where they originated.

Confused? Let me try to clear the air. Blue gramma and buffalo grass are meadow plants that like to roam in the Great Plains. Cross the Rockies, and the native grass du jour is wheat grass. It's a terrific choice for wide-open places like homes on the prairie.

2. Wildflowers. Wild by name, these plants can be readily purchased in seed mixes from reputable mail-order sources. Wildflowers come in a wide variety of colors, heights, and looks. Some like sun; some seek shade. Many also beckon butterflies to your yard! These are great if you have traditional, ranch-style homes. Make your choices from the list of wildflowers in the box "Wildflowers of the Continent." Check with your favorite local nursery or mail-order resource for other plants that will do well in your climate and that suit your tastes.

3. Meadow mixes. This type combines a sort of greatest-hits collection of the best meadow plants. I like the meadow mixes best because they contain something for everyone, from tall wind-blown grasses like little bluestem to flowers like black-eyed Susan. And they don't ask much in return for all the pleasure they give. I like that!

Care-Giving Facts

After the introductions are out of the way, you'll need to know how to take care of meadow mixes. Remember, folks, these are easy growers. Prepare your soil much as you would to plant turf grass — except don't worry as much. Wildflowers and native grasses are mellow and virtually maintenance-free! They need less fertilizer and less water, and you can even sow seeds in fall *or* spring.

GOOD LAWN SAMARITANS

Think of wildflowers and native grasses as your allies. They step in and fill in places in your yard that are too wet or too dry for traditional lawn grasses. They attract butterflies, hummingbirds, and other yard-friendly creatures.

Want to find out what wildflowers will settle in really well on your turf? Call the folks at your closest Nature Conservancy office (for addresses, see www.tnc.org) or the National Wildflower Research Center (www.wildflower.org).

Let Them Be!

Even though they're called *wildflowers,* please resist the temptation to dig them up from the wild — in woods or meadows or along roadsides. Some wildflower plants are at risk of extinction. You also don't know what else (bugs, disease, even car pollution) is mixed in with plants plucked from the wild.

Buy wildflower seeds or cuttings or divisions from reputable wildflower propagators. Seeds are by far the cheapest way to go. You can purchase them in person, by phone, or by mail.

Rock Gardens

Welcome to the Stone Age — of lawns, that is! I'm not talking about the Stone Age as in that Saturday-morning cartoon of years ago. It may surprise you to know that stones and rocks can really spruce up a yard.

Rocks on the Front Lawn?

Who would want a bunch of rocks in his yard? The biggest rock-garden fans are folks who live in parched places like Arizona. Desert climates are ideal for rock gardens because turf grass is just too difficult to start, grow, and thrive. The soil cares more for cacti than for crabgrass. So go with the flow!

Be Creative!

Now, rock gardens don't have to be dull in color. Use your imagination. Color the rocks to accent the trim on your home. Or arrange the rocks in a special pattern or border. Use them to define a little pond or waterfall, and fill it with fish. Add some ground cover or wildflowers. Rock gardens can be designed for flat locations as well as slopes.

SUITABLE STONES

So where do you find suitable stones? Well, you can buy them directly from a local rock quarry or nursery. Or you could harvest them yourself! By that, I mean you can collect stones from public woods (make sure there are no laws banning this). You can even collect stones from a neighbor who is replacing them with a different landscape. Barter back and forth and get yourself a good deal!

Jerry Baker Says

"Once in place, a rock garden is practically maintenance-free. That should appeal to those of you who detest pushing a lawn mower around your yard!"

Flowers That Thrive in Rock Gardens

Amur adonis
   (*Adonis amurensis* 'Plena')
Basket-of-gold
   (*Aurinia saxatilis*)
Bellflower (*Campanula* spp.)
Betony (*Stachys byzantina*)
Blanketflower (*Gaillardia* spp.)
Blue fescue (*Festuca glauca*)
Bugleweed (*Ajuga* spp.)
Buttercup (*Ranunculus* spp.)
Cactus
Campion (*Lychnis* spp.)
Columbine (*Aquilegia* spp.)
Cranesbill (*Geranium* spp.)
Creeping baby's breath
   (*Gypsophila repens*)
Cupid's dart
   (*Catananche caerulea*)
Daylily (*Hemerocallis* spp.)
Dwarf iris (*Iris cristata*)
Edelweiss
   (*Leontopodium alpinum*)
English daisy (*Bellis perennis*)
Fernleaf bleeding heart
   (*Dicentra eximia*)
Ferns
Forget-me-not
   (*Myosotis sylvatica*)
Garden pink (*Dianthus* spp.)
Jacob's ladder
   (*Polemonium* spp.)
Lady's mantle (*Alchemilla* spp.)

Lebanon stonecress
   (*Aethionema cordifolium*)
Meadowsweet (*Filipendula* spp.)
Pasqueflower (*Anemone pulsatilla*)
Primrose (*Primula* spp.)
Purple rockcress
   (*Aubrieta deltoidea*)
Rockcress (*Arabis caucasica*)
Sandwort (*Arenaria* spp.)
Sedum (*Sedum* spp.)
Siberian dragonhead
   (*Dracocephalum ruyschiana*)
Snow-in-summer
   (*Cerastium tomentosum*)
Spurge (*Euphorbia* spp.)
Sweet woodruff
   (*Galium odoratum*)
Thyme (*Thymus* spp.)
Tunic flower
   (*Petrorhagia saxifraga*)
Violet (*Viola* spp.)
Virginia blue-
   bells (*Mertensia virginica*)
Wild ginger
   (*Asarum* spp.)
Woolly yarrow
   (*Achillea tomentosa*)

Decks and Patios

In my Grandma Putt's day, folks called them porches. You know, we just loved those wooden-planked extensions from the exterior walls where you would sit back in a rocking chair, sipping iced tea.

Today's homeowners are big into decks and patios. Small or large, roofed or open to the sky, decks and patios come in all shapes and sizes and serve all kinds of wants and needs. You can install them in the front of your home, on the side, at the back, or anywhere else your little heart desires. They can be connected to your home or even be freestanding.

Raise That Property Value!

Decks and patios give added *oomph* to a house — help it stand out from the rest of the crowd. They provide privacy and a place to relax, gather with the family, and entertain friends. They add value to your homestead by serving as an outside extension to your indoor living area. Decks are among the first items spotted by prospective home buyers. Remember, first impressions do count in the home-buying market.

THE REAL KICKER

But most of all, decks and patios provide a place for happy gatherings. Whether it be with family or friends, I have many a fond memory of enjoying summer cookouts with lawn chairs strewn all over the back patio or around a picnic table filled with lots of good things to eat! Nowadays, folks have hot tubs built into their decks, and there's nothing better to come home to after a long, hard day at work.

Sweet Solution

Want a solution for under those pesky shade trees where it's impossible to grow grass? Surrender and build a deck in that area, then you can kiss your turf troubles good-bye!

Patio Primer

As for patios, you can make them out of brick, flagstone, exposed aggregate, or concrete. Those materials also need sealant, which you can spray on or use a roller brush to apply. Check with your local hardware store or visit some of the do-it-yourself Web sites.

Whoa!

Before you head to the lumberyard with a list of materials or hire a contractor to build a patio or deck, run down my helpful checklist:

✔ Have you considered the weather conditions in your area? Can the materials you're planning to use handle extreme cold, heat, or moisture?

✔ What are your soil conditions? Is your soil clay, rocky, or porous?

✔ Have you planned for a proper drainage system? Does water pool up in your yard? Do you have sinkholes or slopes that are prone to erosion?

✔ Have you weighed the pros and cons of brick, concrete, fieldstone, and other materials?

✔ Are you willing to invest time and money to prolong the life of your deck and patio materials?

✔ Have you squirreled away some money to handle repairs, including unexpected mishaps?

✔ Did you check with your local municipality to see whether you need to get a special permit before building?

✔ Will this addition add to your property taxes?

✔ What are the main reasons you want this deck or porch? As a place for social gatherings? For privacy? For shade? To replace poorly growing areas of your yard?

Penny-Wise

I gotta caution you right up front: Materials for decks and patios cost a whole lot more than a bag of grass seed. But once a deck or patio is in place, maintenance is relatively easy and inexpensive.

Every year or so, you'll need to treat the deck with a sealant or paint to protect against damage caused by the harsh rays of the sun, pounding rain, and, for some of us, mounds of snow. Yes, decks can be adversely affected by the weather, even if you use pressure-treated timber!

The Importance of Contours

Pay close attention to the contours of your property. The slopes, hills, dips, and flat areas all play a role in whether your property drains adequately. Nobody likes to wake up to a flooded basement, wet garage, or pools of ice stubbornly collecting near sidewalks and driveways. So, before you add on a deck, gazebo, or other yard project, make sure your yard is truly "in shape" to handle it, and fix any drainage problems before you start. See Chapter 13 for how to improve your grade.

Jerry Baker Says

"Be selective with the timber you buy for your deck. Make sure the lumber comes with a 40-year guarantee against rot."

Ask Jerry

Q I love my lawn, but I have some spots where a ground cover would mean less work for me during the year. One of these is a narrow slope where I'd like something that has some height and is also easy to care for. I don't want shrubs or trees. Any ideas?

A Fill the area with ornamental grasses like zebra grass or silver grass. You'll get rid of a hard-to-mow area and at the same time have easy-to-grow plants that are a real interesting feature in your yard, even in the winter. Spray the plants regularly with my **All-Season Green-Up Tonic** (page 328) and watch them grow!

Q Part of my lawn near the house is a shady area underneath a big, old shade tree. Nothing seems to grow under this tree, and I don't want to thin out the branches because it's so pretty. What can I do to make the space under the tree more useful and more attractive?

A That shady spot is the perfect place for a low deck or patio that either stands alone or is connected to the house. It'll make that shady area more attractive and easy to maintain, and you'll have a great place for a weekend party or barbecue!

Well, whether your lawn is as big as the village green or the size of a postage stamp, you should now have a good idea about how to give it all the tender loving care it needs. No matter what size lawn you have, I want you to always remember to stop and take time to smell the growing grass. There's nothing quite like it, and I thank God for that.

Part IV

Putting It All Together

USDA Plant Hardiness Zone Map

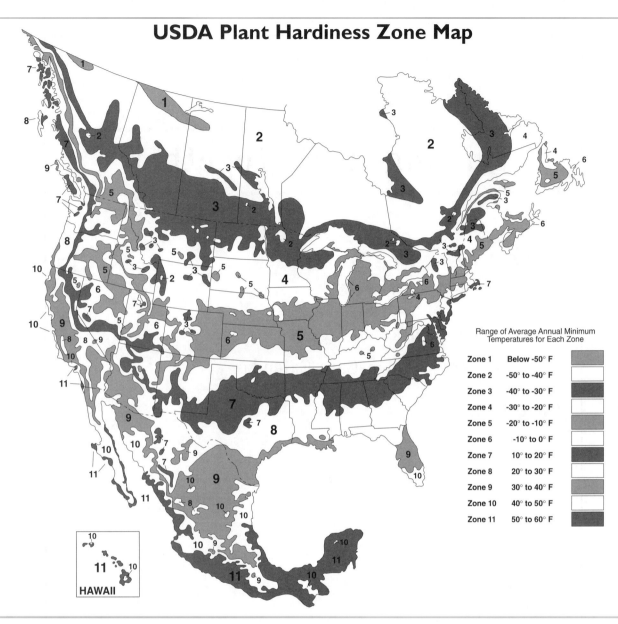

Range of Average Annual Minimum
Temperatures for Each Zone

Zone 1	Below -50° F
Zone 2	-50° to -40° F
Zone 3	-40° to -30° F
Zone 4	-30° to -20° F
Zone 5	-20° to -10° F
Zone 6	-10° to 0° F
Zone 7	10° to 20° F
Zone 8	20° to 30° F
Zone 9	30° to 40° F
Zone 10	40° to 50° F
Zone 11	50° to 60° F

HAWAII

This map, created by the U.S. Department of Agriculture, divides the United States into 11 temperature zones. Find your location on the map, then note the zone number to learn the average minimum temperature where you live. You'll need this information when you choose perennial plants, such as ornamental grasses, so you can select varieties that do best in your climate.

CHAPTER 17

Jerry's Tonics

Throughout this book, you've come across oodles and oodles of my terrific tonics using everyday, common household products. Before you start scratching your head and wondering how beer, cola, *and* the rest of the bunch work, I'll save you some time. In this chapter, I give you the inside scoop on each of these ingredients, plus a handy recap of each of the tonics so that you have them all in one easy-to-refer-to place.

The Inside Scoop on My Terrific Tonics

Ammonia

I like to call it a "thunderstorm in a bottle." It's a readily available source of nitrogen that helps encourage leafy plant growth. If you use it around plants, always dilute it as specified in my tonics, or you may burn your plants. The ammonia you buy at the grocery store is a diluted solution of ammonium hydroxide. It's a clear liquid with a very penetrating odor. Wear gloves when mixing it into tonics and be sure not to splash any into your eyes.

And, *never, ever* combine ammonia with vinegar or bleach (or products containing bleach) because the resulting chemical reaction releases fumes that can be toxic.

Antiseptic Mouthwash

You've heard of Listerine? It was invented by Dr. Lister, a surgeon, to disinfect his operating tools. Well, it does the same thing to diseases in your yard — messes them up before they get a chance to get established. I've yet to determine if it also takes away that stale morning breath smell in lawns.

Beer

Foreign, domestic, stale, or just opened — whatever you want to use — all will work just fine! Beer acts as an enzyme activator to help release the nutrients that are locked in the soil. It also wakes up and energizes organic activity. I like to think of this one as the "captain" of my tonic team!

Cola

The sugar in this carbonated drink helps feed the good bacteria that condition your soil. Skip the diet brands — the sugar substitutes don't work like the real thing. Now you know *why* they call it that.

Epsom Salts

This very effective product is a virtual gold mine for your yard, yet it costs only pennies and it greens up your lawn instantly. The magnesium sulfate in Epsom salts deepens the grass blades' color, thickens the blades, and increases root structures in your grass plants. That's why I always recommend you add a few pounds of Epsom salts to every bag of dry fertilizer before you apply it to your lawn.

Sugar/Molasses/ Corn Syrup

Your choice — any one works to sweeten the deal. These sugar sources stimulate chlorophyll formation in plants and help feed the good soil bacteria. Bet you didn't know your grass had a sweet tooth!

Safety First

As with any household and garden cleaners and pesticides, I want you to always take the proper precautions when you use these products.

• Even though most are safe and natural, some can cause your eyes or skin to be irritated, especially if you have allergies.

• You certainly wouldn't want any of them to be mistaken for something that someone could eat or drink. Be sure to label each tonic clearly, and keep **all** products safely stored out of the reach of children or pets.

• If you reuse containers, stick to the same or similar products. You don't want to use an herbicide container for a fertilizer, as you just might just end up spraying a little leftover herbicide on your prize lawn or pride and joy flowers. And that would be tragic!

Liquid Dish Soap/ Baby Shampoo

These products help soften soil and remove dust, dirt, and pollution on the plants so that osmosis and photosynthesis can occur more easily. Also, bugs hate the taste (especially of the lemon-scented types), so they head for the hills as fast as their little legs can carry them.

Tea

Instant tea granules contain tannic acid, an ingredient that helps seeds and grass plants digest their food faster. Add a little tea, and there'll be no tummyaches for your turf!

Tobacco Tea

This brew poisons bugs when they ingest it, as well as when they simply come into contact with it. It also treats some plant diseases. (See the box below for the recipe.) You heard it here — nicotine kills. Enough said!

Urine

Yours, your dog's, the neighbor's (yikes!) — it doesn't matter. The powerful smell is enough to scare away unwanted critters like moles and gophers from your yard.

How to Make Tobacco Tea

I used to call this "chewing tobacco juice," but one of my loyal readers suggested that I rename it to more accurately reflect what it is and how it is made. That was a darn good idea! So here's how to make my newly renamed Tobacco Tea.

Place a thumb-and-three-fingers worth of chewing tobacco in an old nylon (pantyhose) stocking. Fill a clean milk jug (or similar container) with a gallon of very hot water, then soak the tobacco-filled stocking in the hot water until the mixture turns a dark brown color. Label the container, then use 1 cup of it whenever one of my Tonics calls for it.

My Terrific Tonics

(In alphabetical order; most lawn mixtures listed here are enough to cover 2,500 square feet of turf.)

Aeration Tonic

Use this Tonic regularly to slow down soil compaction and improve spray penetration.

1 cup of liquid dish soap
1 cup of beer

Mix all of these ingredients in a 20 gallon hose-end sprayer; fill the balance of the sprayer jar with warm water. Apply once a month to the point of run-off. (For related text, see page 115.)

All-Purpose Pest Prevention Potion

This Tonic repels most critters, including gophers and moles.

1 cup of ammonia
½ cup of liquid dish soap
½ cup of urine
¼ cup of castor oil

Mix all of these ingredients in a 20 gallon hose-end sprayer and thoroughly saturate the animal runs and burrows. (For related text, see page 165.)

All-Purpose Varmint Repellent

This Tonic repels animals with a keen sense of smell.

½ cup of Murphy's Oil Soap
½ cup of lemon-scented dish soap
½ cup of castor oil
½ cup of lemon-scented ammonia
½ cup of hot, hot, hot pepper sauce
½ cup of urine

Mix everything in a 20 gallon hose-end sprayer. Apply to the point of run-off to any areas that need protection. (For related text, see page 166.)

All-Season Clean-Up Tonic

Use in early evening every 2 weeks to discourage pests and disease and keep plants clean and mean!

1 cup of liquid dish soap
1 cup of antiseptic mouthwash
1 cup of Tobacco Tea★

Mix all of these ingredients in a 20 gallon hose-end sprayer, filling the balance of the sprayer jar with warm water. Soak everything in your yard to the point of run-off. (For related text, see page 202.)

★For recipe, see page 326.

All-Season Green-Up Tonic

Keep your lawn growing great by using this Tonic every 3 weeks, from early spring until fall.

1 can of beer
1 cup of ammonia
½ cup of liquid dish soap
½ cup of liquid lawn food
½ cup of clear corn syrup

Mix all the ingredients in a large bucket, pour into a 20 gallon hose-end sprayer, and saturate your lawn, trees, shrubs, flowers, and even vegetables. (For related text, see page 39.)

Anti-Summer-Patch Tonic

Use this Tonic every 3 weeks to prevent summer patch.

1 cup of liquid dish soap
1 cup of antiseptic mouthwash
1 cup of Tobacco Tea★
1 cup of ammonia
3 tbsp. of saltpeter

Mix all of these ingredients in a large bucket, and pour into your 20 gallon hose-end sprayer. Apply to your lawn to the point of run-off . (For related text, see page 234.)
★For recipe, see page 326.

Aphid Antidote

To keep aphids and other pests out of your yard, mix up a batch of this amazing antidote.

1 small onion (finely chopped)
2 medium cloves of garlic (finely chopped)
1 tbsp. of liquid dish soap
2 cups of water

Put all ingredients in a blender, blend on high, and then strain out the pulp. Pour the liquid into a handheld mist sprayer and apply liberally to all areas at the first sign of aphid activity. (For related text, see page 207.)

Blight Buster Tonic

To fight fusarium blight (also known as frog's eye), apply this Tonic at the first sign of trouble.

1 cup of baby shampoo
1 cup of antiseptic mouthwash
1 cup of Tobacco Tea★
½ cup of ammonia
8 tbsp. of rose/vegetable dust
3 tbsp. of saltpeter

Mix all ingredients in a 20 gallon hose-end sprayer. Apply early in the morning to the point of run-off. (For related text, see page 231.) ★For recipe, see page 326.

Buzz Buster Tonic

Keep mosquitoes out of your yard and away from you by applying this Tonic in the early morning or late evening.

1 cup of lemon-scented ammonia
1 cup of lemon-scented dish soap

Pour these ingredients into your 20 gallon hose-end sprayer, filling the balance of the sprayer jar with warm water. Thoroughly soak any places around your yard where mosquitoes tend to gather. Repeat 3 times each week. (For related text, see pages 214–15.)

Chillin' Out Brew

After a long, hard day in the yard, a few spritzes of this brew will make you feel as cool as a cucumber!

2 tsp. of witch hazel tincture
10 drops of peppermint essential oil
12 drops of lavender essential oil

Combine these ingredients with enough water to fill an 8-ounce spray bottle. Use as needed. (For related text, see page 73.)

Chinch Bug Tonic

This brew is a "cinch" to make.

1 cup of liquid dish soap
3 cups of warm water

Mix these ingredients in a 20 gallon hose-end sprayer, and then saturate your lawn with it. (For related text, see page 211.)

Dog-B-Gone Tonic

To keep dogs away, liberally apply this spicy Tonic to your yard.

2 cloves of garlic
2 small onions
1 jalapeño pepper
1 tbsp. of cayenne pepper
1 tbsp. of hot sauce
1 tbsp. of chili powder
1 tbsp. of liquid dish soap
1 qt. of warm water

Chop the garlic, onions, and pepper fine, and then mix with the rest of the ingredients. Let the mixture "marinate" for 24 hours, strain it through cheesecloth, then sprinkle it on any areas where dogs are a problem. (For related text, see page 159.)

Doggie Damage Repair Tonic

To fix spots caused by dog droppings, overspray the turf with 1 cup of baby shampoo per 20 gallons of water, then apply gypsum at recommended rate. After 1 week, apply this Tonic.

1 can of beer
1 cup of ammonia
1 can of regular cola (not diet)

Mix these ingredients in a 20 gallon hose-end sprayer, and overspray the turf every other week until the normal color returns. (For related text, see page 159.)

Drought Buster Tonic

Minimize drought damage by applying this Tonic once a week in early morning during hot weather.

1 can of beer
1 cup of Thatch Buster
½ cup of liquid lawn food
½ cup of baby shampoo

Mix all of these ingredients in a 20 gallon hose-end sprayer jar and apply to the point of run-off. Water for 10 minutes at noon and again at 4:00 P.M. for optimum results. (For related text, see page 145.)

Drought Recovery Tonic

Once drought is over in the fall, apply a dry fertilizer at half of the recommended rate, adding 1 lb. of sugar and 1 lb. of Epsom salts per bag (enough for 2,500 sq. ft.). Then overspray the turf with this Tonic.

1 can of regular cola (not diet)
1 cup of baby shampoo
1 cup of ammonia

Mix these ingredients in your 20 gallon hose-end sprayer and saturate the turf to the point of run-off at 2-week intervals until the grass returns to normal. (For related text, see page 145.)

Fairy Ring Fighter Tonic

Fight fairy ring with this Tonic.

1 cup of baby shampoo
1 cup of antiseptic mouthwash
1 cup of ammonia

Mix all of these ingredients in a 20 gallon hose-end sprayer and apply to the point of run-off *after* you've sprinkled dry laundry soap over the area. (For related text, see page 228.)

Fall Clean-Up Tonic

1 cup of baby shampoo
1 cup of antiseptic mouthwash
1 cup of Tobacco Tea★
1 cup of chamomile tea

Combine all ingredients in a bucket, and then add 2 cups of it to your 20 gallon hose-end sprayer, filling the rest of the jar with warm water. Overspray your turf, trees, shrubs, and beds when the temperature is above 50°F. (For related text, see page 152.) ★For recipe, see page 326.)

Fall Lawn Food Mix

3 lbs. of Epsom salts
1 cup of dry laundry soap
1 bag of premium, dry lawn food (enough for 2,500 sq. ft.)

Mix all of these ingredients together, and apply at half of the recommended rate with your handheld broadcast spreader. (For related text, see page 147.)

Get-Up-and-Grow Tonic

To energize the dry Spring Wake-Up Tonic (for recipe, see page 338), overspray your lawn with this elixir.

1 cup of baby shampoo
1 cup of ammonia
1 cup of regular cola (not diet)
4 tbsp. of instant tea

Mix all of these in your 20 gallon hose-end sprayer and apply to the point of run-off. (For related text, see page 37.)

Goodbye Gophers and Move On Moles Tonic

Mix up and apply a batch of this Tonic to rid your lawn of unwelcome gophers and moles.

1 cup of liquid dish soap
1 cup of castor oil
2 tbsp. of alum (dissolved in hot water)

Use your 20 gallon hose-end sprayer to saturate the turf to the point of run-off. (For related text, see page 162.)

Gopher-Go Tonic

I've had some amazing results with this Tonic.

2 tbsp. of castor oil
2 tbsp. of liquid dish soap
2 tbsp. of urine

Combine all of these ingredients in cup of warm water, and then stir the mixture into 2 gallons of warm water. Pour it over infested areas. (For related text, see page 162.)

Grandma Putt's Homemade Organic Fertilizer

In a large wheelbarrow, mix:

1 part dehydrated manure
1 part bonemeal
5 parts seaweed meal
3 parts granite dust

Use a spreader to apply mixture evenly over turf. (For related text, see page 42.)

Grandma Putt's Terrific Sunburn Tonic

This Tonic is just the thing for soothing sunburned skin.

2 cups of water
2 fresh garlic cloves (chopped)

Simmer the garlic in a pan of water for 5 minutes. Turn off heat, cover pan, and let steep for 45 minutes. Cool, strain, cover, and store in the refrigerator.

Soak a washcloth or hand towel in the cool garlic tea, wring out the excess liquid, and place the cloth on the sore area. Leave it on for about 20 minutes or so. Replace it with a fresh compress until you feel its cooling relief from the pain. (For related text, see page 180.)

Grass Clipping Compost Starter

Every time you add a batch of grass clippings to your compost pile, spray the pile with this mixture. Toss the mix occasionally with a garden fork.

1 can of regular cola (not diet)
½ cup of ammonia
½ cup of liquid lawn food
½ cup of liquid dish soap

Pour these ingredients in your 20 gallon hose-end sprayer and soak each new layer of grass clippings with this Tonic. This will speed up the decomposing process. (For related text, see page 86.)

Grass Clipping Dissolving Tonic

If you don't pick up your grass clippings, apply this Tonic twice a year to help speed decomposition. It also will help the turf to breathe better.

1 can of beer
1 can of regular cola (not diet)
1 cup of ammonia
1 cup of liquid dish soap

Mix all of these ingredients in a bucket and pour them into your 20 gallon hose-end sprayer. Apply to the point of run-off. (For related text, see page 85.)

Kick-in-the-Grass Tonic

After you've repaired your lawn, apply this Tonic to get it off to a rip-roarin' start.

1 can of beer
1 cup of antiseptic mouthwash
1 cup of liquid dish soap
1 cup of ammonia
½ cup of Epsom salts

Mix these ingredients together in a large container, and then pour the mixture into your 20 gallon hose-end sprayer. Apply liberally to the point of run-off; wait 2 weeks, then apply again. (For related text, see page 131.)

The Last Supper Tonic

This Tonic softens up the dry fertilizer mix so that the nutrients can be easily digested by your lawn all winter long.

½ can of beer
½ cup of apple juice
½ cup of Gatorade
½ cup of urine
½ cup of fish fertilizer
½ cup of ammonia
½ cup of regular cola (not diet)
½ cup of baby shampoo

Combine all of these ingredients in a large bucket, pour into your 20 gallon hose-end sprayer, and apply to the point of run-off. (For related text, see page 152.)

Lawn Freshener Tonic

Before you water a thirsty lawn, strap on your aerating lawn sandals or golf shoes and take a stroll around your yard. Then follow up with this mixture.

1 can of beer
1 cup of shampoo
½ cup of ammonia
½ cup of weak tea water

Mix all of these ingredients in your 20 gallon hose-end sprayer and apply to the point of run-off. (For related text, see page 93.)

Lawn Fungus Fighter Tonic

If your lawn develops brown or yellow patches that eventually die out, fight back with this fix-it formula.

1 tbsp. of baking soda
1 tbsp. of instant tea granules
1 tbsp. of horticultural or dormant oil
1 gal. of warm water

Mix all of the ingredients together in a large bucket, then apply with a handheld sprayer by lightly spraying the turf. *Do not* drench or apply to the point of run-off. Repeat in 2 to 3 weeks, if necessary. (For related text, see page 226.)

Lawn Pest Control Tonic

This is a good, all-around preventative spray.

1 cup of Murphy's Oil Soap
1 cup of Tobacco Tea★

Mix these ingredients in a 20 gallon hose-end sprayer and apply to the point of run-off. (For related text, see page 213.)
★For recipe, see page 326.

Meow-a-lous Tonics

To make cats head elsewhere, overspray the perimeter of your yard with one of these Tonics.

Tonic #1: Mix cup of Tobacco Tea (for recipe, see page 326) or oil of mustard and cup of liquid dish soap in 2 gallons of warm water.

Tonic #2: Add 1 clove of garlic (crushed), 1 tbsp. of cayenne pepper, and 1 tsp. of liquid dish soap to 1 qt. of warm water, and purée the heck out of it. (For related text, see page 161.)

Mildew Relief Tonic

Use this Tonic to rid your lawn of powdery mildew.

1 cup of baby shampoo
1 cup of hydrogen peroxide
4 tbsp. of instant tea

Mix these ingredients in a 20 gallon hose-end sprayer, filling the balance of the sprayer jar with water. Every week to 10 days, apply my Tonic to the affected area of lawn. (For related text, see page 230.)

Mole Chaser Tonic

In a medium-size container, mix:

2 tbsp. of hot sauce
1 tbsp. of liquid dish soap
1 tsp. of chili powder
1 qt. of water

Pour a little of the Tonic every 5 feet or so in the mole runways to make them run away! (For related text, see page 165.)

Moss Buster Tonic

To get rid of unsightly moss and mold in your lawn, mix:

1 cup of Murphy's Oil Soap
1 cup of antiseptic mouthwash
1 cup of chamomile tea water

Combine all ingredients in your 20 gallon hose-end sprayer and apply to the point of run-off every 2 weeks until moss is gone. (For related text, see page 181.)

Plug Feeding Tonic

To feed newly planted plugs, mix:

3 lbs. of Epsom salts
1 bag of dry lawn food (enough for 2,500 sq. ft.)

Apply at half strength with your handheld broadcast spreader. (For related text, see page 287.)

Plug Rejuvenating Tonic

To keep your plugs and sprigs fresh before putting them in, periodically mist-spray them with the following Tonic.

¼ cup of liquid dish soap
¼ cup of ammonia
1 gallon of weak tea water

When you're done planting, sprinkle the leftovers on the newly planted plugs. (For related text, see page 136.)

Pollution Solution Tonic

To give your lawn some relief from the dust, dirt, and pollution that accumulates over the winter, apply this mix with a handheld broadcast spreader as early as possible in the spring.

50 lbs. of pelletized lime
50 lbs. of pelletized gypsum
5 lbs. of Epsom salts

Spread this mix over 2,500 sq. ft. of lawn area. Then, wait at least 2 weeks before applying any fertilizer to the area to give the mix a chance to go to work. (For related text, see page 127.)

Rise-'n'-Shine Clean-Up Tonic

This Tonic will roust your yard out of its slumber in spring, nailing any wayward bugs that were overwintering in the area.

1 cup of Murphy's Oil Soap
1 cup of antiseptic mouthwash
1 cup of Tobacco Tea★
4 oz. of hot sauce

Mix these ingredients in your 20 gallon hose-end sprayer and apply to everything to the point of run-off. (For related text, see page 199.)
★For recipe, see page 326.

Scat Cat Solution

If felines are digging in your yard, send them packing with my All-Purpose Pest Prevention Potion (for recipe, see page 327) or with this Tonic:

5 tbsp. of flour
4 tbsp. of powdered mustard
3 tbsp. of cayenne pepper
2 tbsp. of chili powder
2 qts. of warm water

Mix all of these ingredients together and sprinkle the solution around the perimeter of the areas you clearly want to mark as being "Off Limits!" (For related text, see page 161.)

Seed Starter Tonic

This nifty little Tonic will guarantee almost 100 percent grass seed germination every time.

¼ cup of baby shampoo
1 tbsp. of Epsom salts
1 gallon of weak tea water

Mix these ingredients in a large container. Drop in your grass seed, refrigerate for 2 days, let it dry, and then sow as usual. (For related text, see page 134.)

Slug It Out Tonic

Let slugs drink themselves to death with this powerful concoction.

1 can of beer
1 tbsp. of sugar
1 tsp. of baker's yeast

Combine all ingre-
dients in a large
bowl and let it sit
uncovered for a few days. Then, pour the mixture into shallow, disposable containers. Set the containers below ground level in various areas around your yard, and bid bye-bye to your slug problem. (For related text, see page 216.)

Snack Tonic

My Snack Tonic gets your lawn up and growing in both spring and fall when you need rapid root action and thatch breakdown.

1 can of beer
1 cup of liquid dish soap

Put these ingredients in a 20 gallon hose-end sprayer jar and fill the balance of the jar with ammonia. Overspray your lawn to the point of run-off. The best time to apply this Tonic is around 3 P.M. (For related text, see page 37.)

Soil Prep Tonic

Give your soil this treatment before you sow grass seed. Your seed will establish better and faster.

1 cup of fish fertilizer
½ cup of ammonia
¼ cup of baby shampoo
¼ cup of clear corn syrup

Mix all ingredients in your 20 gallon hose-end sprayer jar and saturate the soil several days before you're going to reseed. (For related text, see page 134.)

Spot Seed Tonic

Once you've reseeded your lawn, get your grass seed off to a run-ning start with this tonic.

1 cup of beer
1 cup of baby shampoo
4 tbsp. of instant tea

Combine these ingredients in your 20 gallon hose-end sprayer and lightly apply the Tonic to the straw covering the area. (For relat-ed text, see page 134.)

Spring Wake-Up Tonic

Get your lawn off on the right root in spring by applying this mix as early as possible.

50 lbs. of pelletized lime
50 lbs. of pelletized gypsum
5 lbs. of bonemeal
2 lbs. of Epsom salts

Mix these ingredients in a wheelbarrow and apply with your hand-held, broadcast spreader 2 weeks before fertilizing. Follow up with a dose of my Get-Up-and-Grow Tonic. This will help aerate the lawn while giving it something to munch on until you start your regular feeding program. (For related text, see page 37.)

Squeaky Clean Tonic

1 cup of antiseptic mouthwash
1 cup of Tobacco Tea★
1 cup of chamomile tea
1 cup of urine
½ cup of Murphy's Oil Soap
½ cup of lemon-scented dish soap

Combine all of these ingredients in a large bucket, and apply with your 20 gallon hose-end sprayer to the point of run-off. (For related text, see page 203.)
★For recipe, see page 326.

Stress Reliever Tonic

To keep your grass growing happy and healthy during the winter months in the mild climates, overspray your lawn once a month with this Tonic.

1 cup of baby shampoo
1 cup of antiseptic mouthwash
1 cup of Tobacco Tea★
¼ cup of ammonia
¾ cup of weak tea water

Mix all of these ingredients in your 20 gallon hose-end sprayer and apply to the point of run-off. (For related text, see page 153.)
★For recipe, see page 326.

Summer Soother Tonic

Water and soothe your plants at the same time with a nice, gentle, relaxing shower.

2 cups of weak tea water
1 cup of baby shampoo
1 cup of hydrogen peroxide

Mix these ingredients in your 20 gallon hose-end sprayer, and spray everything in sight. (For related text, see page 150.)

Super Slug Spray

For slugs that are too small to hand-pick or be lured into traps, try this spray.

1½ cups of ammonia
1 tbsp. of Murphy's Oil Soap
1½ cups of water
Mix all of the ingredients in a handheld, mist sprayer bottle and overspray any areas where you see the telltale signs of slug activity (like their "silvery trails"), even if you don't see the slugs themselves. (For related text, see page 216.)

Terrific Turf Tonic

Keep your lawn looking its best by washing it down with this Tonic once a month after you mow.

1 cup of baby shampoo
1 cup of ammonia
1 cup of weak tea water

Pour the ingredients into your 20 gallon hose-end sprayer and fill the balance of the sprayer jar with warm water. Then apply it liberally to your lawn to the point of run-off. (For related text, see page 75.)

Thatch Control Tonic

Here's a Tonic that helps to control thatch.

1 cup of regular cola (not diet)
½ cup of liquid dish soap
¼ cup of ammonia
Mix all of these ingredients in a 20 gallon hose-end sprayer and apply to your lawn once a month to the point of run-off. (For related text, see page 119.)

Tire-Track Remover Tonic

Wait for the damaged area to dry out a bit, then aerate and sprinkle a little gypsum over the area. Then, overspray with my very special Tonic.

1 cup of ammonia
1 cup of beer
½ cup of baby shampoo
¼ cup of weak tea water

Mix these ingredients in a 20 gallon hose-end sprayer, filling the balance of the sprayer jar with warm water. Apply to the point of run-off. Repeat this treatment every 3 weeks. (For related text, see page 128.)

Weed Killer Prep Tonic

To really zing a lot of weeds in a large area, overspray it first with this Tonic:

1 cup of liquid dish soap
1 cup of ammonia
4 tbsp. of instant tea

Combine all ingredients in your 20 gallon hose-end sprayer, filling the balance of the sprayer jar with warm water. Apply this Tonic to the point of run-off. (For related text, see page 179.)

Wild Weed Wipeout Tonic

Here's a weed killer for those who want to avoid harsh chemicals.

1 tbsp. of vinegar
1 tbsp. of baby shampoo
1 tbsp. of gin
1 qt. of warm water

Mix all ingredients in a bucket, and then pour into a handheld sprayer. Drench each weed to the point of run-off, taking care not to get any spray on the surrounding plants. For particularly stubborn weeds, use apple cider vinegar instead of white vinegar. (For related text, see page 175.)

Winterizing Tonic

Give your lawn and garden a heavy soaking in the fall to zap cutworms and other bugs before winter with this Tonic:

1 cup of Murphy's Oil Soap
1 cup of Tobacco Tea★
1 cup of antiseptic mouthwash

Mix all the ingredients in a 20 gallon hose-end sprayer, filling the balance of the sprayer jar with warm water. Saturate your lawn, and then follow with an application of a pyrethrum-based insecticide for total control. (For related text, see page 211.)

★For recipe, see page 326.

Winter Walkway Protection Tonic

To keep the grassy areas around your walk and driveways in good shape during the winter, first sprinkle the lawn liberally with gypsum. Then, apply this Tonic.

1 cup of liquid dish soap
½ cup of ammonia
½ cup of beer

Combine all of the ingredients in your 20 gallon hose-end sprayer and then apply it over the gypsum. (For related text, see page 126.)

CHAPTER 18

Jerry's Lawn-Care Calendar: A Season-by-Season "To-Do" List

With this book in your hands, you've got all the answers to help you get that gorgeous, look-at-me lawn I promised you 'way back on page 1. But there's one last thing I want to share with you — my at-a-glance calendar that makes it easy for you to plan your lawn chores and apply my terrific tonics season by season, no matter where you live.

Spring's Not the Same Everywhere

You'll notice that I said "season by season." That's because spring doesn't start on the same day, or even in the same week, everywhere in this great country of ours. Why, when those daffodils pop up in my friend's yard out in California, folks are still shoveling snow in Michigan.

But if you're observant, you'll know it's arrived by what's happening around *you*. And if you've lived in a particular area for any length of time, I'll bet you can pretty well predict when that might be, even though it's weeks different from when spring bursts out a few states further south — or west.

Jerry Baker Says

"My Grandma Putt swore she didn't need a calendar to get a fix on just what time of year it was, and she taught me the natural clues she relied on."

Here are some of the things I look for: One of my favorite sounds is the spring peepers. Out of the blue, I'll hear them one night and know that it's early spring. A little later on, I'll see the grass start greening up

In the Long Run

I've put down a few chores that need to be done throughout the growing season. Some you do every time you mow; others you do every 3 weeks or so. I like to keep these chores at the head of my list so that I don't forget them! I call them my "And Don't Forget to . . ." chores.

— that's a sign that it's midspring. Later on, when lilacs are in full bloom, I know that late spring has arrived.

There are many other signs I've come to recognize right on through till the trees lose their leaves and, in cold regions, the first frosts hit us. As each season comes along, I have a new list of things that I've got to get to around my yard.

How to Use My Lawn-Care Calendar

I've set up this calendar for you, starting with "Early Spring," so that you can dive right into it at any time and know exactly what you should be doing at that time of year. And pay particular attention to my special tips for those of you who grow either warm-season or cool-season grasses.

"And Don't Forget to . . ."

✓ Check your lawn regularly for any signs of insect, varmint, or disease damage; if you spot any, treat it right away.

✓ Wear your golf shoes or lawn aerating sandals whenever you're working in your yard.

✓ Keep your lawn mower, mower blades, and all other tools clean, sharp, and in tip-top shape.

✓ **Whenever you mow:** Walk around the lawn before you mow, looking for problems and picking up any debris. After mowing, apply a dose of my **Terrific Turf Tonic** (page 339) to your lawn. (And don't forget to use your sunblock.)

✓ To get rid of grass clippings, apply a dose of my **Grass Clipping Dissolving Tonic** (page 332) after you mow. If you pick up the grass clippings, add them to your compost pile, and be sure to saturate the pile with my **Grass Clipping Compost Starter** (page 332).

✓ Whenever you hand water, use my **Lawn Freshener Tonic** (page 333).

✓ **Every 2 weeks:** Apply my **All-Season Clean-Up Tonic** (page 327).

✓ **Every 3 weeks:** Apply my **All-Season Green-Up Tonic** (page 328).

✓ **Once a month:** Slow down soil compaction by applying my **Aeration Tonic** (page 327).

As snow melts, repair any winter damage to drives and walkways from snowplows and shovels. Remove piles of soil and scraped up grass, rake the area clean, water well to remove any road salt, and reseed as needed, following the directions on pages 132–33.

•••••••••

Test the soil for pH and nutrients, if you didn't do so last fall, and make any adjustments recommended by the tests. (See page 253.)

•••••••••

Give your whole yard a dose of my **Rise-'n'-Shine Clean-Up Tonic** (page 336). This mixture wakes your lawn up from its winter slumber and nails any bad bugs that managed to overwinter there.

Follow my **5-Step Spring Feeding Program** (see also pages 36–42):

Step 1. Apply my **Spring Wake-Up Tonic** (page 337) just as your grass is waking up. Do this before you apply any fertilizers or controls.

Step 2. Follow the Spring Wake-Up Tonic with a dose of my **Turf Builder Tonic** (page 339) to get your lawn up off its grass!

Step 3. Within 2 weeks of applying **Spring Wake-Up Tonic** and **Get-Up-and-Grow Tonic,** feed your lawn with a mix of 3 lbs. of Epsom salts per bag of premium dry lawn food (enough for 2,500 sq. ft.). Apply at half of the rate recommended on the package label, going first north to south, then east to west.

Step 4. Within 2 days of putting down the Epsom salts/dry lawn food mixture, energize your lawn into action by applying my **Snack Tonic** (page 337).

Step 5. One week later, apply the other half of the Epsom salts/fertilizer mix in the same way.

Use a preemergent herbicide to control weeds like crabgrass before they sprout. For broadleaf perennial weeds, use a postemergent herbicide or try a dose of my **Wild Weed Wipeout Tonic** (page 340). Whatever you decide to use, spray the turf with my **Weed Killer Prep Tonic** (page 340) to prepare the weeds for the fateful coup de "grass."

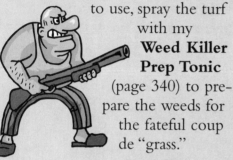

As new grass growth begins, spread screened compost over your lawn, particularly in any weak, thin, or scraggly areas.

Clean up underneath your bird feeders: Remove any debris (which develops into weeds), and reseed if needed, following the directions on pages 132–33.

If you didn't get a chance to sow cool-season grasses last fall, sow them now. Be sure to use my **Soil Prep Tonic** (page 337) before sowing any seed, followed by my **Seed Starter Tonic** (page 336) to get the grass seed off to a quick start.

Lay warm-season grass sod, followed by a dose of my **All-Season Green-Up Tonic** (page 328) to jump-start the green grass growth.

Plant warm-season grass plugs. Apply my **All-Season Green-Up Tonic** (page 328) after planting, and fertilize with a 20-5-10, slow-release, dry lawn food and Epsom salts (3 pounds of Epsom salts to a bag of fertilizer with 2,500 sq. ft. coverage) 5 weeks after planting.

EPSOM SALTS

REMINDER

Don't forget to keep up with your regular feeding, weeding, watering, mowing, and pest patrol. See "And Don't Forget to ..." on page 343.

Overseed to repair any damaged areas of lawn (see pages 132–33).

● ● ● ● ● ● ● ●

Sharpen lawn mower blades and other cutting tools (see page 78), getting ready for the season.

● ● ● ● ● ● ● ●

Remove thatch from cool-season grass lawns. Spread screened compost over the lawn after removing thatch. Apply a dose of my **Kick-in-the-Grass Tonic** (page 333) after dethatching, along with my **Thatch Control Tonic** (page339) to keep thatch from coming back.

● ● ● ● ● ● ● ●

If Japanese beetles were a problem last summer, apply a natural grub control like milky spore to your lawn now (see page 201).

As soon as the weather warms up, look for new mole tunnels, along with the telltale holes that skunks make as they, too, go after grubs in the soil. Apply my **All-Purpose Pest Prevention Potion** (page 327) to tunnels, runs, and holes.

● ● ● ● ● ● ●

Use my **All-Purpose Varmint Repellent** (page 327) to keep dogs, cats, and deer out of your yard.

● ● ● ● ● ● ●

Lay cool-season grass sod, applying my **All-Season Green-Up Tonic** (page 328) after installing it.

REMINDER

Don't forget to keep up with your regular feeding, weeding, watering, mowing, and pest control patrol. See "And Don't Forget to . . ." on page 343.

Late Spring

If dogs have been visiting your yard, apply my **Doggie Damage Repair Tonic** (page 330) to the affected areas. Keep unwelcome dog visitors away by mixing up a batch of my **Dog-B-Gone Tonic** (page 329) and sprinkling it in problem areas.

• • • • • • • •

Sow warm-season grasses now, so they can benefit from the hot weather that's coming up. Be sure to use my **Soil Prep Tonic** (page 337) before sowing any seed, followed by my **Seed Starter Tonic** (page 336) to get the grass seed off to a quick start.

• • • • • • • •

Test for grubs in the soil and apply milky spore or beneficial nematodes, if needed.

> **REMINDER**
>
> Don't forget to keep up with your regular feeding, weeding, watering, mowing, and pest control patrol. See "And Don't Forget to . . ."

Early Summer

Make your time in the yard more enjoyable by getting rid of mosquitos with regular applications of my **Buzz Buster Tonic** (page 329).

• • • • • • • •

Change the oil in your lawn mower before July 4th.

Use your edger and string trimmer around trees and along flower and shrub beds, as well as along walks and driveways.

> **REMINDER**
>
> Don't forget to keep up with your regular feeding, weeding, watering, mowing, and pest control patrol. See "And Don't Forget to . . ." on page 343.

Summer

If a drought threatens, apply my **Drought Buster Tonic** (page 330) to help your lawn remain strong and healthy. Following a drought, treat your grass to my **Drought Recovery Tonic** (page 330.)

• • • • • • • • •

If you water the lawn by hand, use my **Summer Soother Tonic** (page 338). It will perk up your lawn during the hottest months. Before you water, aerate the soil, then spray the lawn with my **Lawn Freshener Tonic** (page 333).

• • • • • • • • •

Test for white grubs in lawn (see page 212) and apply parasitic nematodes if needed. Keep the mosquito population in check with regular applications of my **Buzz Buster Tonic** (page 329).

• • • • • • • •

Check for the fungus among us. Diagnose the problem (see Chapter 12 for advice), then choose the Tonic you need: **Fairy Ring Fighter** (page 330), **Lawn Fungus Fighter** (page 334), or **Mildew-Relief Tonic** (page 334).

REMINDER

Don't forget to keep up with your regular feeding, weeding, watering, mowing, and pest control patrol. See "And Don't Forget to . . ." on page 343.

Early Fall

Sow cool-season grasses now so the plants can establish strong root systems before winter sets in. Be sure to use my **Soil Prep Tonic** (page 337) before sowing, followed by my **Seed Starter Tonic** (page 336) to get the grass seed off to a quick start.

Lay warm-season grass sod and apply my **All-Season Green-Up Tonic** (page 328) after installing to jump-start growth.

Fertilize your lawn with a mixture of 3 lbs. of Epsom salts per bag of premium, dry lawn food (enough to cover 2,500-sq. ft). Apply at half of the recommended rate. Apply my **Fall Lawn Food Mix** (page 331).

Two days after fertilizing, apply my **Snack Tonic** to activate the dry food mix (page 337).

Test the soil for pH and nutrients, and correct any deficiencies by adding lime or sulfur, as needed, along with whatever nutrients the test results suggest (see pages 253–55).

Remove fallen leaves promptly or they'll smother the grass. Chop them up with your mower, add to your compost pile, and saturate the pile with my **Grass Clipping Compost Starter** (page 332).

Tackle big projects like regrading slopes, building retaining walls, and adding gardens in the lawn area now that the weather's cooled down.

If you hear it's going to be a drier-than-normal winter, apply my **Drought Buster Tonic** (page 330) to strengthen your lawn.

Use my **Fall Clean-Up Tonic** (page 331) to prepare the lawn for the cool weather that's about to come.

To zap nasty lawn bugs before they get comfy and cozy in their underground home, apply a dose of my **Winterizing Tonic** (page 340).

REMINDER

Don't forget to keep up with your regular feeding, weeding, watering, mowing, and pest control patrol. See "And Don't Forget to . . ." on page 343.

Wash all jars and sprayers thoroughly with soap and water, rinse well with clear water, then dry and store them in a cool, dry place until next season.

• • • • • • •

Clean up your hand tools by wiping off any dirt with a moist rag. When the tool is clean, wipe it with a lightly oiled rag to help prevent rust from developing.

• • • • • • •

Be sure all lawn chemicals are stored in their original containers. Keep the containers tightly sealed in a secure place away from children and pets.

• • • • • • •

To prevent weeds from going to seed, mow regularly until just before ground freezes.

Inspect and repair your lawn tools. If any need fixing, get it done now so that they will be ready to go first thing in spring.

• • • • • • •

After the last mowing, get the mower ready for winter by draining the gas tank, replacing the engine oil, checking the spark plug for wear, and sharpening the mower blades. You may want to have your lawn mower and other power tools, like your weed trimmer, tuned up (see page 66).

• • • • • • •

After you mow your lawn for the last time, apply my **Last Supper Tonic** (page 333) to keep it happy all winter long.

• • • • • • •

Before the really cold weather sets in, overspray your lawn with an antitranspirant like my Weatherproof. This polymer material seals moisture into the blades of the grass, while locking out the harmful winter weather.

Overseed warm-season grasses with annual ryegrass to keep your lawn green in winter.

• • • • • • •

Look for new mole tunnels before the ground freezes. Pour my **All-Purpose Pest Prevention Potion** (page 327) into tunnels and holes.

REMINDER

Don't forget to keep up with your regular feeding, weeding, watering, mowing, and pest control patrol. See "And Don't Forget to . . ." on page 343.

To zap cutworms and other insect pests before winter, give your lawn and garden a heavy soaking with my **Winterizing Tonic** (page 340).

Winter

In warm climates, apply my **Stress Reliever Tonic** (page 338) once a month throughout the winter.

• • • • • • •

Before Jack Frost comes around in earnest, carefully clean and roll up the garden hose, then store it inside the garage or basement. Be sure to shut off the water to outside spigots so the pipes don't freeze over the winter.

Apply my **All-Purpose Varmint Repellent** (page 327) to drive away deer, raccoons, 'possums, and other unwanted critters.

• • • • • • •

Keep your lawn around walkways looking good and in good shape, even in winter, with my **Winter Walkway Protection Tonic** (page 340).

In warm climates, apply my **Stress Reliever Tonic** (page 338) once a month during winter to keep your lawn growing in the right direction.

• • • • • • • •

Remove thatch from lawns with warm-season grasses. Spread screened compost over the lawn after removing thatch. Apply a dose of my **Kick-in-the-Grass Tonic** (page 333) after dethatching. To prevent reappearance, use my **Thatch Control Tonic** (page 339).

As snow melts from lawns in cold-weather regions, check for snow mold growing on grass blades (see pages 232–33).

• • • • • • •

As weather warms in late winter, skunks become active. Again, look for the telltale holes dug in lawns. Apply my **All-Purpose Varmint Repellent** (page 327) to drive away these unwanted critters.

☆   ☆   ☆

And now we're cycled back to Early Spring once again, and it's time for my **Spring Wake-Up Tonic** and the rest of my **5-Step Feeding Program!**

Index

(Page references in italics indicate charts.)

Buffalo grass
    drought tolerance, 144
    mowing height, 81, 297
    pH range, 253
    plugging with, 136
    seeding with, 268, 270, 271
    slopes and, 137
    sod, 279
    warm-season grass, 14, 149, 154, 297
    watering, 98
Buffer gardens, 150
Bugs. See Insect control
Bulldozers, 240
Bump repair, 129–31
Burclover, 184
Burning lawns, 303
Burnt grass from fertilizing, 28, 29
Butterfly larvae, 201
Buzz Buster Tonic, 214 (recipe), 215, 329
    (recipe), 347

Calcium (Ca), 22, 24–25
Calculating
    composting needs, 257
    seed for sowing, 271
    sod, 30–31, 281
    square footage of lawn, 30–31
Calendar for lawn care, 341–52
California Flex Rake, 110
Carbaryl, 203
Carpet grass
    mowing height, 81, 297
    pH range, 253
    seeding with, 268, 269
    warm-season grass, 154, 297
    watering, 98
Castor oil in tonics, 162, 165, 166, 327, 331
Catch-can test, 94
Cats, 160–61, 168, 334, 336
Cayenne pepper in tonics, 159, 161, 329,
    334, 336

Centipede grass
    mowing height, 81, 298
    pH range, 253
    plugging with, 136
    seeding with, 268, 269, 271
    shady areas and, 148
    warm-season grass, 14, 149, 154, 298
    watering, 98
Chamomile tea in tonics, 152, 181, 203,
    331, 335, 338
Checkerboard sowing, 273
Cheeseweed, 192
Chemical control. See Fungicides;
    Herbicides; Insecticides
Chickweed, 185
Chili powder in tonics, 159, 161, 165, 329,
    335, 336
Chillin' Out Brew, 73 (recipe), 329 (recipe)
Chinch bugs, 200, 201, 203, 205, 209–11,
    329
Chinch Bug Tonic, 211 (recipe), 329 (recipe)
Chinese and lawns, 4, 90
City water, 96
Clay soil. See also Soil basics
    composting, 41, 41, 257
    defined, 248
    improving, 262
    pH adjustments, 255
    testing, 249, 250
    watering, 8, 90, 97
Climate (weather), 140–56. See also Cool-
    season grasses; Drought defense; Warm-
    season grasses
    areas of yard, needs of, 141
    cold weather, 151–53, 154, 155
    heat, 149–50, 154
    map of lawn regions, 141
    rain, 96, 100, 104–5, 106, 146–47
    seeding and, 268–70, 273
    shade, 148–49, 154, 247, 307, 320
    watering and, 92, 98–100, 104

New lawns. See Plugging lawns; Seeding (sowing) lawns; Sodding lawns; Soil basics

Newspaper for killing lawns, 304

Nighttime watering, 92

Nitrogen (N)
disease control and, 228, 231, 232, 233, 234
fertilizing, 19, 20–21, 20–21, 29, 32, 40, 43
soil basic, 251, 252, 256

Nodes of grass, 10, 11

Nonselective herbicides, 177

Noxious weeds in seed, 267

Nurse grass, 90

Oiling tools, 64

Oil in tonic, 226, 334

1-inch watering rule, 93, 95, 97

One-Third Rule, 7, 76, 80, 132, 139

Onions in tonics, 159, 207, 328, 329

Oregon for grass seed, 267

Organic
disease control methods, 223
fertilizers, 6, 27, 41
insect control methods, 200–202
weed control methods, 173–74

Ornamental grasses, 308–11, 320

Oscillating sprinklers, 102

Other crop seed, 266

Oxalis, 192–93

P. See Phosphorus

Patios, 317–19, 320

Peppermint essential oil in tonic, 73, 329

Pesticides. See Insecticides

Pests. See Animal control; Insect control

Phosphorus (P)
fertilizing, 19, 20–21, 29, 31, 32
soil basic, 251, 252, 256

Photosynthesis, 13, 15

pH (potential of hydrogen)

disease control by, 230, 231
soil acidity, 251, 252, 253, 253–55, 260–61
weed control by, 174, 180, 181, 196

Plows, 240

Plug Feeding Tonic, 287 (recipe), 335 (recipe)

Plugging lawns, 284–88

Plug Rejuvenating Tonic, 133, 135, 136 (recipe), 139, 335 (recipe)

Pollution Solution Tonic, 127 (recipe), 138–39, 335 (recipe)

Portable sprinklers, 101, 102

Postemergent herbicides, 176, 177, 184, 185, 187, 190, 194

Potassium (K)
fertilizing, 19, 20–21, 29, 32
soil basic, 251, 252, 256

Potential of hydrogen. See pH

Powdery mildew, 229–30, 235

Predatory nematodes, 165, 201, 209, 211, 212, 214, 218

Preemergent herbicides, 173, 176–77, 184, 185, 193

Property value of lawns, ix, viii

Prostrate knotweed, 193

Pure seed percentages, 266

Purslane, 193–94

Push-type mowers, 49, 50

Pyrethroids, 203, 211, 212, 217

Pythium blight, 230–31, 235

Quaking grass, 311

Quick-release fertilizers, 26, 27

Raccoons, 165, 166

Rain, 96, 100, 104–5, 106, 146–47

Raking. See also Composting
disease control, 224, 226, 229, 233
rakes, 56–57, 110, 240, 282
tips for, 110–11, 121

Rear-bagging mowers, 55

Red thread, 231, 235